Missing in Action
An RCAF Navigator's Story

Missing in Action is a moving personal account of a Canadian Air Force navigator's experiences as a German POW during the final months of World War II, including his encounters with the French Resistance and the Gestapo and his experience as a prisoner at the notorious concentration camp in Buchenwald.

Shot down by Germans over occupied France, John Harvie was the only member of his Bomber Command crew to survive the crash. He was hidden by a French family until he made contact with the French Resistance, who offered to help him get back to England. Betrayed to the Gestapo by a traitor within the Resistance, he spent a month in solitary confinement as a police prisoner in Paris and was then transported by boxcar to Buchenwald. He describes the appalling conditions, the indignities, and the extreme hardship he and his fellow prisoners endured. Later he was transferred to Stalag Luft III prisoner of war camp where, with food from the Red Cross and the comradeship of fellow prisoners, his body and spirit were restored. In the final months of the war, as the Russian army advanced into Germany, Harvie and the other POWs underwent the long march from eastern Germany, first to a camp near Bremen and then to Lübeck near the Danish border, until the Allied forces broke through and he was liberated by the British army.

Both painful and uplifting, *Missing in Action* is an invaluable record of the unforgettable horrors, happenings, and heroes of World War II.

JOHN D. HARVIE is a retired civil engineer living in St Sauveur des Monts, Quebec.

Missing in Action

An RCAF Navigator's Story

JOHN D. HARVIE

McGill-Queen's University Press
Montreal & Kingston • London • Buffalo

© McGill-Queen's University Press 1995
ISBN 0-7735-1350-7

Legal deposit fourth quarter 1995
Bibliothèque nationale du Québec

Printed in Canada on acid-free paper

McGill-Queen's University Press is grateful to the
Canada Council for support of its publication
program.

Canadian Cataloguing in Publication Data

Harvie, John D., 1923–
    Missing in action : an RCAF navigator's story
    ISBN 0-7735-1350-7
    1. Harvie, John D., 1923–   2. World War, 1939–
    1945 – Prisons and prisoners, German. 3. Prisoners
    of war – Germany – Biography. 4. Prisoners of war
    – Canada – Biography. 5. World War, 1939–1945 –
    Personal narratives, Canadian. 6. Canada. Royal
    Canadian Air Forces – Biography. I. Title.
    D811.H37 1995   940.54'7243'092   C95-900442-4

Typeset in Palatino 10.5/13
by Caractéra production graphique, Quebec City

This book is dedicated to my crew:

Gordon Baird	*Pilot,* RCAF
Thomas Jenkins	*Rear Gunner,* RCAF
Robert Longley	*Wireless Operator,* RCAF
Thomas Marler	*Flight Engineer,* RAF
Donald Wilson	*Bomb Aimer,* RCAF
William Winder	*Upper Gunner,* RCAF

They shall grow not old, as we that are left grow old:
Age shall not weary them, nor the years contemn.
At the going down of the sun and in the morning
    We will remember them.

"For the Fallen," Laurence Binyon

Contents

Acknowledgments

I must first acknowledge that the catalyst for this memoir was the anxiety-arousing and provocative questioning by my then teenage children, John Todd, Jennifer, James, and Jessica. This book was written for them.

I would have had difficulty completing my story without the help of Gérard Renault. His research gave me detailed facts about the crews and aircraft shot down in the Eure-et-Loire district of occupied France as well as data concerning Resistance and Gestapo operations in the Chartres area.

Madam Antoinette Baudois (Rothiot), "Venette," supplied the particulars about her family who risked their lives sheltering me; she also identified the location of their wartime home as Chappes.

I wish also to thank Krisha Starker, Executive Director (retired) of The Montreal Holocaust Memorial Centre, for making available the extensive records and documents of the Centre concerning Buchenwald. A concentration camp survivor herself, her office was always open to me and over many a cup of coffee she filled in the missing details which helped make my story more complete.

The post-war research of German documents by Stan Booker, ex-RAF and fellow Buchenwald inmate, allowed me to know why we were sent to Buchenwald and that we were not to leave there alive.

Sally Campbell, my freelance editor, is due thanks for patiently and meticulously correcting my grammar and punctuation. Her suggestions and support were invaluable as this, my first manuscript, was assembled.

Acknowledgement must be given to my long-time friend, John Mappin, who appointed himself my "agent-at-large." His enthusiasm and encouragement helped my manuscript to become a book-in-print.

Finally and most importantly, this book would never have been undertaken had it not been for the gentle urging and persuasion of my wife Elizabeth. Without complaint she patiently listened as I read to her every chapter and then its many revisions. Her constructive criticism and wise counselling helped me uncover buried feelings and emotions which I had long denied.

Introduction

On my sixteenth birthday, September 3, 1939, my mother wakened me with, "Many happy returns ... the war has started." Although we in Canada realized that Europe was headed for a terrible conflict, no one could foresee the manner in which each of us would be affected.

That summer, I had vaguely realized that if war came, my eldest brother Robert would enlist, and perhaps even myself. A few days before hostilities officially commenced, I sat on the curb across from the armoury on Hillside Avenue watching a few soldiers doing whatever soldiers do and being very impressed. I was with my friend Cyril Manhire at the time and I thought he summed up our feelings succinctly with the statement, "I don't want to go to war and have my balls shot off." In my mind's eye I could picture myself in uniform in some foreign land attacking the enemy, and a defending soldier taking deliberate aim at that part of my anatomy and shooting it off. What a horrible thought!

My brother Robert joined the air force. He was navigator of a Lancaster bomber when on January 17, 1943, he was killed on his twenty-first raid. A year later I too saw action as a navigator with Bomber Command in Europe. My early fears proved unfounded; I returned home with all my anatomy intact.

I make no pretense to be a hero. This story is about an ordinary young man from an ordinary family who was caught up and engulfed in World War II. It is the true account of my adventures after my bomber was reported missing in action.

Everyone who saw battle experienced exciting adventures. No two stories are identical; each in its own way is unique. I believe my war story is unusual because of what happened to me after I was shot down over occupied France. These terrible experiences, the worst of which were shared by 168 other Allied airmen, I have tried to keep bottled up. But my wife Elizabeth has wisely persuaded me that I owe it to myself, my children, and friends who might be interested to tell "my war story." Her perception that I needed to get it out of my system has proved valid. Her assistance, not only as a caring and loving partner but also as a professional psychologist, has been invaluable as I dug back into the horrors of this unforgotten period.

Fifty years have passed since I went to war; consequently some of my memories are blurred. However, the most exciting events remain vivid and I only have to close my eyes to relive them. I have used wartime personal diaries and letters to recall certain dates and events. Memorabilia that I collected have helped me reconstruct my adventures. Well-documented research in recent letters from old comrades has been invaluable. I have verified facts whenever possible with my own research of official records.

In my account, I have tried to concentrate on my feelings and impressions as events unfolded for me. Everything I have written is true as I saw it. Others who were there may have slightly different versions. I do not pretend to say that my memory of certain events is the correct one, nor do I necessarily agree with theirs. In many instances their version of terrible events is more devastating than mine. It is more than possible that my mind has blocked them out.

I have tried to make these memoirs flow as a story. To achieve this in the later chapters I have occasionally moved minor anecdotes forward or backward a few weeks.

Flying Officer John D. Harvie, J27573 Royal Canadian Air Force

Crew of "W" Willie, winter 1943–44
Front row (left to right): Bill Winder (upper gunner), John Harvie (navigator).
Back row: Bob Longley (wireless operator), Gordie Baird (pilot), Hugh Fraser
(bomb aimer), Tom Jenkins (rear gunner). Absent: Tom Marler (flight engineer),
Gordon Wilson (bomb aimer on July 4, 1944)

Telegram reporting the author missing in action

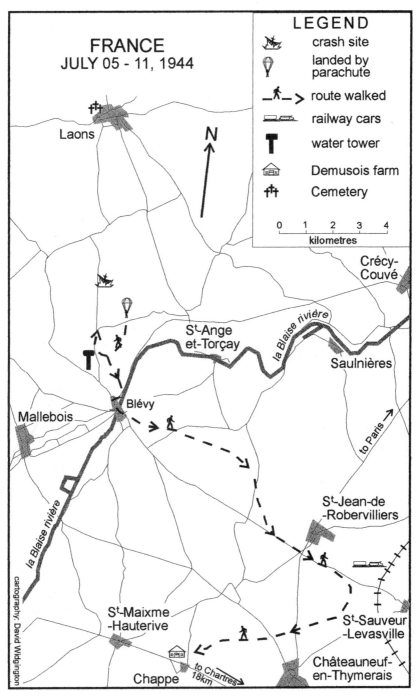

Map of bomber crash site showing route walked and location of Demousois farm

ROYAL CANADIAN AIR FORCE

OTTAWA, Canada, 15th July, 1944.

Dr. Robert Harvie,
355 Metcalfe Avenue,
Westmount, Quebec.

Dear Dr. Harvie:

It is with deep regret that I must confirm our recent
telegram informing you that your son, Flying Officer John Dalton
Harvie, is reported missing on Active Service.

Advice has been received from the Royal Canadian Air
Force Casualties Officer, Overseas, that your son and the entire crew
of his aircraft failed to return to their base after taking off to
carry out bombing operations over Villeneuve St. Georges, France, on
the night of July 4th and the early morning of July 5th, 1944.

The term "missing" is used only to indicate that his
whereabouts is not immediately known and does not necessarily mean that
your son has been killed or wounded. He may have landed in enemy territory and might be a Prisoner of War. Enquiries have been made through the
International Red Cross Society and all other appropriate sources and I
wish to assure you that any further information received will be communi-
cated to you immediately.

Attached is a list of the members of the Royal Canadian Air
Force who were in the crew together with the names and addresses of their
next-of-kin. Your son's name will not appear on the official casualty
list for five weeks. You may, however, release to the Press or Radio
the fact that he is reported missing, but not disclosing the date, place
or his unit.

Permit me to extend to you my heartfelt sympathy during
this period of uncertainty and I join with you and the members of your
family in the hope that better news will be forthcoming in the near
future.

Yours sincerely,

I. E. Ladd s/o

R.C.A.F. Casualty Officer,
for Chief of the Air Staff.

R.C.A.F. G. 32B
500M—1-44 (3778)
H.Q. 885-G-32B

Letter from RCAF casualty officer to author's next of kin advising them that he was
missing on active service

ROYAL CANADIAN AIR FORCE

OTTAWA, CANADA,
September 28, 1944.

Mr. Robert Harvie,
355 Metcalfe Avenue,
Westmount, Quebec.

HARVIE, John D., F/O (Missing)
No. J.27573, R. C. A. F.

Dear Mr. Harvie:

We beg to acknowledge receipt of your letter of September 14 with respect to the effects of your son who is unfortunately reported missing.

Pursuant to your request, we have instructed Overseas Headquarters to deliver his bicycle, radio, record-reproducer for radio and records to Miss Jeannette Harvie of Barrhead, Scotland.

We sincerely hope that your son will return to claim his own effects.

Yours faithfully

E. C. Collins F/L

ECC/TD   for Director of Estates.

R.C.A.F. G. 32
000M—3-44 (3868)
H.Q. 885—G-32

Letter from RCAF to author's family concerning disposal of his personal effects

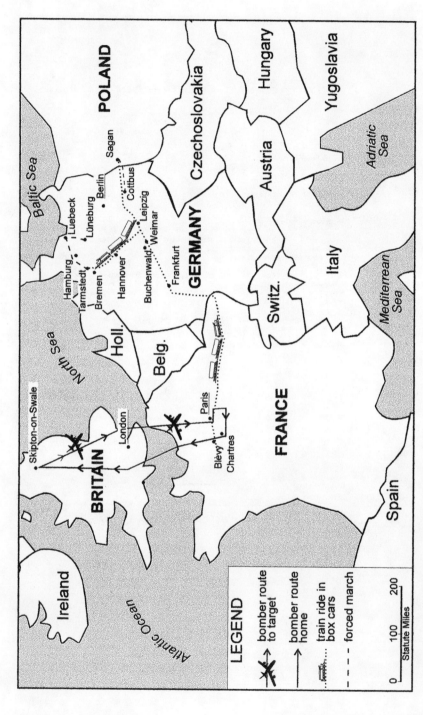

Map showing bomber route on July 4 and route author followed as a prisoner

Author's identity card as a German POW

FORCED MARCH - APRIL 1945

POWs on forced march, April 1945

FOOD PARCELS

ONE PER WEEK PER MAN

RED   CROSS

BRITISH			AMERICAN			CANADIAN		
Condensed Milk	1 can		Powdered Milk-16oz.	1 can		Powdered Milk		1 can
Meat Roll	1 can		Spam	1 can		Spam		1 can
Meat & Vegetable	1 can		Corned Beef	1 can		Corned Beef		1 can
Vegetable or Bacon	1 can		Liver Paste	1 can		Salmon		1 can
Sardines	1 can		Salmon	1 can		Cheese-8 0z.		1 can
Cheese-4 oz.	1 can		Cheese	1 can		Butter-16 oz.		1 can
Margarine or Butter	1 8oz.		Margarine-16 oz.	1 can		Biscuits-soda		1 box
Biscuits	1 pkg.		Biscuits--K-Ration			Coffee-ground-8 oz.		1 bag
Eggs-Dry	1 can		Nescafe Coffee-4 oz.	1 can		Jam		1 can
Oatmeal	1 can		Jam or Orange Pres.	1 can		Prunes-8 oz.		1 box
Cocoa	1 can		Prunes or Raisins	1 can		Raisins-8 oz.		1 box
Tea-2 oz.	1 box		Sugar-8oz.	1 box		Sugar-8 oz.		1 bag
Dried Fruit or Pudding	1 can		Chocolate-4oz.	2 bars		Chocolate-5 oz.		1 bar
Sugar-4 oz.	1 box		Soap	2 bars		Soap		1 bar
Chocolate	1 bar		Cigarettes	5 pks.				
Soap	1 bar							

REICH ISSUE

WEEKLY RATION

Army Bread-1 loaf	2100 grams		Soup-Oatmeal, Barley or Pea	3 times
Vegetables-Potatoes	400 grams		Cheese	46 grams
Other Seasonal	?		Sugar	175 grams
Jam	175 grams		Mare	215 grams
Meat			Salt	
Flour---on occasion				

List showing contents of Red Cross POW food parcels and German weekly food ration
(issued when available)

NOTICE
To All Prisoners Of War

— POSTED IN ALL GERMAN PRISONER OF WAR CAMPS —

TO ALL PRISONERS OF WAR!

THE ESCAPE FROM PRISON CAMPS IS NO LONGER A SPORT!

Germany has always kept to the Hague Convention and only punished recaptured prisoners of war with minor disciplinary punishment.

Germany will still maintain these principles of International Law.

But England has besides fighting at the front in an honest manner instituted an illegal warfare in non combat zones in the form of gangster commandos, terror bandits and sabotage troops even up to the frontiers of Germany.

They say in a captured secret and confidential English military pamphlet.

THE HANDBOOK
OF MODERN IRREGULAR
WARFARE:

" . . . The days when we could practise the rules of sportmanship are over. For the time being, every soldier must be a potential gangster and must be prepared to adopt their methods whenever necessary."

"The sphere of operations should always include the enemy's own country, and occupied territory, and in certain circumstances, such neutral countries as he is using as a source of supply."

England has with these instructions opened up a non military form of gangster war!

Germany is determined to safeguard her homeland, and especially her war industry and provisional centres for the fighting fronts. Therefore it has become necessary to create strictly forbidden zones, called death zones, in which all unauthorised trespassers will be immediately shot on sight.

Escaping prisoners of war, entering such death zones, will certainly lose their lives. They are therefore in constant danger of being mistaken for enemy agents or sabotage groups.

URGENT WARNING IS GIVEN AGAINST MAKING FUTURE ESCAPES!
IN PLAIN ENGLISH:
Stay in the camp where you will be safe!
Breaking out of it is now a damned dangerous act.

THE CHANCES OF PRESERVING YOUR LIFE ARE ALMOST NIL!
All police and military guards have been given the most strict orders
to shoot on sight all suspected persons.

ESCAPING FROM PRISON CAMPS HAS CEASED TO BE A SPORT!

German notice to POWs regarding escapes

Graves of crew members, Laons Cemetery, France

Missing in Action

CHAPTER ONE

The Adventures Begin

The bad weather that had caused last minute cancellation of our scheduled bombing raids on both Sunday and Monday nights began to improve on Tuesday July 4, 1944. The rain stopped and the clouds hovering over the airfield showed signs of breaking up. I found these last minute stand downs very hard on the nerves after I had managed to get myself psyched up to participate in a raid. The question that always ran through my mind was whether a stand down was an act of God that saved our lives on the night that our number was up or it was bad luck because this would have been an easy op.

Our crew of seven was flying Halifax Mark (Mk.) III heavy bombers from No. 433 squadron based at Skipton-on-Swale in Yorkshire, England. We had come together as a crew at operational training unit on November 25, 1943. The air force didn't use a scientific method to assemble the crews who would live or die together – when a new course was starting at the unit, equal numbers of pilots, navigators, and bomb-aimers were brought together in a hangar. Without introduction or prior knowledge of each others' backgrounds, we were told to mix and form crews. I looked around and saw a young man wearing pilots' wings who was eyeing me. We said to each other, "How about it?" He was fair-haired, my height, slender without being skinny, and had a mischievous smile. His name was Gordon Baird; he was twenty years old and came from Calgary. Then we saw a bomb-aimer nearby and asked him if he would like to join us. He agreed, and Hugh Fraser from Tilsonburg, Ontario, became our third crew member. We were doing very well in such a short time. Hugh had blondish hair with early signs of baldness and, at twenty-six, was the old man of our group.

The next day we met the group of noncommissioned airmen from whom we would select the next three crew members. We had heard there was a warrant officer wireless operator with Middle East experience and we decided to try and get him before another crew grabbed him. We were lucky! Bob Longley from Winnipeg was about twenty-two, always cheerful, and never wore his hat if he could avoid it. What I remember most about Bob was how well spoken he was when we first met him – and how after that he could never speak a sentence without injecting "f––king" in front of each noun. We finished by asking two air gunners to team with us as upper and rear gunners. Tom Jenkins, who became the rear gunner, was dark and the only crew member to sport a mustache. Bill Winder, our mid-upper gunner, was full-faced, fair-haired and of medium build. Both were about nineteen years old and came from Vancouver. I was navigator and twenty years old. Tom Marler, the seventh and last member of our unit, did not join us as flight engineer until some time later, when we first started flying the four-engined Halifaxes. Tom was twenty years old and came from Manchester. He was the only Englishman in our crew. Looking back now I realize that all but the "old man" of our team, Hugh Fraser, were just a group of kids, most of us not even old enough to vote.

Six of us completed four months of intensive work at operational training unit at Gamston, on Wellington twin-engine bombers. Then we enjoyed three-weeks leave before a posting to Topcliffe, where Tom Marler joined us. There, four weeks were spent learning to fly the bigger and more complicated Halifaxes. The seven of us then received our final and most important posting to No. 433 squadron, a fully operational bomber unit.

Although we had been at Skipton since May 26, we had only flown together as a unit six times. Three of these flights had been on bombing operations over enemy occupied France. We were rapidly gaining confidence in ourselves as a team, even though we had not yet been tested by enemy fighters nor hit by flak. We realized we were short on training hours in Halifaxes, mainly because we had not flown in over three weeks due to ten days' leave, followed by Gordie's having been grounded for another ten days with hay fever. Whenever we were not flying I was down at the navigation section, keeping up on the latest techniques and intelligence reports and practising with ground versions of air-borne navigation aids. The rest of the crew would be similarly occupied in their respective sections. However, the best way of improving our skills was flying together in a Halifax, learning its every quirk and how to respond instantly and correctly to any unusual situation.

We had not done any flying since June 10. In an attempt to get us back into flying shape our flight commander scheduled a practice cross-country flight that morning. But this chance to get some air time was cancelled when our bomb-aimer, Hugh Fraser, who had been suffering from a strep throat for several days, was grounded by the station medical officer. I spent the morning at the navigation section. Although our squadron was on standby that night, we didn't expect to fly when one of our crew members was in sick quarters, so it seemed like a good opportunity to visit our station dentist after lunch and have a tooth filled.

However, late in the afternoon I was surprised to learn that our crew was scheduled to fly that night. Our squadron, No. 433 (Porcupine), and No. 424 (Tiger) were slated to put twenty-five to thirty Halifax Mk. III heavy bombers in the air as our contribution to the bombing raids on enemy targets. Briefing was scheduled for after supper and take off for 10:15 P.M., at the end of the long summer day.

When I checked in at the general briefing with the rest of my crew, I learned that the squadron senior bomb-aimer, Don Wilson, would be filling in for Hugh. Don needed only one more trip to complete his tour of thirty operations, after which the lucky guy would receive a cushy posting home to Canada. We were not too happy about a "stranger" in our crew for it might mean bad luck. However, we did not have much time to worry as we were soon fully occupied absorbing and digesting all the details of the forthcoming operation.

When I looked at the large map at the front of the briefing room I saw that the target was the railway marshalling yards at Villeneuve-St-Georges, southeast of Paris. As navigator I had to know the route intimately. This included knowing the courses, distances, flying heights, anticipated wind speeds and direction, code words and signal flares if required, alternate bases at which to land in case of bad weather on return, and a host of other details. The route to the target was reasonably direct, but the route home seemed to have us flying over occupied France for an unusually long time. After leaving the target we had to head south, then west past Chartres, before finally turning north for home past Rouen. Total flying time was estimated at six hours.

Our route into and out of enemy territory was planned with frequent changes of course. This was to avoid known concentrations of German antiaircraft guns and at the same time make it difficult for the enemy to predict our ultimate target. Not knowing our flight pattern made it difficult for them to muster concentrations of fighters along our route. I could see that, as usual, I would be very busy with my navigation. The advantage of being fully occupied, however, was that I wouldn't have time to succumb to my fears of enemy fighters, flak, engine failure, or any of the many other dangers which could suddenly bring us crashing to the ground. Unfortunately the weather forecast was for a full moon over France, with no clouds. Our best defence from attack was always total darkness and clouds that hid us from enemy fighters.

In the general briefing we were assigned the height from which we were to bomb. To avoid congestion over the target the other squadrons were assigned bombing heights above and below ours. We were informed that only Lancasters and Halifaxes would be taking part in tonight's raid. Pathfinders in Lancaster bombers would mark the target with ground flares five minutes in advance of the main bomber force. The pathfinder leader would act as "Master of ceremonies," directing the raid as he circled a few thousand feet above the target for the full time that the raid was in progress. His call sign on radio telephone would be the code words "barn door."

Bombing raids required such accurate navigation that the old wireless fixes and star shots were no longer used except in extreme emergencies. I was using two secret navigation devices with the code names "Gee" and "H2S." High frequency signals from ground stations were electronically calibrated by the Gee box, and when plotted on special navigation charts gave me our position within a few hundred feet. The enemy could jam these signals over their territory and hence these sets were excellent over England but useless over France.

H2S was an airborne radar that broadcast and received its own signals, which were then displayed on a TV-type screen. Shapes of cities, towns, and bodies of water were clearly defined in varying degrees of light. It required extreme concentration to correctly identify the landmarks shown on the monitor. These sets were excellent over hostile territory since they could not be jammed. However, the German night fighters were equipped with devices that allowed them to home in on a bomber when its set was in use.

After the general briefing, and the special briefings for each trade, a WAAF driver took us to our dispersal point on the far perimeter of the airfield, away from the main buildings. Meanwhile the other bomber crews were being driven to their dispersal areas, which were widely scattered around the airfield. Our crew had not completed enough ops to be assigned the same bomber each trip. It was the belief of the junior crews that they were always assigned the "leftovers," the older and temperamental planes. Tonight we were assigned to fly "W" Willie, the old crock that had taken us safely to Paris and back on June 7.

The evening was one of those that make you feel it's great to be alive. Standing beside "W" Willie I looked beyond the ugly dark bombers scattered around the perimeter of the base and saw the English countryside at its summer best. The sun setting in the west behind our dispersal area gave a mellow glow to everything. As yet, no harsh roar of airplane engines disturbed the peace of the perfect evening. It was hard to believe that men were at war and that many of those standing around their bombers, engaged in idle chit-chat and smoking a last cigarette before embarking, would never return.

Our ground crew, who would help start the engines with battery boosters, waited nearby. They would stay close by with fire extinguishers in case of fire during start-up and would not leave the area until we had taxied out to take our position in the line of aircraft awaiting their turn to takeoff. One of the ground crew had two navy friends with him, undoubtedly on leave, who wanted to observe the start of a bombing raid. I remember idly wondering if either of them wished they could change jobs with one of us. If the impossible had happened and they could have taken our places, would I have agreed? I believe that any one of us would have quickly given up his position in the plane. In spite of our nonchalance as we lounged by our aircraft, I was sure the rest of my crew were as tense and scared as I was ... a state of nerves that could only be relieved by boarding Willie and immersing ourselves in the task of flying her to the target and back.

All too soon it was time to board and start our deadly affairs. The engines started easily, with no apparent malfunctions that would have given us just cause to abort the trip. We taxied out of the dispersal area on schedule and moved slowly along the perimeter to take our place with the other bombers waiting their turn to take off. We were all maintaining strict radio silence so the enemy would not know that we were mounting a raid. All communication to the bombers was given by a hand-held Aldis lamps aimed in their direction. Every thirty seconds or so the Aldis lamp shutter would open and wink closed on a green light signal, the engines of another massive bomber would be carefully opened to maximum power, and it would start its long thunderous roar down the airstrip. Soon we were next in line for take-off. Gordie, with brakes fully applied, carefully tested each engine to maximum power. Satisfied, he eased back the throttles and taxied to the beginning of the runway. The Aldis winked its green eye at us. Gordie slowly opened the throttles, released brakes, and we began building up speed. We felt the tail lift as the heavily laden aircraft struggled to get off the ground. At the instant when it seemed certain that we had used up all the runway and would not lift off, the change in vibration told us the plane was airborne and we were headed off on a new adventure.

The "battle stations" for the wireless operator, bomb-aimer, and navigator of a Halifax are in the nose, ahead of the four engines and the main wing. Because this is a vulnerable section of the aircraft in a crash on take-off or landing, it was standard safety procedure for these crew members to leave the front and sit in comparative safety behind the main wing spar, midway back in the plane. Accordingly Bob, our wireless operator, Don, the bomb-aimer, and I were buckled into our take-off seats until the plane had climbed a few hundred feet and we could be sure that it was safely airborne.

As we circled while climbing for height, Bob, Don, and I left our seats at the rear and moved forward to our battle stations. We passed Tom, our flight engineer, who acted as co-pilot during take-off and had already folded down the jump seat so that we could pass through the narrow opening into the nose section. All of us except Gordie were equipped with the chest type of parachute. For mobility we were wearing the harness only and carrying the parachute pack, but there were so many protuberances inside the bomber that we still had to be careful not to snag our harnesses.

Bob eased himself down the few steps past Gordie, turned left, and entered his wireless compartment, directly under the pilot. Don was next into the forward section, where he deposited his parachute in the perspex nose beside his bomb sight. He would be helping me with the Gee box and H2S so he came back into the navigator's cabin, carefully closing the blackout curtains behind him. The navigator's work area occupied the full width of the aircraft from the bottom of the steps to the blackout curtains separating it from the nose. The work table projected from the left-hand side of the cabin. From the right we folded down the narrow bench that faced it. Don sat nearest the front while I was towards the back. I put my parachute pack on the floor by my left side where I could quickly pick it up and snap it on my harness if necessary. As usual, I was wearing my parachute harness fully buckled up. For me the extra discomfort of its tightness was preferable to the risk of wasting valuable seconds fumbling for the last two buckles in an emergency.

In the gathering dusk hundreds of bombers from the many airfields were climbing and circling, like us apparently aimlessly. They would only set course for the target at the time given in briefing so that we would all be flying in the comparative safety of a large swarm of bombers.

In "W" Willie I spread my charts and log books in front of me and glanced at the altimeter above my desk to see how far we had climbed. I looked at my watch to check the time left before setting course for target, then at our air position indicator to see if it was functioning properly. I called Gordie on the intercom to tell him what speed and time to pass over base on the first leg of our trip. Beside me, Don was already warming up both the Gee box and the H2S sets. The steady engine roar made conversation difficult except by intercom. Gordie, behind and above us, was adjusting the trim and synchronizing the four engines. Tom was watching gauges for signs of overheating, excessive fuel consumption, or other trouble areas. Bob was fine-tuning his wireless set to hear if there were any last-minute instructions from base. The gunners were swinging their guns and turrets around to make sure they functioned smoothly. Together we did an intercom check and each man checked his oxygen supply.

Gordie timed his orbiting to bring "W" Willie over base at approximately zero hour. I set the latitude and longitude of our base on the Air Position Indicator and switched it on as we passed directly above. Then I noted the exact time that we set course, checked on my gyro compass that we were on the right heading, and noted these items in my log. We headed south for the English coast, about one hour's flying time away. Over the channel I broke intercom silence to tell Bob that we were leaving friendly territory and it was time to turn off the Identification, Friend, or Foe (IFF) set which told our defence forces we were a friendly aircraft. Tom and Bill, in turn, asked Gordie for permission to check their guns by firing a short burst. Up forward we felt the plane shake as each turret fired a few second's burst from its four machine guns.

We droned across the enemy coast, heading inland without incident. In our little cubby hole, hidden from the rest of the crew by the blackout curtains, Don and I heard the rest of the crew calling back and forth to each other as they saw important signs of enemy activity. The two of us seemed to be in a world of our own. Although there were hundreds of our own aircraft all around us headed for the same target, I had the awful feeling that our bomber was flying alone in the hostile skies.

As we headed deeper into enemy territory, a feeling of tenseness began to pervade the confines of "W" Willie. In expectation of a sudden fighter attack we were each at the ready. Tom, in the rear turret, was straining his eyes to the rear as he scanned the sky above and below. Bill, from the upper turret with its more limited field of vision, searched above and alongside while paying added attention to the rear. These two would be the first to spot a fighter attacking from astern, the area from which an attack would most likely come. Tom Marler, in the astrodome, checked all the area above the aircraft, again with extra attention to the rear. It was unlikely that an attack would come from head-on but as Gordie flew the plane he kept a watch forward. He had to be ready to bank or dive instantly on a shouted warning. Bob, in his wireless cabin, had the job of throwing out bundles of metallic paper, code-named "window," which interfered with the operation of enemy ground and airborne radar. Don, beside me, kept passing me position fixes obtained from the H2S set, with which I plotted our progress. At any sign that we were straying off course and away from the safety of the bomber swarm, I would give a course alteration to Gordie. Periodically a crew member would call out the position of a new searchlight battery, flak battery, or an aircraft going down in flames and I would enter it in my log.

Everything had been going well when, shortly before we were due to make our last turn to the east for the run in on target, Gordie called me. He thought his gyro compass was slightly out of adjustment and asked me to make another position check. The possibility that we might have wandered away from the main bomber stream was an ugly thought as we all knew the German night fighters picked off the stragglers first. My fix showed that we had angled off by a matter of ten to twenty miles to the west. I quickly calculated a course alteration that would bring us over target only three minutes behind schedule ... not too serious a matter. When we were only a few minutes away from our target, Don prepared his bombs for release. I updated our ground speed, the latest wind velocity, and direction and gave them to him to set in his sight. He rose from the table and I turned off the lights in our navigation compartment as he parted the blackout curtains to move forward to his bomb sight in the perspex nose.

My navigation skills were hardly needed as the bursting anti-aircraft shells and searchlight concentrations indicated the direction of our target. As we came closer, the green blobs of the target indicators glowed on the ground. These markers had been dropped by the pathfinders, who had arrived a few minutes ahead of the main force and were now circling to one side to guide the bombers onto the target and to replace the markers if they should go out. I kept the blackout curtains closed so that I would not be distracted by the flak, searchlights, and aircraft going down in flames. Besides, I had to have my new courses ready for when we flew away from the target. On our intercom we could hear the "Master of Ceremonies" calling to the approaching bombers, "Main Force ... this is 'Barn Door.' The target indicators are slightly short of target. Aim your bombs about one hundred and fifty yards beyond them." "My God," I thought to myself, "he is a cool one, circling around over the target, exposing himself to flak and fighters as he calmly directs the attack until the last bomb is dropped and he can head home."

In the isolation of the perspex nose Don had a full view of all the action as we headed for the target. He needed several minutes to feed the latest data into his bomb sight, adjust all the switches on his control panel to the proper settings, and open the bomb doors. Only then was he ready to hunch over the sight with the release tit in his hand and guide Gordie over the target. Squinting along the sight he started guiding Gordie towards the green target indicators … "Left, left, steady, right, steady, steady," he called over the intercom. At the instant when the illuminated yellow cross-hairs on his sight coincided with the aiming point he pressed the release button and, as the sixteen thousand pounds of high explosives hurtled downward, called out "Bombs away!" Gordie held the aircraft straight and steady for a few moments more so that our automatic cameras could take photographs of our strikes. None of the bombs had hung up on the racks so the doors to the bays were closed. We had survived the agonizing run over the target during which we had to fly straight and level, making us vulnerable to the curtains of flak bursting over the target.

East of the target we turned south on the first leg of the trip home. We also started descending from twelve thousand feet to eight thousand feet as part of the raid strategy. Now we were well within the range of light flak with several hours of flying over enemy territory still left. However "W" Willie was now lighter by eight tons of high explosives which made the aircraft more manoeuvreable and increased its speed to two hundred miles per hour.

Forty miles south of Paris we banked ninety degrees to the right and headed due west. I was getting good position fixes and consequently was able to give Gordie courses which kept us right on track. Not only had we regained the time lost before we came over the target but we had not been hit by flak nor seen any fighters. We were all beginning to breathe a little easier. On the H2S set we saw Chartres off to the right. I called out to Gordie the new heading to the north and the time to swing on to it.

Soon I felt us banking onto the last leg for home. It was just before two o'clock in the morning and in less than an hour we would be back over England and nearing our base. Beside me Don kept getting me fixes as I monitored our flight. Except for the roar of the engines, all was quiet and peaceful as we concentrated on getting home safely.

Twenty-five miles from our last turn, Tom Jenkins in the rear turret suddenly yelled over the intercom "Fighter ... Starboard Go!" and the peace was broken. This was the dreaded warning that we were in the gun sights of an enemy fighter which had dived in unnoticed from the rear starboard side. Gordie commenced evasive action. He dipped our starboard wing violently as he turned "W" Willie sharply into the fighter and dived away. If we were lucky the small fighter diving at high speed would be travelling too fast to make a tight turn and follow us. Then we would corkscrew in the opposite direction.

Don and I clung to the edge of the navigation table with our stomachs churning from the abrupt change from straight and level flight. I waited for the cannon shells to tear into me and wondered if I would feel anything. The aircraft shuddered several times, which could be caused either by our guns firing or by the enemy cannon fire striking us. In the navigation compartment we could not see what was happening towards the rear. I waited for my stomach to drop to my knees as Gordie pulled the plane out of the dive and corkscrewed to port. But nothing happened. We continued diving. Then Tom from the rear turret called over the intercom, "Gordie, Gordie!" but there was no answer from our pilot. Instead Tom Marler, who was standing in the astro dome directly behind Gordie, replied, "We have been hit ... we had better get out!" Normally the order to abandon ship came from the pilot but Tom must have seen that Gordie was dead or unable to use the intercom. In any case neither Don nor I questioned the decision, for we knew there was very little time left before we would hit the ground.

Without a word we quickly unplugged our intercoms, stood up, and folded away our seat. The space above the main escape hatch was now clear. Don hurried forward to the nose to retrieve his parachute pack. In a matter of seconds I had picked up mine and snapped it onto my harness. A few more seconds and I had twisted the handle of the escape hatch. The hatch came open easily, thank God, and I threw it out the opening to leave the way clear for the crew members who would soon be crowding forward to jump.

Don was still up front getting his chute ready. I sat down with my back to the front of the aircraft so that when I eased myself into the opening I would go out cleanly without hitting the back of the hatchway. My intention was to sit with my legs partly through the hole and wait to see how the others were making out. However, I forgot about the pull from the slipstream as we headed for the ground. First my left flying boot was pulled off my foot, then I was sucked out effortlessly. As I was dragged out I remember seeing our wireless operator's blackout curtain billowing towards me in a strong draft. With it was something large and white which I think was his parachute. Bob must have accidentally pulled the rip cord when he picked it up to put it on. As I slid out into the night, I couldn't see any other crew members coming forward to bale out.

As soon as I was free of the crashing bomber and realized that I was unhurt, a feeling of relief swept over me. It was only some seconds later, almost as an afterthought, that I remembered to reach for the rip cord and pull it. I don't remember any violent jerk as the parachute opened. I do remember how clean and fresh the air smelled and how quiet and peaceful it became as the noise of aircraft engines faded in the distance. It was a marvelous sensation as I gently floated down. In the brilliant moonlight I could see that I was above farmland with occasional small patches of woods. Over my right shoulder I could discern a farmhouse and nearby a large fire burning. It suddenly occurred to me that this could be "W" Willie. I tried to twist for a clearer look but the parachute harness would not allow it. Then I remembered the procedure that we had been taught to spill air from the canopy to change direction. I was about to do this when I realized that I was almost on the ground. I braced for impact and landed uninjured in a wheat field. I tapped the release button. There was no wind and the parachute silently collapsed on the ground. Thinking back, I calculated that it had taken only thirty seconds to a minute for me to come down, although it seemed much longer. I was extremely fortunate to be alive. I knelt down and said a short prayer of thanks for having survived.

Now I had to start thinking clearly and quickly if I was to evade capture and get back to England. The first step was to hide any evidence that there was a survivor from the bomber. Then, in case the Germans still suspected that any crew member was alive, I had to get as far away from the area as possible before they started an intensive search of the surrounding countryside. I had no time to stop and worry about whether anyone else had survived the crash, though I was almost sure that I was the only one alive.

There was no way I could bury the bulky parachute or harness to conceal the evidence of my landing. The best I could do was to bundle it all together and hide it in the tall wheat. However, first I decided to save a piece for a bandage or as a memento of the parachute which had saved my life. The nylon was tough and I had to work hard before I was able to tear off a piece. I could feel my escape kit still tucked into my battledress top and was relieved that it had survived the action of the last few minutes. I had nothing at all in my pockets, since they had been emptied at briefing and the contents sealed in an envelope by the intelligence officer to await my return. We had not been flying at great heights so I was lightly dressed in my standard RCAF battledress.

Since I imagined that hundreds of Germans had watched me float down on my chute and would shortly be converging on me in trucks and tanks, within minutes of touching down I started off at a fast trot without wasting time to get out my escape maps and compass. I was in such a hurry to get going that I was hardly aware of the fact that I was missing my left flying boot and had only my heavy sock to protect this foot when walking. I went south, away from where I had seen the fire burning. In the distance I could hear the sound of traffic on a highway, probably German military vehicles moving under cover of darkness. Otherwise the countryside seemed peaceful and quiet. As I hurried along I came to a small road at right angles to the line of my route which I quickly crossed to enter another large wheat field. Shortly after I came to another, larger, country road that angled across my path. I retreated a safe distance back into the cover of the waist-high wheat to rest and plan my next moves.

The blackout was complete, without a light to suggest any sign of human habitation. Occupied France was under German curfew and I could easily stumble into an enemy patrol. Germans were certainly around, as evidenced by the sound of vehicles some-where ahead. I asked myself if I should keep blundering along in the dark without being sure of where I was or where I was going. Although the moon allowed me to make out the prominent features of the landscape, it was not bright enough for me to study the map in my escape kit. I could see that the tall field of wheat surrounding me would give ample cover until daylight, when I planned to make my next move. Already it was after 2 A.M., so it was not hard for me to decide to lie down and await daybreak.

The ground was warm and I stretched out, although I slept only fitfully thinking of all that had happened. I was working on nervous energy and had not yet fully comprehended that I was in enemy territory and perhaps my friends were all dead.

CHAPTER TWO

Evasion

Sleep did not come easily as I anxiously awaited my first daylight view of France. Soon the darkness of night changed to the brightness of day. My eagerness to see where I was and to plan my next moves temporarily obliterated the events of the last few hours, with their fear-filled moments. Gone was the realization that I had not had a real sleep in the last twenty-four hours and that in normal circumstances I would soon be sitting down to a good breakfast. Forgotten, too, was the fact that I had been lying uncomfortably on the damp earth of the wheat field for several hours listening to the noise of enemy vehicles in the distance.

As the sun climbed into a cloudless sky, revealing the foreign countryside to me, I knew that I was no longer hidden from curious or hostile eyes. I crouched lower in the protecting wheat before I carefully raised my head to study the surrounding fields glistening in the hot summer sun. I was at the crest of slightly rising ground and, judging by the position of the sun, I was facing south. The sparsely settled farmland was gently undulating, with a scattering of small woods among the largely unfenced fields of grain. I thought I could make out a river flowing from west to east about a mile south of me and, beyond, the ground gently rising again. Behind me and to my right was a small wood. A country road originating somewhere to the north came through the wood to pass close by on my right as it curved down the slope in front of me onto lower ground and then continued directly to the river. Where the road crossed the river, houses nestled against each other to hug both sides of the road and form a small village. Each house appeared to have a yard, back and front, surrounded by high masonry walls. Above the walls rose the upper parts of the houses: red brick or whitewashed stone surmounted by tiled roofs and chimneys. Smoke spiralled from several of these chimneys and this, together with the crowing of roosters signified, the start of another day for the farm community. On the near side of the village, secondary roads branched off both to the east and west, following the general direction of the river, and a few houses were scattered along them. I studied very carefully a tower on the near side of the village that stood adjacent to the road leading towards my place of concealment. Was it an enemy lookout or simply a water tower or mill?

I was surveying the lay of the land when a farmer with a horse and cart came towards me from the direction of the village. When he passed me, about fifteen yards away, he was whistling a cheerful tune, while a dog trotted beside the farm wagon. The trees were green, the fields of wheat had a golden lustre, and overhead a hot sun shone from a cloudless blue sky. This was enemy-occupied France as I saw it for the first time on the morning of July 5, 1944.

From inside my battledress top I brought out my escape kit in its waterproof container. Inside was a small-scale map of France printed on waterproof silk, a miniature compass, French francs, a plastic water bottle, tablets for purifying water, a tiny razor with shaving soap, malted milk tablets as a source of energy, and photographs of myself in civilian clothing to be used on forged passports. With the razor I cut off and discarded all insignia from my battledress that would identify me as an enemy airman. I kept my dog tags, however, as required by the Geneva convention. As near as I could determine from the small-scale map I was about twenty miles northwest of Chartres, between the small villages of Blévy and Laons. The river south of me that flowed through the village was probably the Blaise, working its way in a northeasterly direction towards Dreux.

The escape briefing the previous night had instructed us that if we ended up in France we should try and make our way to neutral Spain, since the Allied armies had not yet broken out of their Normandy beachhead, some one hundred and fifty miles to the northwest of where I was. I estimated that Spain was about five hundred miles to the southwest and that it would take me at least until the end of the year to walk there, dodging major cities, crossing rivers and other obstacles en route. I was quite sure that before I arrived at the Spanish border the Allies would have broken out of Normandy and drastically changed the course of the war. Consequently I decided to head for Spain but not try to break any speed records walking. My plan was to walk only at night, inspite of the German-imposed curfew, and to be content with a slow but steady progress towards my destination. As I worked my way across France I thought there was a good possibility of making contact with either a friendly French family or even the Resistance. Then perhaps I would be able to remain hidden in one place until I was overtaken by the advancing armies.

As I deliberated on the options open to me, an automobile with two occupants came from the direction of the village, passed about forty feet from my hiding place, and disappeared up the road behind me. A short time later the car and its occupants returned the same way. Because fuel and vehicles were strictly rationed for the French, I assumed that the occupants were Germans who had perhaps gone to examine the wreckage of my bomber, which I guessed was not too far away to the north behind me.

My decision to travel at night meant that I had a full day ahead of me before I could skirt the nearby village, cross the river, and start my long journey south. Until darkness fell I decided I would explore the relatively open and uninhabited farmland behind me, away from the threatening tower and the chance of encountering unfriendly villagers. Perhaps I might even find an isolated farm where I could get something to eat. If I used the waist-high wheat as cover no one would be likely to see me.

As soon as I moved off through the grain I began to feel that hostile eyes were watching me. It seemed to me that enemy soldiers were stationed at every farmhouse window, at hidden places around the fields, and especially on top of the tower, sweeping the area with binoculars as they searched for escaping airmen like me. Consequently I started off on my hands and knees, keeping well hidden. I may have crawled twenty feet or one hundred and twenty before I realized that I would not cover much ground in this manner. I rose to my feet and tried walking in a crouch. This time I covered a lot more distance, perhaps even five hundred feet, but faced the prospect of being permanently crippled if I attempted to walk like this every day until I reached Spain. I sat down and had a council of war with myself. "Look here," I said, "the German army has millions of men fighting in Russia, Italy, and now in France. It is very unlikely that they have assigned a few hundred men to watch just for you around this peaceful village. In fact, they probably don't even know you are here. If you are going to encounter the enemy, it will likely be around villages, towns, military areas, bridges, crossroads, and railways, as we had been told. So why draw attention to yourself by crawling through fields like an escaped convict? Instead, walk along the roads in isolated areas as though you belonged instead of drawing attention by acting suspiciously. If you keep alert you will have time to hide if someone happens along."

I continued my side foray in relative comfort, walking upright along the road. Although walking with one flying boot and only a woolen sock on the other foot did not bother me very much, my footwear would have seemed odd to anyone I met. But I encountered no one and soon came upon the crash site of a large airplane near the edge of the road. Close by was a solitary house. Something seemed to draw me to the wreckage and, when I saw no one nearby, I risked being reported to look more closely. There were no signs of bodies and the partly burned wreckage was in such small pieces that I could not positively identify the type of plane except that it had been large enough to have been "W" Willie. A charred piece of paper caught my eye and I picked it up. It was the corner of a navigation chart, perhaps even the one on which I had done calculations only a few hours ago. The nearness of this wreckage to the place where I had landed by parachute made me feel quite certain that this was all that remained of my bomber. When I had jumped we were so close to the ground that it was unlikely anyone had time to follow me. I was no doubt looking at the funeral pyre of my crew.

Before I left the area I asked a woman from the nearby farm, in my best high school French, if she could give me something to eat. Although she did not want to risk being seen giving me food, she volunteered the information that the Germans had already taken away the bodies of the bomber crew, including one who had jumped too late for his parachute to open, most likely Don Wilson. I had already lingered dangerously long near the crash site so I hastened back the way I had come to await nightfall at my hiding place in the wheat.

When darkness slowly settled on the countryside I walked down through the fields in a southerly direction. My intention was to cross the river to the left of the settlement, thereby avoiding the tower, which I still feared as an enemy outpost. I hoped to find a place where I could wade across, not only because I had never learned to swim properly but also because I did not wish to get all my clothing wet, even on such a warm night.

It was cloudless and the continuing full moon gave good visibility as I crossed the road that ran parallel to the river. Keeping the village off to my right, I arrived at the river bank. Other than distant sounds of truck traffic similar to those of the previous night, and the occasional barking of a restless dog in the village, all was quiet. I guessed that the sluggish river was forty feet wide and six feet deep near the middle. Turning towards the village I worked my way along the bank searching for a shallow place to ford. Luck was not with me and I was soon close to the backs of the houses clustered along the eastern side of the village. I decided to try my luck on the other, westerly, side. This meant that I would have to circle back around the northern limits of the hamlet. Turning my back on the river, I climbed fences and moved stealthily between houses on the eastern outskirts before I was finally walking along the western side road from the village. Becoming bolder by the minute, I stayed on the road until I came to an apple orchard on my left. I turned into it in an attempt to get down to the water. On the river side of the orchard I encountered wet, marshy ground. I did not fancy walking with wet feet so I made for a communal wall at the back of the houses on the western side of the main street, hoping that I would perhaps find a path leading down to the river bank. No such path existed and I did not want to scale the wall and get trapped in vegetable gardens among aroused watch dogs.

There was no doubt that my plans would have to be revised. Already I had wasted a considerable amount of the available hours of darkness in the short summer night and had made virtually no progress. In all the time I had been searching for a river crossing I had not seen or heard anyone moving on the roads in the area, nor had any motor vehicles passed in the vicinity. So I decided on the bold approach of quietly and slowly walking down the sleepy main street and across the bridge. I retraced my steps through the orchard to the side road, then back to the main road leading into the village and to the bridge. My "footwear" made no noise as, heart pounding, I inched my way down the narrow street into the heart of the village. I kept to the right-hand side where the shadows were darkest. Every few paces I stopped to listen for sounds that might signal danger. As I progressed, the houses and walls, built to the very edge of the road, formed a walled canyon with no doorways or niches in which to hide should danger threaten. My heart rose to my mouth and I stood stock still when, not far ahead, I heard water being pumped from a well behind a house. When all was quiet again I continued tiptoeing down the narrow street towards the bridge, beyond which was the far end of the village and the comparative safety of the open fields.

Suddenly I heard the sound of a truck approaching along the road behind me. There was no time for me to race back out of the village before it would be upon me ... I could only run forward. Silently I ran towards the stone bridge ahead, all the time scanning either side for a place to hide. I could see nothing as I came to the bridge with the truck close behind. Fortunately its headlights were only small slits of light, as required during wartime blackout. I dashed across the bridge, and on the left-hand side spotted an opening where I could duck down to the river between the nearest house and the abutment. I slipped into the gap and then into the shallow water at the edge. I hid under the bridge as the truck crossed overhead and came to a stop. Cautiously I eased myself out from underneath and peered around the edge of the bridge. In the bright moonlight I saw that an army truck with a trailer had stopped two houses up on the right-hand side. The driver shut off the motor, left his cab, and went around to talk to someone who had been standing in the shadow of the doorway. After a few minutes' conversation in a guttural language that I did not understand, the driver returned to his cab, started the engine, and drove off. I am quite sure that the two men were Germans and that if I had continued running along the street I would have stumbled into the man awaiting the arrival of the truck. I waited a few minutes, then left my hiding place under the bridge and waded eastward at the edge of the river where it lapped against the house. As soon as I was clear of it I climbed out of the stream, crossed some marshy ground, and headed south.

Now that I was in open country again, I considered it safe to walk along the road. It must have been well past midnight when I noticed that a railway ran parallel to the road. In the distance I could see the silhouettes of freight cars. Railways, with the possibility of Germans around them, made me nervous, so instead of continuing I struck off at an angle through the fields on my right. Soon I was at the side of a small forest which stretched south into the distance. I did not enter the trees but skirted the edge towards the right until I came to a road which disappeared into the forest. The night was well advanced, so it was time to find a hiding place, preferably well into the trees. I followed the road into the woods for about a quarter of a mile before leaving it for a path that crossed at right angles. I had chosen to turn left on the path and, unfortunately it led to the nearby edge of the forest. I backtracked, then lay down to sleep in some brush near the edge of the path.

When dawn was breaking, something disturbed me. I opened my eyes to see a fox trot by a few feet from me, then I slipped back into a sound sleep. A tremendously loud explosion woke me with a start. I was quite confused as to what was happening. The sun was well up, and overhead I heard the sound of airplane engines. Then from very close by, more loud explosions. I realized that a German antiaircraft battery must be hidden a few feet away in the trees and firing at the airplanes. Soon the noise of the aircraft engines faded and the heavy guns fell silent. Some stroke of luck must have caused me to turn onto the path the previous night just before I stumbled into the enemy battery hidden in the trees another hundred feet along the road.

I did not dare stay where I was for fear of discovery, but which way to go? If I continued south along the road I would walk right into the middle of the antiaircraft guns, and if I returned north along it I would be seen by the German soldiers. The path to the east would take me out into the open fields where I would be spotted. My only choice was to cross the road and head west along the trail into the denser woods.

I crept along to the edge of the road and looked to my left. About two hundred feet away I saw a German soldier pacing up and down. He was the first unmistakable enemy I had seen. I studied his movements for several minutes. My best plan would be to walk, not run, to the far side. Anyone running into the woods near an enemy gun position would be cause for suspicion. When the sentry was walking away from me, I stood up and sauntered nonchalantly across to the other side without looking towards him. I entered the wood fully expecting to hear a shout or the sound of a bullet fired at me, but nothing happened. When I was out of sight of the soldier without being challenged, I broke into a run. The woods were extensive and I ran or jogged for more than a mile before I felt safe.

It was now Thursday morning and the last meal I had eaten was on Tuesday night before leaving England. Although I had tried some of the concentrated food tablets from my escape kit, I was beginning to feel very hungry. Our training for evasion had taught us that the French were sympathetic towards downed Allied airmen. However, we had been warned never to compromise their safety by directly asking for food or assistance in a situation where they could be seen by prying eyes. The best method was to contact a farmer away from his house where he would not be observed talking to you by those who might favour the German cause. Of course the ideal would be to make contact with the French Resistance, who were actively fighting the German occupation by sabotaging their military installations and, on occasion, ambushing German troops. The Resistance at that time had networks of supplies and hideouts that were often used to smuggle downed airmen out of the country.

At one stage of my journey that day I tried out my evader's skills in asking for food. When I came to an isolated farmhouse, I concealed myself in the vegetable garden at the back. My patience paid off when eventually an old man came out of the house and passed close to my hiding place. I called out to him and asked if he had anything to eat. He was quite startled to find that a part of the war had reached even into his vegetable plot. He returned to the house and a few minutes later came back with half a loaf of bread and some cheese. He wished me good luck and I left. I was feeling more confident now, so I continued walking in daylight.

At dusk that evening the countryside was peaceful, without sight or sound of humans. While I was crossing a large field I heard a rifle shot from the woods behind me and then a noise like the buzz of an angry bee as a bullet whizzed by me. My first impulse was to drop flat on the ground. But I controlled myself, for I realized that if someone were watching me it would be a very guilty reaction. In fact the person who had fired the gun was perhaps testing me to see if I would do just that. I hesitated a second, then continued walking across the field without further incident.

During my travels through the country I frequently found pieces of "window," the long narrow strips of silver paper thrown from Allied bombers to confuse enemy radar. It gave me a feeling of comfort in this foreign land to see something that came from home, even if it was only bits of tin foil.

That night, Thursday, I was caught in a short, sudden, summer thunderstorm. Unable to find shelter, I was soon soaking wet. By dawn I was chilled and shivering in a field behind a large farm-house. I decided to try and make contact with someone from the farm during the day, so I searched for a hiding place near the house. Then if someone passed I would have a chance to call out. Behind the house were apple trees with low leafy branches. I climbed into one of these trees because the ground was too wet to lie on. Wedging myself in the crotch of a lower branch, I dozed off.

When the sun came up my clothes began to dry and I felt warmer. As I waited in the apple tree a middle- aged woman came from the house with a small dog running beside her. Her path took her close enough for me to call out to her; I said, in my best high school French that I was hungry and needed help, explaining that I was an Allied airman. She was surprised to hear a voice coming from an airman hidden in her apple tree and hesitated for a few minutes before refusing any assistance. Continuing on her way, she disappeared from view. There was always the possibility that she would alert the authorities and turn me in, so I waited only a few minutes before climbing down from my perch to continue another day's journey.

The surrounding countryside was peaceful and I decided that at the first opportunity I would again try for help, not only food but shelter as well. A prosperous looking farm in the distance, without neighbors, presented a good opportunity. I hid in the ditch beside the road which passed in front of the house, waiting patiently for someone to come by. Presently two girls in their twenties left the farm, walking in my direction. When they were abreast of me I startled them by calling out from the ditch. They were surprisingly friendly and, telling me to stay there for a few minutes, they hurried back to the farm.

I decided to wait for them to return; if their actions appeared suspicious or hostile when they came back, then I would take to my heels across the fields. Everything seemed normal when they returned a few minutes later and asked me to accompany them to the house. We entered the yard through a doorway in a high stone wall. I could see various stables and sheds as we crossed to the kitchen of the main building. Here I was greeted by the other members of this fine household and given my first real meal in more than two days.

Regrettably, I have forgotten how many people lived there, but I have the impression that there was more than one family unit. They told me that they would very much like to hide me until the end of the war but that it would be very risky. Their large farm had people continually coming and going, increasing the chances of my being spotted by an unsympathetic person. However, there was a family living close by who they knew would be honoured to shelter me; would I consider it? The house was small, they said, but no one ever went near it. I accepted the offer without hesitation.

After dark Marthe and Venette, from my prospective new home, came for me. It took only a few minutes to walk down a side road to their house. The single-storey dwelling was set back a short distance from the road. A path led from the road through a small parcel of lawn and garden to the front door. This whole area was enclosed by a hedge that blocked the view from the road, as well as access to the back. The door opened into a large kitchen-living section that stretched the full width of the front of the house. Windows in this room overlooked the gate and path. Behind this room, to the right, was a bedroom with a back window facing onto a plot of grass and a run-down vegetable garden. Shrubs enclosed this section on all three sides. Beyond were open fields and further still in the distance were some woods. These features were important to me because I had to know my escape routes in case of danger.

We had to be alert at all times. Should I be found by the Germans, all members of the household would be shot. We expected that the most likely threat to our safety would be German soldiers arriving at the front door. If this should happen the plan was that I would move into the rear bedroom and shut the door. If they did not leave immediately, I was to jump out the window, cross the garden, and head for the woods.

Four generations of the family were living in the grandparent's house, which I believe was somewhere between Senonches and Chateauneuf-en-Thimerais. There was the grandmother who, I presumed, was a widow, and her daughter, Madame Demusois. My generation was represented by Madame Demusois' daughter, Antoinette ("Venette") Rothiot, and daughter-in-law, Marthe (Demusois). The husbands of these three women were all in Germany working at forced labour. Last were the children, Venette's daughters, Jeanine and Simone, and son, "Bibi." The fourth child was Marthe's son, Jean-Claude. I guessed that the children's ages ranged from two to six years old and that the two mothers were in their twenties. They had only come to live there within the last year to escape the severe food rationing and shortages in Paris.

I lived in that tiny house with four adult women and four small children for the next three days, Saturday, Sunday, and Monday, July 8, 9, and 10. (I still chuckle when I tell people that I slept in the kitchen with grandmaman.) Food, a prime concern in occupied France, was not fancy, but there was enough that none of us went hungry. There was little or no meat but plenty of vegetables and dairy products, available no doubt because out-of-the-way farms were able to hide produce for themselves and their friends. "My family" was not farming the property and kept to the house except when Venette or Marthe set off on foot for food or other necessities.

None of "my family" spoke English and I was hard put to recall my high school French. However, in order to survive I learned quickly, helped by my new friends who were always excited when I used new words or spoke a sentence without error. Had I stayed with them a month, I am sure I would have become fluent.

The hot sunny days continued as we sat around and chatted or dozed in the sun at the back of the house where we were hidden from passersby. One day Venette or Marthe, I forget which one, produced a French pocket novel and asked if I could read it. With the words in front of me and the verbs in the proper conjugation, I was soon able to read the story aloud, and with a passable accent. This brought cries of delight and I had to repeat my performance in front of the others.

Apparently I was known to the small children as "Baton Jean" because I used to play some kind of a game with them using a stick. I have forgotten what the game was. Perhaps it was a modified game of baseball.

One day I heard a noise in front of the house, so I peeked out the window. To my horror two German soldiers were coming down the path to the front door. The prearranged plan was put into action and I ran into the back room, closed the door, and stood near the window, ready to dash for freedom. I overheard some kind of a discussion going on and then the sound of the door closing. Venette came back to tell me that everything was safe again – the off-duty intruders were looking for fresh eggs. The two women told them they had none in the house and the men left.

On at least two other occasions strangers came to the house and I retreated to the safety of the bedroom. When it had been established that the visitors were trustworthy Frenchmen I was invited out by "my family" and shown off with great pride. I had to tell the story of my escape from the crashing bomber which, after much repetition, I was able to repeat in fairly good French. "My family" and their friends never tired of hearing this story. Sometimes I had to go through the performance of reading aloud from a French novel. I felt very foolish on these occasions but my presence obviously meant a great deal to them.

I was embarrassed to be the centre of so much attention and to be considered some kind of a hero by these courageous people. I thought about the possible reasons for their "hero" worship. Since the invading Nazi armies had swept unchecked into France three years previously, the French had been subjected to German rules, regulations, and propaganda. Most of their able-bodied young men had been taken away to work at forced labour. They had few means at their disposal to stand up to their oppressors. But now the tide was turning and here, in their quiet part of the country, one of the hundreds of thousands of Allied soldiers fighting their hated foe had arrived unexpectedly. He had asked for their help so that he could get home and continue the fight against the enemies of France. They considered it an honour to help him.

They wanted to learn about the war from the other, the Allied, viewpoint. They wanted to hear my opinions of battles that had been fought and in what direction I thought new attacks or retreats would be made. They wanted to learn about various Allied leaders and what I knew about them. They knew that a month earlier the Allied armies had landed in France, about one hundred and fifty miles northwest of where I came down. I was afraid this attack would be similar to the Anzio beachhead, where the Allies had landed halfway up the Italian coast and months later were still contained there by the German armies. I was quite sure that our armies would break out of Normandy and advance into the heart of France, but I secretly thought that it might not happen for some months yet. However, I did not share this reservation with them.

At times my personal thoughts and feelings dominated. Perhaps I should have been more shocked by the probable deaths of my crew members, but we had been living in a world of sudden death for so long that we knew deep down inside that our turn to be killed could come at any moment. After all, bomber command statistics proved that, with an accepted casualty rate of four percent, the odds were against completing the required thirty trip tour of operations. I wondered what my companions had really been like. We used to think of ourselves as a great bomber crew, but outside of flying we knew very little about each other, and had seldom discussed our personal likes or dislikes before joining the air force. We didn't know each others' real interests, or perhaps even our own; we were all so young. Nor did we know each others' plans or goals for the future. When we were not involved in flying duties we were often together, but no one talked about after the war because we couldn't see the end of it. Instead we joked and kibitzed about flying, drinking, girls, and leave. I somehow think that if it had not been for the war we would not have chosen each other for close friends. Perhaps this is why I wasn't more upset when I realized they were dead. But I did do some serious thinking as to why I should have been the only one to live. I told myself it was just the luck of the draw: if we had been flying Lancaster bombers someone else would have gotten out instead of me, because in that aircraft the navigator did not sit above the escape hatch. In the meantime I had very immediate and pressing things to do if I were to continue to survive.

I kept wondering whether there were some way to let my family in Canada know that I was very much alive. I remember thinking, a few hours after the crash, that at base the squadron would soon realize that "W" Willie had gone down. Then the telegrams would be sent off to the next of kin. I wished I could have relieved my mother and father from the shock of knowing their second son was missing in action, so soon after their oldest son had been killed and on the very day that their third son was to report to the air force for air crew duties. I remembered that when my brother Robert was reported missing we had hoped he was able to parachute to safety. Our hopes were kept alive by well-meant letters from his squadron mates who said they had seen many parachutes during the raid. Then, agonizing months later, the word came that he was dead. Would my family think I was dead too, even though the telegram would say "Missing in Action?" I became obsessed with the idea of leaving a message to let them know I had at least survived the crash.

I still had many dangers to face in my attempt to get back to England. There seemed to be only two options open to me. The first, the easy one for me, was to lie around the farm and wait for the invading Allied armies to arrive. This would greatly endanger the lives and friends of the family sheltering me. The second plan was to rest for a few more days and then make a concerted effort to reach Spain. As it happened, events soon occurred that helped me with my decision.

On Sunday afternoon, July 9, a stranger came to the house so I went into hiding. I heard a prolonged discussion taking place in the front room before I was eventually asked to come out and join in. I was introduced to the visitor, an older man in civilian clothes. He was Colonel Lecointe and he was from the French Resistance. He explained that Mme. Guyot, the woman with the dog whom I had asked for help when I was hiding in the apple tree a few days previously, had thought that I was a German "plant" sent to trap sympathetic Frenchmen. After leaving me she reported the incident to the local French Resistance, who had decided that my story was most likely genuine. However, by the time Madam Guyot had come back to get me I had disappeared. Since then the Resistance had been trying desperately to locate me without arousing the suspicions of the local authorities or German supporters. For the last few days the Colonel himself had been discreetly scouring the area for me until his search had brought him to Mme. Demusois' house. Colonel Lecointe had had a most difficult time persuading "my family" that he was from the Resistance before they would finally admit that I was hiding in the next room.

The Colonel said he would make arrangements for me to travel to Paris, then south to a safe hiding place. There I would remain for awhile before flying back to England from a secret flying field. On Tuesday someone would come to take me to a safe house nearby. He or she would be a link in the Resistance chain where for security each member knew only the person above and the person below him.

The house was buzzing with excitement at the thought of my departure. The next day the Resistance produced a brown suit, a shirt but no tie, and a pair of snug brown shoes for me ... I was only too happy to discard my one flying boot and well worn sock! However, it was with some misgivings that I shed my now grubby but familiar battledress and donned the ill-fitting French civvies. I kept my dog tags as proof of my true identity as an escaping airman, should I be unlucky enough to get caught.

Not expecting to have need of my escape kit, I gave "my family" the remains of it. I thought that the French francs would be the most useful item and were small compensation for all that they had done and risked for me. I also gave them a piece of my parachute as a souvenir, keeping a piece for myself. They gave me photographs of themselves and we exchanged addresses. I hoped they would write to my parents when they were liberated in case I never returned home. They kept telling me about a large German ammunition dump in a nearby forest at Senonches that I should arrange to have bombed on my return to England. When I did not seem to fully comprehend, they wrote the details and location on a piece of paper which was then stitched into the shoulder pad of my suit. I promised to send them a message on the free French radio when I arrived safely in England.

On Monday night, July 10, the farm family who had directed me to Mme. Demusois' invited me back for a farewell dinner. I was pleasantly surprised and pleased at their kindness because I doubted, given the tough German food rationing, that they had much to spare for farewell dinners. After dark Venette, Marthe, and I walked over to their large farm. It was a truly sumptuous feast when thirteen of us sat down to what was probably the best meal I had eaten since leaving Canada more than a year before. There were innumerable courses of soup, fowl, and meat, accompanied by various side dishes. Dessert consisted of strawberries and cream, something I had never eaten in England. All of this was in my honour, and yet I could hardly carry on a prolonged conversation in French with my friends. They had even seated a girl about my age beside me, but unfortunately she came from Belgium and I had great difficulty understanding her accent. Champagne was served and various toasts were drunk before the party broke up. Should the unforeseeable have happened and the Germans stumbled upon us, I am sure they would have been stunned to find the conquered French wining and dining an Allied airman under their very noses.

CHAPTER THREE

The Resistance

About 9:00 A.M. Tuesday, July 11, two "farmers" arrived on bicycles, with an extra one for me. Emotional farewells were said to all the "family" and the three of us set off. My instructions from the two Resistance men were simple. They would lead the way by riding a short distance ahead. If they stopped, I was to immediately turn around and casually pedal back to Mme. Demusois's farm. They assured me that there was little to worry about as we would only be travelling about six or eight kilometers along back roads.

Nevertheless I was very nervous as soon as I left the safety of the farmhouse. However, nothing untoward happened during the short ride. I followed right behind when the two from the underground finally wheeled their bicycles into a farmyard facing a house, various outbuildings, and a barn. We rode to the barn. When one of the two "farmers" opened the door, I found myself face-to-face with three disreputable looking men in poorly fitting clothes. We carefully studied each other for a few tense moments until recognition dawned. Then we started laughing and hugging each other because the men were none other than Pat Scullion, Stan Hetherington, and Léo Grenon, members of a bomber from my squadron. Their plane, I learned, had been shot down the same night as mine, in the same area. What a surprise and what stories we had to tell! They were not sure what had happened to the rest of their crew, but thought perhaps one other member had jumped. When they baled out of their crashing bomber they had landed far apart. Consequently each had different adventures before making contact with the Resistance.

After wandering around France alone, then living among those who did not speak my language, it was like heaven to be able to converse effortlessly in English. We were able to share our feelings of being alone and hunted in a foreign land. I had wondered if our bomber was the only one shot down that night, but I learned that the Luftwaffe had been very busy. We compared notes and ideas on how best to evade capture and return to England. Should we trust the Resistance to get us back home? Were their plans plausible or should we strike off on our own? The only interruption to our discussions and planning was at midday when food was brought to us in the barn.

That afternoon I reflected on my good fortune so far in evading capture. However, I realized that I could still end up in German hands if my luck ran out. Should this happen my captors would find the names, photographs and addresses of my French "family" that I carried with me, as well as the piece of parachute. I did not want any harm to come to my benefactors, so I reluctantly destroyed my tangible links to them; besides, I felt that after the war we would somehow be able to contact one another. I kept only my good luck piece of parachute. I was extremely worried about the scrap of paper on which was written the damaging information describing the location of the German ammunition dump. My "family" had told me that they had sewn it into the shoulder-padding of my jacket. If it were found, I could be accused of spying and shot. I carefully probed inside the lining of each shoulder but I could find nothing. Then I tried squeezing the material in my hands, hoping that I could hear it crumple or feel its outline. Over and over again I searched for the incriminating paper without success – the message seemed to have disappeared.

I noticed that Pat was wearing a pair of low, black, fleece-lined shoes. I recognized them for what they really were ... the lower part of a pair of the latest RCAF flying boots. This new style differed from the older issue in that below the ankles the black boots were stitched and shaped to look exactly like civilian shoes. If one was unlucky enough to parachute into enemy territory, as we had, they provided an excellent set of footwear when the uppers were cut away. A knife was provided for that purpose in a pocket on one boot. I thought it would be quite a lark to arrive back in England wearing a pair of these shoes, so after some hard bargaining I was able to swap my snug brown ones for this special escaper's footwear. My new shoes had a removable inner sole under which I hid my souvenir piece of parachute. I now felt satisfied that I was better prepared for whatever might come next.

When darkness set in our host invited us to the main house for dinner. It was an excellent meal, accompanied by champagne toasts all around. A special toast honoured the nineteenth birthday of one of the Canadians. During the course of the conversation our hosts casually told me that as late as that morning I had been suspected of being a spy. My enthusiastic reception and identification by my compatriots had convinced them otherwise and saved my life. This was indeed a sobering thought. It was announced that arrangements had been completed for us to drive to Paris the next day. There we would be hidden until we were moved south to an airfield for the clandestine flight back to England.

Later that night, in the seclusion of the barn, the four of us discussed the merits of the plans for our return home. We had begun to live one day at a time – because we were so few among so many, and so much could go wrong, we tried not to look too far into the future. It seemed that our only other option to the risky journey to Paris was to strike out on our own again. After weighing the pros and cons, we decided to commit ourselves to the care of the underground.

Early the next morning, Wednesday, a man driving a large four-door automobile arrived at the farm accompanied by a redheaded woman. We had breakfast in the farm kitchen before we four escapers entered the car with the driver and his lady friend. I was filled with mixed emotions: fear of capture, but also excitement at the idea of seeing Paris, some one hundred miles to the east.

We Canadians sat in the back, immersed in our own fantasies of what could happen that day. Paris was reputed to be teeming with Germans. I wondered whether we would be able to stay hidden among so many of our enemies. I wondered if we would be stopped at a roadblock or in the busy city itself. We carried no forged identity papers, none of us spoke German, and only Léo spoke French fluently. Were we not taking one hell of a risk leaving the safety of isolated farm country? In the front seat, the two people from the Resistance seemed very unconcerned as they carried on a desultory conversation in French. They showed no sign of understanding English, or of being distracted by our chatter in the back.

We travelled along isolated farm roads before turning onto the main highway through Dreux and Versailles to Paris. The prewar highway was only wide enough for one lane of traffic in each direction. My eyes almost popped out of my head when I realized that the narrow highway was crowded with German military vehicles. The road was almost devoid of civilian traffic, which made our car all the more conspicuous.

Judging by the number of antiaircraft guns with crews at the ready that were hidden under the trees or camouflage nets, the Germans were expecting to be attacked at any moment by Allied aircraft. In fact most of the military vehicles had pulled off the road to hide from strafing fighters. Any trucks which were moving had soldiers clinging to the front mudguards and standing on the truck platform at the back. These men were the lookouts for hostile planes. Until that time I had forgotten that we four Canadians ran a very real risk of being killed by our own aircraft.

As we drove east I saw the dreaded German Tiger tanks for the first time. I saw the black uniforms of the Panzer corps, the grey-green of the Wehrmacht, and the light blue of the Luftwaffe. These were all front-line, battle-ready troops. I was so enthralled with what I was witnessing that I almost forgot that we were outnumbered a thousand to one by our enemies. So far I had not been in close enough contact with any Germans to know what they looked like. Now I saw that they were of various heights, builds, and complexions, differing in appearance from our fighting men only because of the uniforms they wore. Certainly they were not tall, blond supermen as Nazi propaganda would have had us believe. I could see them only a few feet away, watching us indifferently as we drove by. Their lack of interest in us quelled some of my fears of discovery.

Loaded with troops, munitions and supplies, the vehicles were headed towards the battle for France now taking place in the west. I am sure the others were thinking, as I was, about the stories we would have to tell when we got home. Would anyone believe me when I told them that four Allied airmen had casually driven along the main road to Paris when it was crowded with enemy troops without ever having been stopped and detained?

Abruptly our incredible journey was halted when a German military policeman standing in the middle of the road signaled us to stop. My heart stood still for I thought we were caught. I wondered what we could do when they searched our car and asked for our papers. However, I breathed a sigh of relief when I realized that the policeman was merely preventing us from continuing on into a bombed section of road. Courteously, he directed us through the field around the damaged highway. Soon we were entering a more urban area. I watched as we drove through Versailles on the western outskirts of Paris and looked in vain for a glimpse of the famous palace. We entered the city and shortly afterwards arrived at our destination, a house in what I judged to be an upper-class residential suburb.

Our car drew up at our new refuge, a vacant three-storey home set in spacious walled grounds. Our Resistance companions walked to the front door, unlocked it, and told us to make ourselves at home. They cautioned us not to be seen at the windows and not to leave the house because to a casual passer-by the premises must appear to be uninhabited. I imagined that the owners had abandoned their home in haste, since it was still partly furnished and there were many personal effects lying around. I remember leafing through a snapshot album of family members at the seaside in happier times. I wondered who the owners were, where they were now, if they were still alive, and whether they would ever be back. Thank God my native land had not been invaded by foreigners, our homes entered and private effects tossed about while our families were imprisoned or scattered to the four winds. At the time it did not occur to me that I myself was invading someone's private domain.

The next day a new link of the Resistance arrived. He spoke fluent English and confirmed that we were to move out of the city in a day or two to a secure country hideout. Then, when the RAF could make a small plane available, we would be flown home from a secret airfield. In the meantime the underground was concerned that, should our present location be discovered, all four of us would be captured in one fell swoop. They thought it would be better to take at least one of us to another secure house and that the transfer should be done at once. I volunteered to go since Léo, Stan, and Pat were all from the same crew.

I left immediately with this new helper. He drove while I enjoyed seeing the sights of Paris. After a mile or two we came to a run-down area of working-class housing and small shops. My driver parked the car and then led the way through an archway into the inner courtyard of a three storey building. People were continually passing back and forth from the courtyard to the street.

I missed the company of my fellow escapers and felt very vulnerable again. I dreaded being stopped and asked a question in French. How would I reply without giving myself away? The place seemed so public – how could someone like me, who obviously did not belong, hope to remain hidden from curious and prying eyes? Perhaps the secret of success was the very boldness of the idea. So I told myself that no one would ever think that an escaping airman would brazenly dare to live in such close contact with the public.

I followed my contact across the courtyard, through a doorway, then up a flight of stairs to a sparsely furnished second-storey room. A single window looked down onto the courtyard. This was to be my secure hiding place. My companion told me to keep the door locked at all times and to open it only when I heard the secret knock he then proceeded to demonstrate. I was to stay confined to the room at all times except when I had to use the communal toilet located at the head of the stairs we had just climbed. He would bring me food during the day, he said, and left.

The oppressive heat of the last week was still continuing so that my throat was parched and I longed for a glass of cold water. The tiny washroom didn't have a tap and there was nowhere that I could get a drink without risk of showing myself. I passed the time looking out the window, watching children at play and adults coming and going. The building seemed to contain mainly single rooms or pairs of rooms for working-class people. Finally, when I thought I was going to die of thirst, I heard the secret knock on the door. I opened it to find my contact with a bottle of warm red wine and half a loaf of bread. He stayed only a moment, saying that he would be back the next day. I drank the wine, which only partly slaked my thirst. I would have preferred a long, cold drink of fresh Canadian water.

The next day was July 14, Bastille Day, France's national holiday. My contact arrived in the morning with more warm red wine and the news that I would be on my way with the others late that day as planned. I may have imagined it, but to me the people passing through the courtyard seemed to be a little more cheerful on their national day. Several times in the distance I distinctly heard singing and shouting as though celebrations were taking place.

Late in the afternoon came the series of secret taps on the door. My same guide was there and I was happy to quit my latest hideout. An automobile with my three fellow escapers, was waiting for me at the curb. My guide climbed in the front seat beside a civilian driver as I squeezed in the back with my air force friends. We said little to each other as we started across the city on the way to the next stop that we believed would bring us much closer to home.

I enjoyed the sights of Paris as we drove through the streets without incident. Our route took us around the Arc de triomphe, which I recognized, then down a major thoroughfare and right onto another wide street. Looking ahead I had the impression that we were entering a canyon because on either side the tall buildings joined each other and touched the sidewalks. My heart skipped a few beats when I realized that there were more German uniforms in the street than I had yet seen in Paris. Midway down on the left side were fully armed sentries. Perhaps the enemy was preparing to carry out a snap search and identification check. If this was true we were in terrible danger. Our driver seemed to have great presence of mind because just before reaching the sentries he swung the car ninety degrees to the left through an archway. I was instantly impressed by this clever manoeuvre which seemed designed to evade the sentries and soldiers. But then to my shock I realized that the enclosed courtyard was filled with German soldiers and military vehicles.

Bigger surprises were in store when our driver slammed on the brakes; then he and his companion dived out of the car, one on each side, pointed ugly revolvers at us and shouted in English, "Hands up!" The whole event, which happened in a matter of seconds, was like a B-grade movie. I was so shocked by our erstwhile helpers that it was several moments before it hit me that we were in Gestapo headquarters and that these last two Resistance members must be Gestapo agents.

Although we were undoubtedly frightened at ending up in Gestapo hands, I distinctly remember feeling rather flattered by the size of their guns and the fear of us that the two Gestapo agents showed. This in spite of the fact that we were unarmed and out-numbered ten to one. They carefully shepherded us through a doorway and up the stairs to a third floor office where two of their senior officers awaited us.

Before they holstered their revolvers, we were checked for arms and carefully searched. I was extremely relieved that I had had the forethought to destroy the photos, names, and addresses of my French "family." My lucky piece of parachute was not discovered in its hiding place in my shoe. However, my watch was confiscated. We were allowed only to keep our dog tags.

Our interrogation was carried out in fluent English. Each of us in turn was asked for our name, rank, serial number, place of birth, and squadron number. I was the last to be questioned and when my turn came I gave the interrogator my name, rank, and serial number only. I then boldly reminded him that by the rules of the Geneva Convention governing the treatment of prisoners of war I was not obliged to give him any more information. The Gestapo agent standing next to me reacted quickly to my little speech by hitting me across the face; he followed this with the snarled threat, "It does not matter anyway, you will all be shot within the week."

We were then escorted down to the courtyard where we joined a group of civilians who had been arrested, possibly due to their Bastille Day activities. We airmen were ordered into an enclosed truck that stood near-by. Once inside we were locked into tiny individual cubicles, much like broom closets, which were along each side. The centre corridor was packed with the less "dangerous" civilian prisoners before the rear door was locked. The driver started his engine and the truck moved off.

There was total darkness in our cubicles and consequently we could not see where we were being driven. Perhaps an hour later the truck came to a stop. The prisoners standing in the truck corridor were unloaded first and marched away. Then the doors to the compartments were unlocked one by one. I climbed down to join my air force companions and other men who had also been given special attention. We were in the courtyard of what appeared to be a penitentiary, with armed sentries patrolling the walls towering above us. Around us were massive prison buildings with heavily barred windows. We were soon to learn that we were now in the famous Fresnes prison.

The guards assigned to escort us to cells in the heart of the prison were German soldiers. I was most impressed by the number of steel doors that had to be unlocked before we could pass through, as well as by the number of sentries positioned at key stations. The four of us were locked up with one of the civilian prisoners. From the single barred window we looked across a courtyard to more prison blocks and the exterior high walls with their watch towers and patrolling sentries. I thought to myself that it must be next to impossible to escape from this place.

CHAPTER FOUR

Fresnes

As soon as the guards left us alone in the cell with the civilian, we Canadians tried to sort out where the "rot" had set in with the underground. I was upset, of course, that we had been so easily deceived. I agreed with the others that perhaps the driver with his redheaded girlfriend had been the first weak link. Stan, Pat, and Léo said they now believed that all those who had supposedly helped us in Paris were traitors. They had come to this conclusion because, after I had left, one of the "Resistance" members had come by to ask them a few questions about their home country. He had written on a piece of paper that they were Canadians and had spelled Canada with a "K." The use of a "K" instead of a "C" should have tipped them off that perhaps the man was of German origin. One point on which we all agreed was that, given a second chance, we would accept food and shelter from any local person for only a few days. Then, no matter how friendly and trusting they seemed, we would leave suddenly without good-byes to strike off on our own again.

The fifth inmate of our cell spoke English but was reluctant to volunteer much information about himself. I suspected that this was because he was from the Resistance and had learned to trust absolutely no one if he was to survive. He did tell us that he had been held in Fresnes for some time as a Gestapo prisoner and was being questioned daily. He said he expected to be shot. This piece of information, given to us unemotionally, did not help to allay our fears in view of the threat the Gestapo had made to me at their headquarters.

From what I saw during my visit with the Gestapo, it appeared that they had commandeered a large group of office buildings in central Paris for their headquarters. Because the premises were not constructed to hold prisoners, only those undergoing intensive interrogation were held there overnight. Otherwise the suspects were imprisoned in Fresnes and brought in daily as required. The fact that we were in Fresnes did not necessarily mean that they were finished with us.

Although I did not know it at the time, Fresnes was one of the largest and most famous prisons in Paris. The huge complex of buildings, located in a suburb, had been taken over by the German occupation forces and was operated by their military personnel when I arrived there on July 14, 1944.

The morning after our arrival, after our civilian had been taken away for his daily interrogation, I took stock of our surroundings. We had not walked very far from the reception courtyard before reaching this cell the previous night so I guessed that we were confined somewhere near the front of the penitentiary. The sole window in our cell had heavy steel bars set in the main frame with hinged glass windows on the inside. We kept these open so that we could listen to other prisoners shouting messages and news back and forth.

Only a few of the shouted messages were in English, with the majority in French. Surprisingly, Léo, our French Canadian from Chateauguay, had great difficulty with the Parisian accents. We learned that most of the prisoners were French civilians held principally for sabotage and other crimes against the occupation forces. There were, however, a few British, American, and Canadian flyers. We made our contributions to the limited pool of knowledge that was circulated, but had to be careful not to be caught yelling out the window. The first time we were caught, a guard had rushed into the cell making threatening gestures and yelling that it was *streng verboten* to do this.

As airmen flying over enemy territory, we realized that there was always a high risk that, we would be shot down and captured. With this in mind our instructors had explained that, by the rules of the Geneva Convention, captured enemy military personnel could be confined in a civilian jail for only two or three days. The German system was that air force prisoners were handled by the Luftwaffe, navy by the Kriegsmarine, and army by the Wehrmacht. During the day I discussed with the others what we thought it would be like when we were transferred to the Luftwaffe interrogation centre and then to a prisoner of war (POW) camp. From all accounts, being a POW was not too bad; you were among friends, you could send and receive letters and parcels from home, and you were on the same food rations as the garrison troops. If the Gestapo no longer wished to question us, then we should soon be on our way.

Our civilian cell mate again left for Gestapo headquarters on the morning of our second full day, July 16. Then we four airmen were taken under heavy guard, through many doors which were unlocked for our passage, to a large room in the prison interior. I guessed that in normal times it was used as some sort of a high security court room. Seated behind tables at the front were German clerical staff sorting through papers. At the back were individual small cubicles into which we were locked. In due course I was brought forward to have my name, rank, and serial number checked off a list. These were the only questions which I was asked. Perhaps this meant that I would now be recognized as a POW so that the Red Cross and my family would be notified that I was alive. I hoped this would happen before someone reported to the Allies that all the crew of my bomber had been killed.

Then I was marched away under guard. My escort and the many sentries we passed were all in German army uniform and appeared to be older men, perhaps no longer fit for front-line duty. They wore revolvers, and it was clear there was nowhere I could run to escape. As we passed down countless corridors, with sentries unlocking steel doors for our passage, my spirits could not help but flag. It seemed as though I was being taken to a very secure back part of the penitentiary complex.

In due course I arrived in the wing which was to be my "home" for what I believed would be only a few days. In front of me rose five tiers of cells on each side of a central open space. Balconies, which ran in front of the cells at each level, were joined at intervals by short connecting bridges to those on the opposite side. At each end of the building, stairways provided access to the balconies.

All of these were fitted with high wire mesh sides to prevent potential suicides from jumping to the floor far below. Having never been incarcerated in my life, I found this an intimidating sight indeed.

With my guards I climbed the narrow stairs to the third level. A heavy steel door was swung open and I was motioned into my new "residence." The door clanged shut behind me and the key grated in the lock. I was alone in a six-by-fifteen-foot cell with dead white walls and ceiling. At the far end, the outline of vertical steel bars could be seen against the double frosted glass windows which were hinged on each side to open inwards. These were nailed shut. The steel door through which I had come contained a one-way spy hole and a small trap door through which food could be passed.

The sparse furnishings consisted of a bed, chair and table which were all securely bolted to the wall or chained to the floor. This was no doubt so that I could not express my displeasure by throwing one of these objects at the guard or relieve the tedium of a long confinement by rearranging the furniture. In the corner was a flush toilet. A shallow saucepan and a spoon which I used at meal times were the only movable items in the cell. The exposed light bulb in the ceiling was operated from outside the door.

I couldn't stand the stuffiness of the cell, so it didn't take me long to decide that the opaque glass French windows should be opened to let in the fresh summer air and allow me a view of the outside world. Furthermore, I could keep in touch with the other prisoners by calling back and forth. On close examination I found that one flat-headed nail was holding both windows shut. If the wood surrounding it could be loosened, then perhaps it could be extracted. I searched my cell to see if I could find anything sharp that could be used for this purpose. To my surprise, I found a rusty nail lying on the floor in a corner, which for some reason had been overlooked by the Germans. I used it as a primitive chisel to pick away the wood around the flat headed nail. Unfortunately for me, the sentry chose to look in through the spy hole while I was working. He quickly unlocked the steel door and entered, shouting at me that what I was doing was *verboten*. After he left, I made certain he was no longer watching, then compromised by picking a small hole in the wood at the lower corner of one pane. When finished, it was not noticeable to a casual glance.

With my eye pressed tightly against this tiny aperture I could see a minute segment of the outside world. As time went on how wonderful that view turned out to be! I could see over the nearby prison wall into a quiet residential street. It was almost as though I was looking onto the stage of a theatre where I sometimes saw normal people walking by and children playing in the street. I could see if the sun shone or if the cleansing rain fell, things which were becoming more difficult to believe in while alone in the harsh confines of Fresnes prison.

I had always been bothered that I had been unable to find the slip of paper in my jacket lining that contained information about the German ammunition dump. I had a nagging suspicion that it was still somewhere in the padding, even though it had eluded both my careful search in the semidarkness of the barn and that of the Gestapo at their headquarters. To put my mind at rest once and for all, I decided to do one final, painstaking check. Poking around methodically I examined the stuffing of the padding bit by bit. In what seemed only a matter of a few minutes I uncovered it. I felt sick. I immediately shredded the incriminating paper and flushed it down the toilet to be rid of it forever. I just couldn't believe the Gestapo experts had missed it! I could not help feeling that – Whoever – or Whatever – was in charge of my destiny was continuing to favour me.

When darkness came, the grubby straw mattress on the bed did not look too appealing. Nevertheless I decided that I would be more comfortable sleeping there than on the floor or the bare bedsprings. I was too naive to appreciate the hazards of this decision or I would have avoided it like a plague. Prison mattresses were invariably the home of fleas and other vermin. I was lucky because this one was not too badly infested and I do not remember suffering greatly from bites.

There was seldom any variation in the near starvation food ration. Each day started with a saucepan of warm, unsweetened, clear brown liquid that I was later to learn was called acorn coffee. At midday there was a watery soup with a one-eighth inch thick slice of black bread. If there was meat in the soup, it was not discernible either by smell or taste. The final "meal" of the day was another saucepan of acorn coffee. The food was prepared in a central kitchen, then taken around in large wooden barrels on trolleys. These trolleys had small steel wheels which ran on tracks set in the floors of the corridors and balconies. I knew well in advance when food was coming by the approaching clanking sounds. I would wait impatiently for the sounds to come closer and then suddenly my cell door would open to herald the arrival of the biggest event of the day.

During my stay in Fresnes I never enjoyed the luxury of a wash or a change of clothing. Toilet paper was a daily ration of one small sheet of printed paper torn from a book. Before using it I read each page in the vain hope that it might form part of a continuous story, but the pages were never from the same book. This was the only reading material I ever saw.

More than once during my first week I thought I heard rifle shots and on other occasions what sounded like yelling or screaming. It occurred to me that perhaps the Gestapo were working over some of their prisoners. However, my first and second weeks in prison passed slowly by without the Gestapo coming for me. I began to think the threat that I would be "shot within the week" was perhaps not going to be made good, although I wondered why I had not been turned over to the Luftwaffe.

I tried exercising to keep in shape, but it seemed futile. Four paces up, turn, four paces back, turn, repeat over, and over, and over again. How long could I keep this up without going out of my mind? Besides, the more I exercised, the hungrier I became.

There was never enough food to satisfy my hunger and each time I longed in vain for second helpings. Shortly after my arrival a piece of a cheese-like substance that smelled like rotting fish was delivered with my noon meal. It looked so putrid and stank so vilely that I quickly flushed it down the toilet before it could stink up my cell. A few weeks later another piece was handed in with my midday meal. By then I was always so hungry that I managed to eat all of it.

I fell into the habit of dreaming and reliving the past few years of my life ... the excitement of winning my wings at Portage la Prairie, embarkation leave in Montreal in June with my new pilot officer's uniform to swagger around in, farewells to family and friends and the train ride to Halifax, blackouts for the first time, midnight sailing on the *Louis Pasteur* with mysterious vessels and searchlights all around us, arrival on the Clyde, and disembarkation at Gourock in a country really at war with all the rationing, shortages, blackouts, and constant threats of attack from the enemy. Such adventures for a young man of twenty!

Periodically during the day I would hear the scraping noise at the door made by the sentry peering in the peephole on his routine check. Often at night I would awaken to find the light full on and the same noise at the door. Sometimes the guard would warily enter the cell, keeping a good distance from me, to check that I had not sawn through the window bars or cut a hole through the wall in an escape attempt. It gave me great satisfaction to see how nervous and scared of me he seemed. It was not as though I was wearing an intimidating enemy uniform ... only my crumpled civilian suit. Had he been told that I was a saboteur, spy, or other sort of dangerous prisoner? Perhaps the Germans also watched thriller movies in which the hero jumps the villain guarding him and makes good his escape against horrendous odds. In my situation, the odds against an escape were indeed horrendous.

Because my watch had been confiscated by the Gestapo I could not keep accurate track of the time. I had difficulty becoming accustomed to this after my time-bound military training, especially since in air navigation time is measured to the nearest second. I never saw a clock while in Fresnes, nor did any bells or chimes signal the hour of the day. My sole means of measuring the passage of time was by the rising and setting of the sun. I quickly learned that under prolonged imprisonment it was important to keep track at least of the days. As prisoners have done since time immemorial, I scratched on the wall beside my table, one line for each day completed.

It soon became apparent to me that although I was not locked in a dark, dank dungeon I was nevertheless in solitary confinement. I had absolutely no contact with the outside world. I had no one I could talk to, no radio, no newspapers or books to read. I was not free to look out an open window to see the world beyond the prison. I could not write letters or receive mail. The German guards could not speak English and in any case I'm sure they had been forbidden to speak to me other than to give orders. I had no playing cards or other such things with which to occupy myself. In other words, I had nothing with which to stimulate my mind during the long hours of the day. I was extremely frustrated at not knowing how the war was progressing and whether I would be freed in days or years. I could not understand why I was not moved to a proper POW camp among my own people. I felt as though I had been hidden away from the sight of other human beings and my existence forgotten.

I could only daydream for so long at a time. I had to keep busy in other ways. I decided I would invent games and puzzles to occupy myself in the hope that the hours would pass more quickly. One of my first pastimes was to try and remember all the popular songs I knew. Each time I thought of a tune, on the chance that I would be overheard, I whistled it as loudly as I could to give the impression that I was still in good spirits. Over the course of many days, I whistled more than 165 popular songs before my memory let me down.

Another time consumer was a game which required pencil and paper, neither of which I possessed. I had already discovered that I could make legible marks on the white walls with the end of my spoon. These could be erased by wetting and rubbing with the sleeve of my shirt. The object of my game was to make a square box with three horizontal and three vertical rows containing the numbers from one to nine, using each number only once. Each vertical, horizontal, and main diagonal row had to add to the same total. After successfully solving this puzzle, I then tried it with four, five, and six rows of numbers until I became bogged down with cumbersome arithmetical sums. But more hours and days had gone by.

Then I returned to my memory exercises ... quoting poems that I liked, passages from the Bible, and even Latin translations from high school days. I also tried to think ahead to events that might happen and create the scenarios that would occur. When I arrived home, would my family know I was coming? Perhaps I could surprise them by casually walking into the house when they weren't expecting me. If I was given the opportunity to go to university, what course of study would I follow? Engineering? Medicine? Law? Without sketches or drawings I could close my eyes and plan the complete layout of a dream house or how I would remodel an existing one with which I was familiar. I passed many hours in this manner and would come back to the harsh reality of the real world with a start to find that a morning or an afternoon had flown by. Perhaps this mindless daydreaming was a bad habit to get into, but it certainly helped save my sanity.

Sometimes I would think about beautiful England, the good times and the bad. There were so many good times that it seemed unfair to have to fly, because flying brought the bad times. Flying was great fun ... after you had landed safely. I was never comfortable before a flight because I could not help but think of what could go wrong, even on a training flight. I thought of the dreary Advanced Flying School in Millom, Cumberland. Soon after I arrived the ground staff had casually mentioned that hardly a week went by without the loss of one or more training planes! And what about Operational Training School at Gamston, the night Cameron's crew crashlanded at the edge of the runway when the engines stopped – all because the bomb-aimer had accidentally turned off the fuel! And the time another plane overshot the runway and crashed into a sunken roadway because the brakes were not working, fortunately with no loss of life. And the night the fog moved in early over our base when we were low on fuel and we couldn't pick up the beam to guide us down. Even the co left the comfort of the mess that night as he made a special trip to the control tower to take command. Fire trucks and ambulances were ordered to stand by, fortunately unnecessarily. And what about McKinnon's crew flying Halifaxes at Conversion Unit in Topcliffe. They were flying that day while we practiced on ground radar sets. No one knows why their plane climbed a hundred feet into the air and then crashed to the ground near the hangar in which we were working, killing all the crew. And we hadn't even started ops yet!

After I had been in the solitary confinement of my cell for about three weeks, my morale was at a very low ebb. By the time the midday bowl of soup and slice of bread were delivered I was feeling desperate. When I finished it I seemed to be hungrier than ever, yet I now had another twenty-four hours to wait for the next "real" meal. The situation seemed so hopeless that I broke down for a minute and cried, "Oh God, I am so hungry still, what am I going to do?" A few minutes later I heard the soup trolley returning towards my cell. The door opened and for the first and only time that I was in Fresnes I was given a second helping of soup. At the time I really believed that Someone up there heard my plea.

Twice during my month's sojourn at Fresnes I was taken outside to an area adjacent to my cell block where there was a row of individual exercise pens. Alone and confined by high stone walls, I was supposed to walk around and around in circles while I renewed my faith in life and human compassion as heavily armed soldiers watched my every step. I felt like a caged animal. About a dozen prisoners at a time participated in these short walks. We were kept well apart as we were hurried out from our cells and were given no opportunity to speak to one another.

I found it very strange that I continued to be held in Fresnes. Perhaps it was because I had been captured in civvies by the Gestapo, who observed few rules of the Geneva Convention and therefore did not consider me a bona fide POW in spite of my dog tags. I was their prisoner until they decided to shoot me or hand me over to the proper military command. I was confident that if the Luftwaffe had known about my plight they would have insisted that I be immediately released to their custody.

Early in August the occasional distant explosions that I had been hearing, and wondering about, seemed to become more frequent and closer. Then I heard, muffled through the closed windows, someone from another building shouting about Allied troops. A noticeable change occurred in the daily routine of the prison. There seemed to be more activity on the part of the guards – orders were shouted, cell doors opened and closed. This made me think that perhaps prisoners were being moved about.

My morale began to rise perceptibly when I realized that the explosions were probably Allied long-range artillery fire. Or it could have been retreating German troops blowing up important facilities which they did not want to have fall into Allied hands. Our troops were no doubt approaching Paris.

I began to worry that perhaps the Germans had not notified the Red Cross that I was alive. There was a strong possibility that I would be moved to Germany with the retreating forces. I assumed my family in Canada had been informed that I was "Missing in Action." I imagined their delight and confusion were they to receive a letter from my French "family" indicating that I was alive and on my way back to England. However, because no official confirmation would follow, leaving word as to my whereabouts became very important to me. In the hope that when Paris fell the Allies would search all the prisons for traces of missing

Allied military personnel, I decided to leave a message on my cell wall. With the end of my spoon I scratched the following message:

F/O John D. Harvie
J 27573
R.C.A.F
Prisoner here
July 14/44 – Aug. 10/44
God Save the King!
Long Live the Allies!
Oh to be in Canada!

I added the last sentence of the inscription because I was desperately homesick and tired of the war.

Two days later I was moved to a cell in a block near the front of the prison. There Pat, Stan, Léo, and I were reunited. My friends had also been through solitary confinement similar to mine. What a reunion! What excitement! People to talk to! We didn't sleep a wink that night as we talked, and talked, and talked with the pure joy of companionship. The windows of this cell were not nailed shut so we kept them open all the time to get fresh air and keep up with the news. The good news according to the shouted grapevine was that the Allied troops were nearing Paris and were on the verge of surrounding it. The bad news was that the Germans were planning to leave with all their prisoners.

Apparently there were more Allied airmen in Fresnes than I had surmised. The big question was, did the enemy have sufficient troops and transportation to move us east to Germany? If not, surely they would not allow us to be freed to continue the fight against them. Perhaps the Gestapo would give orders that we all be shot? This speculation went on endlessly.

Late in the afternoon of August 15 we were herded down to the large outer courtyard, just inside the main prison gates. Here hundreds of prisoners were being assembled under the watchful eyes and machine guns of sentries. The new soldiers now in charge were wearing a slightly different army uniform. Their actions were more threatening, so I studied them closely. They wore the forked lightening symbols on their collars, the insignia of the fanatical SS troops. These men were young, fit, front-line troops, sentries of whom to be wary, soldiers who would shoot first and ask questions later. They were not at all like the elderly soldiers of the Fresnes garrison.

As we waited in the hot sun a group of female prisoners were brought into the courtyard and lined up separately. They were pushed and shoved indiscriminately by the male guards. To my horror one of these girls appeared to be in the late stages of pregnancy. When she was given no favourable treatment by the Germans because of her condition, she had to be helped by her friends. In due course commands were shouted and we were packed into the back of waiting covered trucks. The ss troops piled into other vehicles and surrounded us to form a convoy. The massive gates of Fresnes prison swung open and we started off for an unknown destination. I wondered where we were going and how many days it would take. In the distance I could hear the noise of battle as the Allied armies moved to encircle Paris.

CHAPTER FIVE

Eastward by Boxcar

The convoy drove briskly through the streets of Paris. As the forbidding walls of Fresnes faded into the background, I fervently hoped I would never again be locked up in such a place. I could see that we were driving far too fast for me to jump out and make a successful bid for freedom. If only our truck would break down – then maybe I could make a short dash down one of the nearby alleyways, find a safe house, and stay put until Paris was liberated!

In what seemed like no time at all we arrived at our immediate destination, some railway sidings in a suburb. Having always had a good sense of direction, I was fairly sure we were in the eastern part of the city. The trucks drew up beside a long string of waiting freight cars. Our guards piled out of their vehicles and some hurried to reinforce armed soldiers who, with police dogs, were already surrounding the area. The remaining sentries shouted, *"Raus! Raus!"* and indicated with their machine guns that we were to jump down and line up along the edge of the track.

The boxcars on the siding beside which we assembled were intended for transporting livestock. On some could still be seen the old French army lettering *10 Chevaux – 40 Hommes* showing that in other war-time emergencies they had been used to carry either ten horses or forty men. Solidly built of wood with steel framing, the cars were about twenty feet long, nine feet wide, and seven feet high. Each was about half as long as its North

American counterpart and had only one set of wheels at either end instead of two. It appeared that fifty or sixty of them had been assembled to transport both prisoners and guards. Compared to trains back home, this string of boxcars looked to me like a toy.

I hoped wildly that the POWs would now be called out and assigned to a passenger train destined for a Luftwaffe interrogation centre or camp. These hopes were quickly dashed when, with more shouts and gestures, we were ordered to climb aboard. Towards the rear of the train I saw the female prisoners scrambling aboard. Every second car was left empty, presumably for the guard troops. I suspected that the SS did not care whether any of us were POWs. Their prime concern was undoubtedly to evacuate Fresnes and move everyone to a new destination as quickly as possible. The military prisoners weren't going to get favoured treatment. Because their actions and movements were so threatening, we airmen realized that they would tolerate no nonsense. We dared not demand our rightful treatment as POWs for fear of what might happen.

With the others I clambered aboard through a centrally located side access door and moved towards the rear. The door on the other side, directly opposite, was already sealed shut. Outside the guards shouted and cursed as they forced more and more prisoners inside. As a child I always imagined that it would be fun to ride in a freight train. But after ninety of us were finally packed like sardines into the small space I quickly forgot my boyhood fantasies. Each person had only inches of space between him and his neighbour and could move about only by pushing or shoving. Almost as an afterthought, a large metal washtub was pushed in from outside to be used for human waste disposal and the door was rolled shut and locked. By late in the afternoon of Tuesday, August 15, 1944, the load of human cattle was ready for shipping.

Early in the summer evening the train started off towards an unknown destination. Every second car was filled with SS troops travelling in relative comfort. I imagined those on guard duty sitting on the floor in the open doorways with their legs dangling over the side, enjoying a leisurely ride through the summer countryside. Their guns would be always at the ready, cradled on their knees. Those who were off duty would be stretched out on their bedrolls or enjoying a snack from their food rations. No doubt all of them would be glad to be moving away from front-line action and back towards home. Probably they were already thinking of leave with their families or girlfriends.

I looked around and saw that fortunately ventilation and daylight could enter the car through narrow, horizontal, "windows" at eye level on each side of the two access doors. Two horizontal steel bars, intended to stop would-be escapers, ran across the windows and provided excellent handholds. However, care had to be exercised when taking hold because barbed wire laced the openings in all directions. With barred windows and locked doors, there seemed to be no avenue for escape.

The occupants of my car all looked the same, wearing ragged clothes and unshaven. But as we got to know each other I learned that about a quarter of them were Allied airmen. We soon congregated in the back while the French grouped themselves at the front. No two of us had had the same adventures when shot down. The only similarity was that after miraculous escapes from crashing aircraft we were still alive. The common bond was that we had overcome horrendous odds and survived. Of those near me I can only remember two names. One was "Whitey" McLaughlin, an American whose father owned a hotel in Miami. The other was Tom Hodgson, from a Canadian bomber squadron. It struck me as perverse that my situation was completely reversed from that of only a few days ago. Then I was alone in a cell, with room in which to walk around. Now I had many people with whom to talk, but no room in which to move.

With the summer heat the stench of unwashed bodies, stale perspiration, urine and feces soon became overpowering. In such cramped quarters, only a few at a time could sit down to rest. Like most of the prisoners, I was already in poor physical shape from lack of proper nutrition and I wondered how long I could remain standing. Such conditions were inhuman for even a very short trip, but obviously the men of the ss could not have cared less. Those nearest the walls leaned against them. Some grasped the window bars to steady themselves. Others tried to support themselves against the car sides by reaching their arms over heads or shoulders. The remainder tried to spread their legs to brace themselves or simply leaned against their neighbours.

Dusk turned to night as we moved through eastern France. We were in darkness. Looking out the windows of our cattle carrier,

I realized that the ss cars ahead and behind us were well lit, the illumination from them casting ghostly shadows on the ditches and hedges as we headed eastwards. The train crawled slowly through the night, almost as though someone was walking in front of the locomotive with a lantern, checking to make sure the track had not been sabotaged. I wondered if the engineer kept imagining that he had spotted damaged track ahead because every few miles he would stop the train with a jolt. Then, after a few minutes, it would just as unexpectedly jerk into motion again as though he had been reassured that it was safe to continue.

Perhaps those in charge of the transport were worried about a sudden attack from the Resistance. I hoped fervently that there was some chance of this. Undoubtedly some of us would be killed in the ensuing fight, but almost anything was better than being locked in this stinking car. I was sure we were still in France, although behind German lines. Having learned from our previous experiences, we could surely evade capture, find a hideaway, or make our way back to Allied territory. I desperately wished that my physical condition were as good as when I had first been shot down so that I could cope with any eventuality.

Each time the train stopped the sentries jumped down to patrol the embankment on either side, flashlights or lanterns in their hands. Certainly their bright lights would quickly reveal anyone who, by some miracle, managed to escape from a car. I wondered if the ss guards were worried that a sudden burst of Sten gunfire from the darkness beyond the stopped train would signal the start of an ambush. To me the patrolling guards seemed so jittery that I thought they were liable to shoot on the slightest provocation. Each time the train started without warning, they made a mad dash to climb back on board as it picked up speed. I suspected this wild scramble was partly because they were afraid of being left behind in hostile France.

Inside the cars the difficulty of sleeping standing up was compounded by the constant sudden stops and starts. That first night we had not yet organized ourselves to allow even one or two people to sit down in turns. At first we chatted incessantly with our neighbours about flying, the only topic of conversation common to us all. But gradually the excitement of being able to talk with people wore off. As the night progressed we became too tired to talk and instead simply leaned against the walls, or each other, in dulled silence. I was exhausted but could not sleep standing up. I tried half crouching, but after only a short period my knees ached. Sometimes, when I was able to squeeze close to the side, I leaned against the wall or hung onto the window bars. I was so distracted by the events that were taking place that I could not even escape into my dream world.

Wednesday finally dawned as the train crept across eastern France. Now that it was daylight I worried that Allied reconnaissance aircraft looking for moving targets might strafe us, with devastating consequences. About midday the train drew to a stop on the outskirts of a small French town in hilly country. It sat there for some time as the guards outside, seemingly disturbed about something, shouted back and forth. They climbed back on board when it started slowly backing up and stopped a few minutes later at a station. The doors were rolled open. Then to impatient shouts of *"Raus! Raus!"* and the intimidating gestures of machine guns, we jumped down. There was no convoy of trucks to transport us as there had been when we left Fresnes so I thought we would not be going any great distance. We were formed into a column and began to walk down the road towards the centre of town. I wondered what was in store for us – perhaps confinement in a large prison there.

Down the middle of the road in front and behind me stretched the long column of prisoners. At either side ss soldiers walked at thirty-foot intervals, with machine guns slung over their shoulders and hand grenades dangling from their belts. Many of them were accompanied by police dogs, restrained on short leashes. To the left of us were scattered houses, but there were no signs of their inhabitants. On the right was a steep drop down a scrub-covered bank to a medium-sized river.

I weighed the possibilities of escape as I studied the positions of the nearest guards. I realized that the best time to try it was while still in France where there would be a better chance of encountering friendly people. Besides, I was still outside prison walls in the relative freedom of open country. I was probably insane to think that I could escape successfully, but I considered it anyway. If I took the sentries completely by surprise I might have a few seconds in which to get out of sight and beyond accurate machine-gun range. The only way to do this was to charge recklessly down the steep slope on the right and into the bushes. There, if I was lucky, I might find rocks or a depression to shelter me from the ensuing gunfire as I scrambled down to the edge of the river. If they tossed hand grenades after me or put the police dogs on my scent I would be finished. Furthermore, if I reached the river unharmed there would be even more difficulties to face. I could not see any safe escape routes along the bank and could not swim across because it was too wide. The odds seemed to be stacked against me. I decided it would be certain suicide and reluctantly continued on without breaking pace.

As we neared the town I saw an increasing number of houses and buildings on either side of the road, frequently surrounded by trees, shrubs, or flower gardens. To the right there were villas nestled into the steep banks on each side of the water and I thought this would be a pretty area in which to holiday after the war. I came out of my pleasant reverie to find that the road in front curved to the left to follow a bend in the river. Within a few hundred feet the column swung sharply to the right, then crossed to the other side on a high road bridge. The town straddled the river and our route veered to the right, away from the built-up areas. I was very tired and hungry when we finally arrived at a new string of cattle cars at a station on the eastern side of the town. I was surprised that our enemy had used this time-consuming process of having us change trains. I could only guess that this complicated manœuvre was necessary because the railway bridge had been sabotaged.

Waiting on the station platform were a number of people wearing Red Cross arm bands. They gave us fresh water to drink and bread to eat. To my surprise there was even a spoonful of *confiture* to sweeten the taste of the rough-textured bread. All this food was beyond my fondest expectations, especially since the last meal I had eaten was the "big" midday meal at Fresnes twenty-four hours before. I suspected that the ss had not planned to feed us but that somehow the Red Cross had heard about the transport and was there. Perhaps the Germans had even requested their assistance. I could not have cared less how it had been arranged now that I had something to eat.

We were not allowed to dawdle after eating. Again we were packed into the cars, the doors shut and securely locked. In no time at all the train pulled out of the station to continue another "start and stop" journey eastward through France. As darkness descended at the end of the second day we faced the prospect of standing all night without sleep. While there was still daylight, a group of us talked things over and decided to organize an arrangement so that all could rest. This was achieved by having one row of prisoners sit down with their backs against the side of the car and their knees drawn up to their chins. Then a second row sat down in a similar manner with their backs tight against the drawn up knees of the first row. This procedure was repeated until everyone was able to sit down. Although we were by no means comfortable, and could not stretch out, we at least had the possibility of dozing off without falling over.

That night most of us were so tired that we slept. But inevitably sleep was abruptly disturbed when someone got up to use the waste tub in the centre of the car. It was quite a procedure to untangle ourselves so that he could get there without stepping or falling on anyone. We could still not relax until the person answering the call of nature had found his way back and managed to get into his sleeping position. Of course I, too, had to take a turn at the tub and did my share of disturbing.

Thursday morning the string of cattle cars continued its monotonous journey. From what signs I could read at railway stations or on buildings that we passed, I gathered we were still in France. Packed like sardines, we often lapsed into silence. At these times I would think about home. I speculated about such things as whether Bert, my sister's fiance, was now flying over Germany. I said a silent prayer that he would come back safely to her. I wondered about my younger brother David and wished the war would end so he would not have to fly on operations. I hoped my folks at home knew that I had beaten the odds and was alive.

Late on Thursday afternoon the train stopped at a station in another small town. Again a number of French civilians wearing Red Cross arm bands were waiting for us on the platform. The door of each boxcar was opened in turn. Then, under the supervision of the ss guards, the Red Cross workers were allowed to pass fresh water and food in to us. The large metal can which held the fresh drinking water was left inside for some time before all ninety of us were able to get a drink. When it was empty, a group of three or four Frenchmen close to me quickly appropriated it. This aroused my curiosity. I could not understand what they planned to do. As they crouched over it in the shadows of the car, their bodies largely concealed their actions. Whatever they were doing, as they pushed and twisted it this way and that, their exertion caused them to utter muffled grunts. Others close to the activity did not seem to be as upset by the jostling or as curious about it as I was. Fortunately the press of the people around the door hid the activities from the view of the Germans outside. Suddenly I heard a suppressed exclamation of excitement that meant that the French had succeeded in whatever it was they were trying to do. The empty water can was then nonchalantly passed out to the Red Cross workers. Shortly afterwards, our door was shut and locked. When all the cattle cars had been attended to, the journey continued.

As another summer day faded into darkness, I could sense an undercurrent of quiet excitement among the members of the small group of Frenchmen nearby. For some time now they had been having heated discussions in subdued undertones. Obviously something was afoot, so I quietly edged up beside them. In the darkness I could see that they were again bent over the area where they had been manipulating the water can. Then to my surprise I saw them lift out a wide floor board and study the track below through the opening. With the plank lifted out and carefully placed to one side, I could see that there was a twelve-inch wide space stretching transversely from the edge to the centre of the car. As I watched they pushed the board sideways so that it dropped easily back into place. Only a close examination would reveal that it was not nailed down securely. Now I knew that they had apparently used the steel handle of the water can as a lever to pry loose the plank.

This potential escape route was known only to those few standing close by. I could see that for it to be successful many problems would have to be solved. First, it could not be used when the train was stopped because the patrolling sentries would see anyone who dropped down onto the track. Nor would it be wise to use when the train was in full motion for its speed would throw an escaper off balance and under the wheels when his feet touched the ground. The safest try would be right after the engine jerked the string of cars away from a stop. At this time the ss guards would be too busy scrambling back on board to notice anyone exiting through the floor.

Before he jumped to the ground an escaper had further decisions to make. Should he flatten himself between the rails, hoping that he would not be injured by the train as it passed overhead, or should he drop on the outside of the rails and lie down, praying that he would be hidden from view by the overhang of the cars? While lying still he would not be likely to attract the attention of the ss troops sitting in the open doorways of their cars. However, were he to roll sideways towards the ditch, he would most certainly be spotted.

The first escape attempt was planned for soon after dark. As the train jolted to a stop, the ss jumped down, as expected, to patrol on either side. The first escaper, one of the Frenchmen, and his helpers were tense as they crouched, ready to lift out the loosened plank when the train started. I admired and envied him his chance to try the escape route beneath the moving train. Around us, idle chatter continued since most of the others were not aware of the dramatic events about to take place.

The seconds ticked by for me with agonizing slowness as I waited for the train to start again. I began to think that we were going to be stopped all night. Suddenly the train jerked into motion and the guards raced to clamber back on board. A few feet from me the plank was lifted out of place. As we increased speed the first escaper disappeared into the black void below. We were moving too fast for a second man to try his luck, so the plank was carefully slid back into place. No alarm was raised. I could only assume that our man had not been spotted lying on the track or rolling down the bank. I dared not think of the other possibility, which was that he had been mangled by the wheels and was now behind us, either dead or dying.

Not long afterward the train stopped again. When it moved off the escape procedure was repeated and another prisoner disappeared into the night. I realized that as each Frenchman dropped into the blackness a new helper joined the group. One of those now around the hole straightened up and turning to me said that he was Stevenson, a Canadian airman. He truly surprised me when he went on to say that he had arranged to be the next one to leave. I told him my name and wished him luck. Up to now I had considered that the French, who had dared to loosen and remove the plank, had the sole rights to this escape route. After all, as civilians accused of crimes against Germany, their chances of survival were minimal compared to ours as prisoners of war. Consequently they were more desperate to get away. Now that I knew that others besides the French were going out, I decided that the attempt might be well worth the risks involved. However, I would have to wait my turn since there were already two or three men ahead of me.

Another stop and Stevenson was gone. Then on the fourth stop another Frenchman took off. Everything had worked like clockwork, so far. Four men had escaped with no alarms raised by the Germans.

The next time we stopped, the ss moved to within a few feet of the train and played their powerful flashlights upwards along the sides. Within, I saw the flashes of light from their torches move slowly and deliberately around each window and then each door. It was obvious to me that they were suspicious of something; no car escaped their scrutiny. I held my breath because I was worried that they would next look under the floor. They had barely finished their inspection of the normal exits when the train jerked into motion without warning. As they rushed to get back aboard a fifth man disappeared through the hole in the floor. Now there was only one more ahead of me.

Crouched around the opening we speculated on why the ss were so suspicious. Did they know that escapes were taking place? Perhaps they were just making an extra security check, although they had not done this before during our two days of travel. Perhaps one of them thought he had seen a suspicious object rolling down the bank, or lying on the track, and wanted to reassure himself that it was not an escaper.

A short time later another halt occurred. Now, the ss troopers purposefully headed directly to check the underside of each wagon. Inside the car, our little group was confident that from underneath "our" plank would look no different from any other. Suddenly, to our horror, we realized that one edge was hung up on the adjacent board. We dared not lift it out to reset it for fear the hole would be spotted.

Already we could hear the ss checking the next car. In minutes they would be under ours. Desperately we fumbled with the offending plank trying to ease it sideways into place. We pushed and shoved without success. Perhaps the emergency made us altogether too anxious. Time had run out for us. I could hear the

Germans crawling around under our car. Abruptly, a triumphant exclamation came from one of the men below. The break in the otherwise level floor had been spotted. Our escape route was doomed.

A few barked commands sent two or three husky young ss to push upwards on the suspicious looking floor board. Inside, we were not prepared to passively surrender our route to freedom. Three of us stood with our full weight on the plank so that it would seem immovable. Furthermore, to increase the pressure, we braced our hands against the roof and pushed down hard. We hoped against hope that our efforts would make it seem as though the large board was well spiked in place. With a twist of grim humour, I thought to myself that it would have been amusing for an outsider to have seen the Germans pushing up while, unbeknownst to them, we were pushing down.

When they moved out from underneath it seemed to me that we had convinced them that the plank was firmly in place. And, I thought, we had gained a reprieve when the train suddenly jerked into motion. But these hopes were short-lived when a few bursts of gunfire in the air signalled the locomotive driver to stop. The door of our car was rolled open. Menacing machine-gun nozzles motioned us back tight against the walls. Then soldiers carrying planks, spikes, and sledge hammers climbed in and moved to the cleared area around the escape hole. In no time at all the opening was boarded over and spiked down. The ss left. The door was rolled shut with a clang. I did not have to look at the sealed opening to know that even if I still had my rusty nail from Fresnes, I would never have been able to work the nails out of these heavy new planks.

From the moment that our escape route was discovered until it was closed, the occupants of our car had been subjected to a torrent of shouted threats and abuse. An older Dutch civilian among us, who understood German, translated for us when we were again by ourselves. If another escape took place, the ss said, everyone from that car would be shot.

As we rolled through the night, I am sure that we were all thinking about the ss threat to indiscriminately shoot everyone. Again I wondered if any of the five escapers had been successful or whether there were five maimed bodies lying uncared for in the darkness on the track far behind us. I calculated that we were still in occupied France so that if any of them got away without injury, their chances of reaching home were excellent.

When the sun was well up in the sky the following day, the train stopped in the middle of a forest. The doors of our cattle car were opened and we were ordered to jump down. Facing us was a line of grim-faced, tough, young ss troopers with submachine guns pointed at us. I felt sick. I was certain this was the end and thought we were to be ruthlessly gunned down in the middle of this quiet forest as an example for any others who had ideas of trying to escape. I waited for the order that would send a hail of bullets into us. Commands were shouted in German but no gunfire followed. Instead we were ordered to remove every stitch of our clothing and to put it in a pile.

"The bastards," I thought, "they are going to shoot us naked so that our clothing can be recovered with little effort and without bullet holes and blood stains!" I was angered that we had stripped so meekly and waited in agony for the bullets to tear into me. Unlike the popular assumption, my whole life did not flash by my eyes in an instant.

Only when we were ordered back on board did I realize, with unbelievable relief, that we were not going to be shot after all. The doors were secured and the train started off, one of its cars full of naked men. Apparently the ss were making us suffer mildly for daring to help the others escape, because the occupants of no other car suffered this indignity. And being naked would certainly make it harder for any of us to escape. As an afterthought I wondered if I would ever get back my clothes and my shoes, which concealed my lucky piece of parachute.

Late that afternoon one of the frequent halts occurred in a wooded area. Outside, as usual, the guards patrolled back and forth. Inside, as I remember, everyone was standing casually, leaning against the walls. As casual, that is, as any crowd of stark naked, semi-strangers could be. A few used the window bars for support as they chattered amongst themselves. Suddenly the relative quiet was shattered by the sharp crack of a rifle fired from a few feet away into the front of our car. Instinctively everyone dropped to the floor.

I wondered if anyone had been hit. We anxiously waited to see if there would be more bullets shot into our midst. We heard the guards talking excitedly and the door was rolled back. An ss officer standing in the opening bellowed out a question in German. When no one answered, he repeated the same question several times. Again there was dead silence. Then some Frenchmen near the front spoke insistently to an adolescent crouched between them. After a few moments the boy reluctantly held up his hand, which was bleeding badly.

A curt order, accompanying a swift hand motion, indicated that the boy was to come forward to have his injury examined. The grimacing youngster, only a few years younger than myself, stumbled through the mass of huddled bodies to the door. After a quick glance at the bloody hand, the officer told him to jump down and run to the front of the train. Presumably his wound was to be cleansed and bandaged in another car. From where we crouched on the rough wooden floor we watched the naked boy hesitate before jumping down. No doubt he was looking for a spot to land which would not be too cruel on his bare feet. He disappeared through the opening and those nearest it saw him start towards the front of the train. The tension was shattered by a burst of machine gun fire from a few feet away. Within seconds another burst followed. There was no doubt in my mind that the body of this defenseless lad lay a crumpled bloody mess on the ground. I was sure he had been shot in the back, murdered in cold blood.

Approaching the doorway, the ss officer ordered the two nearest people out. Once outside they were handed shovels and a thrust of the officer's head towards the bullet-torn body indicated that they were to be the burial party. In the cinders at the edge of the track, they began to dig the youngster's grave. Before long their bare feet were bleeding where the sharp edge of the shovel bit into them. Save for the sounds of the digging, all was deathly silent. Only enough time was allowed for the men to scoop out a shallow place, hardly deep enough to receive the corpse. Once the few scoopfuls of earth were thrown over the body, the two prisoners were hurried aboard. The spot was left unmarked.

I will never forget the look of revulsion and fear on the ashen faces of the two men when they rejoined us. Even today I can clearly visualize the horror in the eyes of one of them, another young Canadian airman. The car door had to have been closed and locked, but I cannot remember this happening. The train must have started with its usual jerk. Nor do I remember that. Gradually we resumed standing positions. We all stayed well clear of the windows, although the train was in motion and guards aboard. For quite some time we seemed to be in some kind of a daze.

Little by little talk resumed. Here and there small groups chatted in hushed tones, as if frightened that they were doing something forbidden. Finally everyone learned the story that lead up to the death of the boy, who, we were told, was only sixteen years old. Apparently when the train had halted the last time he had been holding on to the window bar for support. Seeing this, a soldier outside sadistically took aim and, without any warning, fired a bullet through his hand. It was a wonder that no others were hit or killed. Instead of trying to heal the boy's minor wound, these ss bastards found it easier to shoot him in the back. I could not understand the senseless killing of this hurt, frightened, naked youth. There was no way he could have caused the slightest harm to these so-called soldiers. How could the Nazis consider themselves supermen? They were worse than common criminals. They were savages.

This was the first time I had ever felt real hatred towards anyone. Until then I had thought of the Germans as human beings fighting for a cause in which they believed, although through a twist of fate it was completely different from the one in which I believed. I had often seen photographs and read about wartime atrocities, but they had always been too distant and impersonal to seem true. After what had just happened, I felt sick because I realized for the first time that man can be worse than any wild animal. Very few animals kill for the sake of killing. I despaired because I feared that, given certain conditions, any one of us could behave like an animal.

We discussed among ourselves whether this boy had paid with his life for the five men who had escaped from our car. Was murder the price for this insult? Was there anything we could have done to prevent this atrocious act? Should we have known that a hand on a window bar would be considered an escape attempt? When the ss asked if anyone was hurt, how were the boy's friends, or any of us, to know that those madmen would find it so easy to kill? The ss were barbarians we concluded, whose primitive minds we would never be able to understand. Needless to say, the shooting of the boy gave us deadly warning that they belonged to a vicious organization that certainly did not believe in the Geneva Convention. If we were to survive, they should not be provoked in any manner whatsoever.

After all that had happened up to that point, the remainder of the train journey seemed almost anti-climactic. I do not remember being given food or water during the rest of the trip but, because I don't remember being any hungrier or thirstier than usual, these needs presumably were attended to. Somehow the night came and went. Now that we were into the fourth day of our trip, the train seemed to be moving faster and there were fewer stops. I sensed a change in the behavior of our guards, who now seemed more confident. I speculated that we might well be in Germany. My assumptions were confirmed when, standing well back from the windows, I began to see the occasional German sign on stations or buildings.

At one time during the day the train journey took us close to the edge of a wide river, which I believed to be the Rhine. Particularly after the horrors of the previous day, I enjoyed seeing the picturesque villages nestled on its banks, while farther out boats passed slowly up and down. Endless vineyards covered the steep slopes on each side. Occasionally we stopped at small stations, which invariably had window boxes overflowing with flowering red geraniums. I found it hard to believe that this peaceful land could breed creatures such as ss troopers.

During the stops I was intrigued and delighted by the flute-like sounds coming from whistles used by the railway men. Different rising and falling notes signaled the locomotive engineer when to stop, back up, or go forward when shunting cars onto the various sidings.

We passed through several large cities which showed evidence of severe Allied bomb damage. I had a feeling of vindictive pleasure at seeing firsthand the damage our side had wreaked on German centres in return for what they had done to ours. I caught the name on the station in one bomb-ravaged city – Frankfurt. Adjacent to the railway yards, I saw barbed wire enclosures which I soon learned held forced labour gangs who worked in nearby factories. The sight of these slave work crews became very common. The forced labourers were thin, famished-looking men with close-shaven heads who wore loose-fitting pants and tops striped vertically in blue and white like prison garb. Most of them were barefooted but a few wore straw filled wooden *sabots*. I was very disturbed by the sight of these poor souls. ss guards were always close at hand with their inevitable machine-guns, hand grenades, and watchdogs.

At about noon on the fifth day our cattle train stopped on sidings in a fairly large town. On the station, some distance off, I read the name Weimar. Here considerable activity took place while our train was shunted back and forth. The rear cars holding the female prisoners were unhooked and shunted to a siding in a different section of the yards. Our original clothes were thrown back into our car. We retrieved our secondhand wardrobes and dressed quickly to regain a little dignity. I checked in my shoe and was relieved to find my lucky piece of parachute still in its secret hiding place.

Soon afterwards our now shortened train pulled out of Weimar and started northward, struggling up the steeper grades of what must have been a branch line. We passed through sparsely settled farmland and occasional wooded areas. I saw more and more slave labour work gangs, closely guarded by ss troops. After we had been travelling less than an hour – I guessed perhaps about twenty miles – the train slowed, then stopped, at what proved to be our final destination. The doors of our cattle wagons were rolled open and I could see that we were on one of several sidings. Orders were shouted. Eighty-four prisoners remained of the original ninety in our cattle car; we jumped down to join the others from the train. Our whole tired, filthy, hungry horde was ordered to line up and shouts, curses, and waving machine-guns set us hurrying away from the railway sidings down a stony road between low buildings. ss troops in their green-grey uniforms were visible everywhere.

We halted in front of a formidable, multi-tiered gate structure surmounted by a clock tower. Long, low wings reached out on each side. Beyond the gate I could see people dressed in the now familiar blue and white striped prison garb of the work gangs. To me, this looked more like a place of internment than a Luftwaffe-run POW camp. At that time I knew there were civilian internment camps in Germany, although I didn't know any of their names. Perhaps this was one of them. Perhaps it would only be a temporary stopover before the POWs were transferred to a proper camp. This certainly couldn't be Stalag Luft III, nor any other prisoner of war camp of which I had heard, not with people in striped prison suits and SS guards everywhere.

Five days after having left Paris, our terrible journey had ended at a prison camp. The date was Sunday, August 20, 1944.

CHAPTER SIX

Buchenwald – Arrival

I stood outside the main gate with my disheveled companions awaiting how many of us had arrived on that cattle train, but I would have guessed somewhere between fifteen hundred and two thousand. We were a mixed lot and hardly knew who was English or French, let alone each other. Consequently there was little attempt at conversation, especially with the menacing machine guns close by.

For the first time in my life I was standing on German soil, deep inside the homeland of my country's enemy. In front of me was my first example of an establishment built by Hitler to hold his enemies. I imagined this place must be for civilians because I saw no sign of Luftwaffe guards or air force prisoners. I hoped this would be only a temporary stopover for us. It would be terrible to spend the rest of the war here where I feared we would be less well treated than in a Luftwaffe POW camp. Of course the Allied armies might still be sweeping unchecked through France and into Germany, so our stay here might be short-lived.

As we awaited the next move I took a few moments to study all that I could see of the complex. A ten-foot-high fence built of closely laced barbed wire, supported on concrete posts, stretched off into the distance from either side of the gate structure. To make it even more impassable, thick coils of barbed wire had been laid on the ground against the inside. Even with sharp wire cutters, it would take an escaper a long time to work his way through to freedom. No one could approach this perimeter fence without being seen from one of the solidly built guard towers that were spaced every hundred yards along the outside. The sentries, when at their posts, were about another ten feet above the fence with an unobstructed view along its line. When on duty in wet or cold weather they could stand inside the tower, completely sheltered from the elements but able to see on all sides through large glass windows. Otherwise, they could patrol on an outside balcony. I caught a movement and the glint of steel from the platform of the nearest post. There was no question that it was manned by an alert guard ready to use his machine-gun if necessary.

Behind us on the hilltop stretched woods that appeared to shelter numerous buildings. The whole area seemed to be part of the complex, which perhaps explained why it was busy with ss soldiers. Many were guarding work parties of slave labourers. All were armed with machine-guns; some were accompanied by police dogs on tight leashes. My hopes sank as I realized it would be almost impossible for anyone to get out and away from this place.

I turned my attention to the inside of the camp, studying what I could see of it through the ugly barbed wire. Immediately inside the big gate was a large open space that I guessed was most likely used as a parade ground or assembly area. Around the three sides were various buildings, solidly built of stone or brick as though they had been there for some time and were intended to last. Many of these structures had very high, sharply peaked roofs that allowed them to have a second or third floor. To me they seemed too large to be family residences, too small for barracks, and yet not suitable for factories. I presumed that because of their size and location they were used to house the administration offices necessary for the everyday camp operation. Over towards the right I noticed the high peaked roof of a building that differed from the others in that it had a fat chimney, about thirty feet tall, from which thick black smoke was pouring. Perhaps this was a power house, or a kitchen, for the complex. Between the structures that surrounded the open space were provisions for access to the interior parts of the camp. Nowhere in the open areas was there any sign of grass or flowers. It was a bleak looking place. Inside, I saw prisoners in striped suits. To my surprise only a few ss were to be seen and in each case they were lightly armed with only a holstered revolver on the hip. This contrasted markedly with the heavily armed guards to which I had become accustomed.

My first quick survey was abruptly interrupted when the steel gates were opened and our familiar machine gun-waving ss soldiers shouted at us to move inside. This we did quickly before anyone was shot. Our guards remained outside when the gates were shut behind us. Presumably their assignment had been only to ensure that no one escaped from the train that had brought us here.

The absence of heavily armed sentries inside the wire should have lessened my uneasiness. However, it had the opposite effect. Somehow it did not seem right that this apparently large internment camp could be so easily guarded from within by such a small show of arms. I had an uncomfortable feeling in the pit of my stomach about this place – which might be my home for some time to come. I sensed that there was something quite different in the behaviour of the guards from what I had known in Fresnes and in the early days of our boxcar ride here. Suddenly I realized what it was – the Germans no longer seemed to be afraid of their prisoners. I believed it was because they were in their own country, surrounded by their own people.

A solitary German NCO, assisted by several stripe-suited prisoners who seem to have some position of authority, took charge of us. Like sheep we followed their instructions to assemble outside one of the larger buildings bordering the right-hand side of the parade ground. About fifty of those nearest the door were summoned inside. I guessed that we were now to be processed as new arrivals. During the short wait before the next lot entered we learned from one of the stripe-suited prisoners that we were in the Big Lager, (main compound) of Buchenwald concentration camp. I had heard the name before but little else about it.

Eventually my turn came to go in as part of the next group. Inside we were instructed to strip naked and pile our clothes to one side. We moved along in a line to be disinfected with chemicals. Then we were handed bars of rock-hard grey soap and motioned through the far door to a shower room. It was large, with a low ceiling out of which numerous shower heads projected. As soon as it was full of naked bodies, the stripe-suited internees shut the door from outside. When the water came it was not very hot, but I welcomed this first opportunity to wash off six weeks of grime and sweat. I scrubbed feverishly. All too soon the cleansing flow ceased and a door at the far end was opened.

As I entered the next room I saw a large number of naked men standing or squatting along one side. They were calling rude remarks to another half dozen naked men sitting on upturned crates across from them, having all the hair removed from their bodies by barbers equipped with electric clippers and straight razors. It made me think of what a sheep-shearing station must look like. It took a moment for me to recognize the shorn men. They were all from my crowd of new arrivals. In no time at all I was receiving the full treatment from one of the barbers. I thought that this indignity was an extreme measure, a terrible invasion of personal privacy. I felt degraded, as though we were being treated like livestock. I wondered if the next step would be branding or tattooing. Perhaps Buchenwald was riddled with disease-carrying vermin and shaving was a sanitary measure. Unfortunately it made us look like the bald-headed slave labourers that we had seen. Surely this was not the next step for us.

When all of our lot had been shaved, our clothes were brought in and dumped in a pile. I am sure that we airmen were all relieved that we were not handed the striped prison garb to wear. Poking through the pile I found my well-worn brown suit and shirt without tie. While our clothes were there, no footwear was returned. Presumably they were of value to the German war effort, whereas our ragged clothes were not. With the severe clothes rationing in Germany, shoes may have been needed for the slave labourers working in war production factories or even for the civilian population. I felt bad about losing my special cut-down flying boots with my "lucky" piece of parachute still hidden under the inner sole. I wondered if the new owner would find it and realize what it was.

We dressed quickly and left by a door which led us outside the back of the building to join the new arrivals already gathered there. It took only a moment for me to find out that the English-speaking airmen had gathered in one group and the French-speaking in another. I felt that now that the military were in a single body we could use our training and discipline to function more effectively. It was not often that any rank above flight lieutenant flew on operations in our bomber command. Consequently the chances were that all the airmen in our group would be NCOS or junior officers. So I was quite pleased to find that we were fortunate to have a squadron leader from New Zealand as well as an even more senior American colonel. These two had already assumed command of the British Commonwealth and American airmen respectively. Now that we had leaders, I hoped that we could function as an organized body with a better chance of trying to establish our rights as POWS.

I squatted in the afternoon sun chatting with the others as I waited for the last of our group to come out from the reception building. While we were talking it suddenly occurred to me that not once during the admitting procedure had I been asked for my name, rank, or number. This seemed most unusual. In all my military training, and also in civilian life, all those in charge of feeding and housing large groups of people needed, in fact demanded, this information. So this deliberate lack of interest in recording who we were and where we came from was most disconcerting. Did this mean that the camp authorities considered us nameless bodies who could die or disappear without trace or concern on their part? The inevitable conclusions to which these thoughts led were definitely disturbing.

When the last of our new arrivals had assembled we carried out a head count. We numbered about eighty Americans and ninety British. One of the stripe-suited inmates, who seemed to be in charge, signaled that the airmen should follow him. We learned that these men were called *Kapos* and that they were assigned to positions of authority over other prisoners. "Good," I thought to myself, "We're going to be allotted space in a barrack and given our evening meal."

We moved off from our location near the right front corner of the complex, heading down the gently sloping ground towards the far end. We straggled along behind the Kapo because our unaccustomed bare feet were sensitive to every pebble or sharp object along our path. Walking gingerly, we followed a road on either side of which were numerous low, flat-roofed, rectangular wooden buildings. On the right, they separated us from the southern perimeter with its barbed wire fence and guard towers. Beyond this boundary were the green trees of a thickly wooded area. On the left, over the top of these structures, I could see the greater part of Buchenwald spread out.

In the late afternoon sun, numerous prisoners lolled outside the single-storied buildings, which made me assume they were barracks. These men watched our slow and painful progress with lustreless, sunken eyes and I could not help but return their gaze with curiosity. Many of them had taken off the tops or bottoms of their striped uniforms and were meticulously picking at the seams for some reason unknown to me. These hollow-cheeked wretches were painfully underfed – they were nothing but skin and bone. I was shocked. I had never seen anyone so thin. Other prisoners whom we passed at close quarters on the road had a piece of cloth with a number on it stitched to the breast of their jacket. Beneath this was a small coloured triangle, also of cloth. I supposed that the upper label must be the prisoner's number and the lower coloured triangle some sort of additional classification.

Our route took us by a squat, rectangular, stone building on the left, from which came the overpowering stench of human waste. Instead of windows, it had long narrow horizontal openings just below the eaves. The entrance that I saw had no door. There was little doubt that this was a huge communal outhouse. I fervently hoped that we POWs would be assigned a decent barrack with its own washrooms. Further down the hill we came to a vast compound, devoid of buildings, which was divided from the rest of the camp by an unguarded fence. From the gate through which we passed I saw, well down the slope ahead, the formidable back outer perimeter with its guard towers. This and the right-hand boundary that we had been paralleling formed the northeast, back corner of Buchenwald. Extending down the hill on the left-hand side was a high unguarded fence with an open gate, beyond which was the concentration of buildings I had already observed.

We followed our Kapo when he veered left towards the gate leading into this busy part of Buchenwald. Just short of the fence, however, he stopped, and beckoned to our leaders to come close. The heated exchange which followed was accompanied by much use of arm waving and hand signs. Our two senior men were obviously upset by what they were being told. They remained where they were standing as the Kapo strode off and disappeared into the next compound. We crowded around the two men to learn that, unbelievably, the camp authorities presently had no space for us in any of the barracks. Until such time as they did, this patch of hard ground was to be our quarters. There would be no shelter from the weather, no groundsheets to lie on, no blankets. This was where we would receive our food rations and be counted during the two daily roll calls. On top of everything else, we had missed our evening meal.

I joined in the heated and furious discussion that followed this news. How we cursed the Germans and the unfairness of our situation! We were airmen who had fought honourably. This was not the way fighting men treated each other. We were volunteers, not conscripts. I assumed the Germans who had been captured and imprisoned in Canada were living in cozy barracks with books to read, and radios and movies to entertain them; they were sending and receiving letters from home, all the while eating like kings on ample Canadian food. In all the weeks since I had been captured by their bloody Gestapo, the bastards hadn't even let me write home, or receive mail, or given me a decent meal. Damn it all, just wait until we won this stupid war!

We stood in groups, then joined with others or broke into twos and threes, circulating and mingling as we discussed the situation. If we were not considered soldiers, would we be forced to work as slave labourers? How would we survive if there was no shelter when winter came? Would we get enough to eat? Was this place disease-ridden? Were there any doctors to provide medical care? Was there any chance of escape? Did our forces back in England know we were here? If the Allied armies were not too far away, would they drop paratroops to free us in advance of their armies? We discussed how we thought barrack space might be found. Perhaps people were being shipped out on permanent work assignments, which would create room for us. Were there other groups waiting for space and, if so, would we have priority? Footsore, tired, and weak with hunger, we settled into small groups on the hard ground, each with his own private fears and worries. Sometimes these would be shared with the others. I know I worried most about whether I would get enough to eat and, if not, how long it would be before I looked like one of the wretches I had seen. I also wondered how I could endure rain, or even snow, without shelter over my head. Inevitably I worried that we might be forced to wear prison garb and work for the Germans.

Our senior officers, who obviously knew little more than we did about Buchenwald – and our future – issued their first orders.

We were not to trust the ss who, as we had already seen on the train ride, could be very unpredictable. We must be careful not to provoke any of them for fear of unexpected retaliation. The best course of action was to keep as far away from them as possible. This meant we mustn't explore the camp because of the chance of breaking unknown rules. Tomorrow, acting on our behalf, they would try to find out from the Kapos more about the functioning of this place and how to approach the German authorities for recognition of our rights. All of this made sense and I was quite relieved that we had older men to lead us.

As I looked around it seemed to me that the Americans had congregated in one group and the rest of us in another. This was pretty much to be expected, considering that the American approach to military training and discipline, although achieving the same ends, was quite different from ours. For me, I was glad to be with the British because they had been at war longer and understood the problems of survival better.

I was sitting with a group that included Harry Bastable, a Canadian who had been on a battle course with me in Sidmouth, and Tom Hodgson from Winnipeg, whom I had met in the box car. As we chatted we watched the French prisoners from our train arrive in the charge of a Kapo. They had been allotted the stony patch of ground next to us. Looking further down the slope I now realized that there were other groups of prisoners lying or squatting on the ground, apparently sharing our fate. Inside space was indeed at a premium.

As evening fell there seemed to be a large increase in the number of people cutting through our compound and circulating throughout the camp as a whole. Some stopped to chat with us. Few of these other inmates spoke English or French, which should have posed a major communication problem. But fortunately many in our group were from immigrant families and the vocabulary they had learned, accompanied by much gesticulating, enabled them to act as interpreters.

The question we were most frequently asked was why we were privileged to wear civilian clothes. I saw that the majority of the men who talked to us had their prison numbers tattooed on their forearms. They told us they lived in the camp but went outside daily in work parties. Most spent their long days in war-production factories located in woods close by the main gate.

Others travelled by train to local sites. A number worked inside the camp at menial tasks or in small shops. They told us terrible things about belonging to the labor gangs that slaved from dawn to dusk. Many, they said, died each day from starvation or beatings. Only on rare occasions were the extremely sick excused from their assignments. This explained the men we had seen earlier sitting outside their huts. Now I knew why they were nothing but skin and bone.

The sun, my only way of approximating the passage of time, was beginning to sink in the western sky. I heard the shouts of, "*Zum Appell! Zum Appell!*" The long-term inmates immediately hurried back to their various compounds. Those living in our area quickly lined up in files of ten for the impending roll call. We were slower at falling in, which greatly disturbed the veteran residents who were obviously terrified of displeasing the Germans. A non-commissioned ss officer and a private appeared and counted the files of men. Anyone not properly in line was kicked into position with a jack boot. This roll call procedure was going on simultaneously all over the camp. No group was dismissed until the totals from each parade ground had been combined to form the count for the whole camp. Only when the grand total was correct were the individual *Appells* dismissed. We were lucky this first time, when we only had to stand on parade for about an hour.

Darkness was approaching – it was time to prepare for "bed." There was really little to do. First a trip to the foul-smelling *Abort* … the latrine which we had passed on our way here. We could not wash ourselves because the Abort had no water. Besides, none of us had soap, towels, washcloths, toothpaste, or toothbrushes, which effectively eliminated these normal civilized preparations for bed. We had no blankets or sleeping bag to spread out and lie on. All there was left to do was to stretch out on the bare earth, avoiding stones or sharp objects. I lay down next to Tom, to whom I had taken a liking, so that we could chat. Thus began my first night in Konzentrationslager Buchenwald.

I lay thinking about the things that had happened to me in the past few days. Last night I had been crowded into a stinking boxcar with little room to move among the other naked men. I had a roof over my head should it rain, and a dry but rough wooden floor on which I could rest when doubled up. Tonight, twenty-four hours later, I had lots of room in which to lie down, plenty of fresh air, but no roof over my head should it rain, and rough, bare ground that would be cold and wet in all but the finest of weather. What a mixture of contrasts!

An idea occurred to me and I discussed it with Tom. Perhaps it had been by accident that we had been sent here. With the Allied armies about to encircle Paris and transport at a premium, German High Command in Berlin had sent an order to evacuate all of Fresnes immediately to Germany. In the rush to obey the orders, no thought had been given to separating the POWs from the other prisoners. Hence we ended up here. Tom and I talked about it, then lapsed into silence again. Around us the others lay in various positions. Here and there subdued conversations were going on, but for the most part our companions lay quietly immersed in their own thoughts.

Lying on my back, I raised my head slightly to look down the hill. The brightly lit perimeter fence stretched across the bottom, then turned at right angles to continue back up past me over on my right. It contrasted sharply with the darkness of the blacked-out countryside. I wondered if the lights were turned off when our bombers came over. With this new thought I looked up to study the heavens. There was no moon on this cloudless night. Locating the big dipper, I followed the line of its lip to pinpoint the north star. With my directions established, I calculated that England was at about 280 degrees, or slightly north of due west. The skies and stars were beautiful to behold. I named to myself all those that I could remember. It was midsummer, so my favorite constellation of Orion was not visible. I wondered if some of my friends or family were at that moment looking up at these same stars and constellations. How I longed to be up there, free, flying high above earth with my crew, flying as we pleased whichever way we fancied. But then, with an involuntary shudder, I remembered how quickly and violently death could catch the unwary flying in those same skies.

I was brought back to earth by a persistent ache in my back. I shifted sideways a few inches to be free of the sharp stone on which I had been lying, only to feel new bumps pushing into me. No matter how I stretched out, a stone was always under a tender part of my body. I tried lying on my side. There were fewer lumps now but my hip began to ache from lack of proper support. When I could stand it no longer, I rolled onto my other side. After only a short interval this side began to ache too. I became angry that I could not get comfortable and sleep would not come. What was wrong with me? Many other times I had been able to sleep soundly in uncomfortable circumstances. Perhaps I was no longer fit and healthy. Perhaps after eating minimal rations while in the hands of the Gestapo I had little excess flesh left to pad my bones against the stones. Gradually another form of torture set in. The night had rapidly cooled and damp from the bare ground permeated my thin clothing, chilling me to the bone. I sat up, then stood up and moved about to get some warmth into my cold body. But when I moved I felt hungry, tired, and weak, so I lay down again and longed for sleep.

All through the night I was aware that those around me were also suffering from the same miseries. Here and there prone bodies shifted position, sat up, stood up and moved around, then lay down again. I heard the murmur of voices. I saw shadowy figures going to and from the Abort. Periodically the glare of the searchlight beam from a watchtower swept the area of the outer fence. And so the first night passed.

At last, when I thought I would never get rid of the chill in my bones, I noticed a perceptible lightening in the sky to the east. In no time at all the sun was rising above the horizon to warm our chilled bodies. Now it was shining on the fresh beauty of the rolling countryside beyond the fence at the bottom of the hill. I could see farmland and villages nestled in the folds of the ground. A church spire pointed toward the heavens. Nowhere in that direction could I observe signs of war.

CHAPTER SEVEN

Buchenwald – The Early Days

In the half light of the new day Tom and I moved around stretching our stiff muscles as we chatted with others doing the same thing. I did not know what time it was, perhaps five or six A.M. Most of our crowd were already awake, grouped here and there in ones and twos, busily comparing thoughts and voicing complaints about their problems trying to sleep the previous night. Through the nearby fences I was aware that the rest of the concentration camp was already active. Outside the perimeter wire ss soldiers were coming and going from the watchtowers as the guard was changed. I was idly watching one of them walk along by the wire when I spotted something sinister about the perimeter fence which I had not been alert enough to understand the day before. Each strand of wire suspended on the concrete posts was fastened to a ceramic insulator, which could only mean that the wires were charged with high voltage electricity. I thought it inhumane that the ss would erect harmless-looking wires that would instantly kill anyone who unwittingly happened to touch one.

In the other compounds prisoners were coming from the upper camp carrying big wooden tubs between them, which I hoped contained the morning meal. Soon four of our men were directed to the camp kitchen to carry back food for us. My stomach was crying for something to eat and I could hardly wait for their return. As I waited for breakfast I watched two stripe-suited prisoners cut through the corner of our compound on their way towards the upper camp. Between them they carried a stretcher over which a coarse blanket was thrown. I shivered when I realized that there was a form under the blanket, probably the remains of some wretch who had not survived the night. In the short time that I waited for our food to arrive I counted some half-dozen bodies carried out; sometimes there was no blanket covering them. If this many died on a summer night, I was horrified at the thought of how many might die in the cold of winter. There must be a huge cemetery to bury the dead. Was there a record kept of the names of those who died and were the next of kin notified? Was any kind of a service said for them to mark their passing in this place, far from their homes and loved ones?

Finally our four men arrived back with two tubs of rations for breakfast. Finding that our meal was a shallow saucepan of tasteless acorn coffee, I seethed with rage and disappointment. I could have gorged myself on a big plateful of bacon and eggs together with hot buttered toast spread with fresh strawberry jam or marmalade. I was extremely hungry and this was the first food of any kind I had received since early yesterday. This phony coffee only increased my hunger pangs!

After the wooden tubs had been returned to the kitchen, a meeting of our group was held under the leadership of Colonel Powell, the American, and Squadron Leader Lamason, the New Zealander. These two had apparently been planning a strategy that they thought would be best for our survival and possible recognition as prisoners of war. First, as they had said last night, they were going to scout around the camp to try and make contact with the German authorities. If successful, they would demand that we be given proper food, clothing, shelter, recognition as POWs, and removal from this place. If our representatives were unable to meet with the Germans today, they would search for any other Allied prisoners in camp and see how they were being treated. While doing this they would, of course, try to learn everything they could about Buchenwald that might be of help to us.

They had decided that we must behave with military discipline at all times, even if we did look like a ragtag bunch of undisciplined civilians. They were sure word would soon spread that we were soldiers who did not belong here. If we had to go anywhere in groups, we were to march in a military manner. We were to fall in smartly for roll calls and for issue of food rations. At such times we would not break ranks until the parade was dismissed or we were ordered to step forward. They repeated their instructions of the previous day that we were not to go exploring around the camp. We were to stay in this area and leave it only to use the Abort or for such things as fetching food rations. If we did have to leave for any reason, it should never be alone. It was permissible to fraternize with other internees, but we must keep clear of political discussions. We must avoid encounters with the ss if at all possible. There were to be no escape attempts for the time being.

I thought all these orders were very impressive, but whether they would help us get away from here was a different matter. At least it was a morale booster in that we would be united in trying to do something about our present plight. I watched the Colonel and Squadron Leader set off through the nearby gate, then turn left up the hill towards the central area of the camp. For all who cared to notice, they marched side by side in military fashion, trying to maintain a brisk pace. The proper effect was hard to achieve though, what with their tattered clothes, shaved heads, and bare feet that forced them to step gingerly.

I took stock of my own situation. I was not nearly as healthy as I should have been because of the lack of food for the last few weeks; I was also tired from lack of a sound sleep. However, I was no longer chilled from sleeping on the bare ground. Even my bruised bare feet, although still sensitive to any sharp objects, were no longer cold. The weather was shaping up for a sunny, hot day. Our leaders had gone to fight for our rights. For the moment, my prospects were not yet desperate.

Through the wire of the inner fences I could see large numbers of men in the striped suits leaving their barracks and heading towards the main gate and upper parts of the camp. They must be the slave labour parties reporting for daily work assignments with Kapos in charge. Seldom did I see German uniforms.

Stomach cramps warned me that it was time for a visit to the Abort. I made my way towards it with two or three others of our group. I was becoming unpleasantly familiar with the disgusting place and the mere thought of having to go there sent shudders of revulsion down my spine. The Abort, entered by one of the end doors, was used by both the healthy and the sick. Even before entering one was greeted by an overpowering stench. This rose from a large seemingly bottomless concrete pit in the centre of the building filled with the stinking urine and feces of the thousands who used it each day. The edges of this opening were bounded by a curb topped by a rounded wooden rail which served as a seat.

On many people the effect of the poor food was a loss of control and their bowels often emptied on the rail or the concrete floor beside it. Consequently it was quite common to find that there was no dry spot to sit so that one had to crouch with one's rear end extending over the stewing, simmering mess. Adding to the horrors of this place was the ever-present fear that one might slip on floor spillage and tumble into the pit to most certainly drown in the filth. The Abort also differed from normal washrooms in that there was neither toilet paper nor water with which to clean oneself or to wash spillage from the floor or seats. As far as I knew, the cesspool was never emptied nor the rails cleaned. The facilities were always in use, day and night, because the runs eventually afflicted everyone.

By the time I returned to our "home ground," the bustle of workers leaving the camp on their assignments had subsided. I joined a group of our people gathered around two stripe-suited prisoners who had stopped to talk to us. At first they seemed wary of saying too much, almost as though for some reason unknown to us we could not be trusted. However, when they discovered that we were airmen we became instant heroes and their hesitance vanished.

These first two were followed by others as the word spread that there were Allied airmen in Buchenwald. We answered their questions and in turn asked many ourselves. It was not a quick, easy exchange of queries and replies because of the language problems. Words and sentences tried in various languages had to be explained with hand signs and gestures. But we soon discovered that where there is a will there is a way if one really wants to understand or be understood by someone from another culture. Most important to our new contacts was our opinion on how soon we thought the war would end. They wanted to know where we came from, if there was lots to eat there, and what was it like flying over Germany. They could not understand why we had not been issued with striped suits and assigned to work parties.

From them we learned that Buchenwald had been built before the war to hold political prisoners. From what I had already seen, and from what I now heard, I got the impression that the place was huge, with thousands of people interned in it. Our visitors warned us not to go near the perimeter fence because the guards shot anyone who came near. Furthermore, the fence itself was charged with sufficient voltage, they said, to kill anyone who came in contact with it. They told us that the barracks were very crowded, very little food was available, and many people died each day from malnutrition. Those who died or were killed were disposed of in a crematorium which worked night and day. The chimney belching smoke that I had seen yesterday must have belonged to it and not to a powerhouse or kitchen! Squatting, sitting, or standing in the summer sun, we listened dumbfounded to the incredible things they had to tell us. Surely this place could not be real and I was only in the midst of a bad dream from which I would shortly awaken. These things could not happen in the world that I had always considered to be civilized.

The morning passed quickly as we chatted with these people. It seemed to me that in no time S/L Lamason and Col. Powell were back and we were eagerly gathering around them. Unfortunately, they had not been able to make any contact with the German authorities. Other than having met and talked to some Kapos, who conceded that we were probably POWs, our leaders had little of encouragement to offer.

Our senior officers said that the Kapos had promised to try and arrange a meeting with the German commandant. In the meantime, however, the Kapos advised that we maintain a low profile while they tried to use their influence to keep us from being assigned to any work details. For the moment, because of overcrowding, there was no inside space available and more trainloads of prisoners were arriving daily. If they could arrange it, they would try and allot the first empty barrack space to us. Sometimes workers living in barracks were shipped away on permanent assignments to factories, thereby freeing inside accommodation. I could see that there was little we could do except wait and hope for the best.

About noon, judging from the position of the sun, four of our men went off to fetch the midday food. When they arrived back, we fell in with the pre-arranged military precision to receive our midday rations, which consisted of a saucepan of soup and a slab of bread without butter or margarine. The bread was similar to the tasteless wartime variety which I had known in Fresnes. The soup was reasonably warm and contained several root vegetables, probably swedes or turnips. There was also meat in the soup, even though I could not taste it, because I found a stringy morsel of it and an occasional small bit of bone. There were no second helpings. As usual, I wolfed down my food and still felt starved. It was almost as I though I had been given just enough to tantalize me.

That afternoon some inmates explained the position of the internees who held the title of Kapo. It was a political appointment by the Germans, often given to criminal elements, to run certain sections of the camp. If no German was present, the Kapo was the senior authority and had to answer for the discipline of the men assigned to him. For example, Kapos were in charge of work parties, barrack blocks, or sections of one of the factories. This delegation of authority perhaps explained why so few uniformed Germans needed to be visibly involved with the internal day-to-day operation of the camp. Our informants said that a Kapo usually had a small room to himself at the end of a barrack block and that he sometimes received mail and parcels from home. I was not sure whether to believe this last bit, because it seemed contrary to the treatment that I had so far come to expect here.

Somehow that first afternoon passed quickly. Quite a number of the men, including myself, managed to doze a little in the hot sun, catching up on the sleep that we had missed the night before. There were frequent visitors with whom to talk. Generally, I noticed that there was much more gabbing among ourselves. No doubt we welcomed the opportunity to chat in relative freedom with others of the same background and language after weeks of isolation in Fresnes. Invariably, most of the talk was still about flying.

Our first supper in Buchenwald proved to be nothing more than a saucepan of acorn coffee. My hunger pangs were worse than ever. As I drank the brown liquid I despaired of ever getting enough to eat in this place. All day, with the thought of another night in the open, I had been keeping an eye on the western sky for any sign that the weather might change to rain. I tried to remember all that I had learned in my meteorology course at navigation training school in Portage la Prairie. With a feeling of relief I decided there would be no precipitation. So at least tonight I would not be soaked to the skin as well as chilled to the bone.

When the time came for the evening Appell, we lined up in military fashion to be counted. One day was nearly over and we were no nearer to leaving. None of us had provoked unwanted attention from the Germans, been beaten, or shot. But we were just that much hungrier. Now it was time to think about sleeping outside for the second night. Various theories were presented about how best to avoid the aches of the previous night. For sleeping on the side, there were two schools of thought. One maintained that it was best to scoop a small depression in the ground in which the hip would rest. The other argued that it was better to tuck a stone under the waist line, like a pillow, for support.

That night nothing seemed to help my aches and pains very much. I found that both the damp coming up from the ground and the cold of my bare feet dominated any other feelings. Luckily my private weather forecast proved correct and no rain fell. As time wore on, I was even more aware of the many trips made by our men to the Abort. The trips were so frequent that I realized they, like myself, must be suffering from bladder problems caused by the damp or from the runs. Twice I had to go there myself, although the place revolted me.

Our second day started much like the one before. As we stretched the cramps and chills from our bones, the grisly parade of stretchers with the night's harvest of dead passed on its way to the crematorium. The acorn coffee was brought and quickly drunk. It seemed to me that moving around to get warm consumed more energy than we derived from this liquid. I wondered if we were fighting a losing battle.

Soon there was no question that I had the runs. I feared that being a more frequent visitor to the Abort greatly increased my chances of picking up disease or infections, especially if I had any cuts on my feet. On one such trip with some of my buddies, we found we had to wait our turn. We chose to use what seemed like one of the less filthy sections of the wooden rail, at the moment occupied by an old man in tattered clothes who seemed to be taking an abnormally long time. Finally one of my friends, who could hardly wait any longer turned and said, "I wish the old bugger would hurry up and get off the pot." Whereupon, to our astonishment, the bundle of rags turned to us and said in perfect English, "I beg your pardon!"

After the acorn coffee breakfast, the Colonel and Squadron Leader again departed for the main camp area. With their bare feet, shaved heads, and dirty civilian clothes they certainly did not look like the senior officers of a group of Allied airmen. Most of the Russian prisoners we had seen here still wore their army uniforms and looked far more important. As I watched our men go their way I thought I noticed something a little different about their bearing. Was it my imagination, or were they walking better now that their feet were becoming toughened? I wondered if they would have more success today than yesterday.

During the morning we again had visitors to divert us from our discussions and private thoughts. Some of our group were now beginning to venture away from "home ground" to chat with people at nearby barracks. Obviously it was going to be impossible to keep such a large number of intelligent men with nothing to do, herded together like sheep in a pen. That morning we learned the significance of the numbers and patches of coloured material that we had seen on the striped prison uniforms. The numbers, which were often tattooed on the forearm as well, were the internee registration numbers. Nationality was indicated by a letter beside each person's number. For example, P = Polish; R = Russian: U = Hungarian (*Ungarn* in German).

Each prisoner was further categorized by a coloured cloth triangle, sewn below the number and letter on his jacket, that defined his social status. The most common were red for political, green for criminal, gray for murderers (with the letter "K" superimposed), pink for homosexuals, and the Star of David for Jews. If a prisoner was wanted for some reason, only his number would be called out. In the German war machine you were a number, not a name.

Now that I understood the significance of the badges, I soon noted that there were prisoners in Buchenwald from almost every country in Europe. I even saw a few orientals. It seemed to me that the German prisoners were in better physical shape than those of the conquered nations. Germans also seemed to make up the largest proportion of those who remained in camp each day.

When our senior officers returned at noon, they again reported little success. Because they had not been able to meet with any of the German authorities, no arrangements had been made for us to leave or for any improvements in our living conditions. Nor had they been able to find any other Allied prisoners of war with whom to compare treatment. On this foray, however, they had met with several Allied civilians, one of whom was Canadian. These men had been convicted of spying and sent to Buchenwald to be executed. They said they expected to be killed any day now. It was very important to them that we let the world know that they had met their fate here.

The French partisans from our cattle train were still occupying the ground next to us, still wearing their civilian clothing. Like us, they were making new contacts, especially among their many countrymen who had been in Buchenwald for some time. By evening Appell I noticed that a large influx of new arrivals had increased the number of people living in the open in our compound. I do not remember ever having watched so anxiously and prayed so much for cloudless skies as I had these past two days. Fortunately the weather continued to hold in our favour. With no sign of rain in the offing, we settled down for the night after evening Appell. I do not know what we would have done if it had rained. I suppose we would have just stood all night and let it soak us through as we wiggled our toes in the wet mud.

I didn't fall asleep for a long time after I lay down because as usual I started thinking about home. I wondered if my family would ever find out that I had been in this terrible concentration camp. I hoped they never would. I thought the shock would be too much for them if my message on the wall of Fresnes got home, yet I didn't survive this place. This third night was still bad, even though I was becoming tougher now and a little less bothered by aches in my back and sides. The major irritant was the number of times I had to join the procession of people to and from the Abort. I was surprised that it was as busy at night as in daytime. It seemed impossible to me that people given so little food would have to empty their bowels so frequently. In one of our discussions that afternoon someone had said that dysentery was just an extreme case of diarrhea. He said that a person who had contracted dysentery first emptied all the contents of his stomach through his bowels and then passed his own mucus, blood, and body fluids as he died a slow death. This was great food for thought as I crouched over the pit in the filthy Abort wondering whether I had diarrhea or dysentery.

Our third full day in Buchenwald started with the sun breaking through a few scattered clouds and warming the restless group of men occupying our "home" ground. As we stretched aching muscles, stamped around to get rid of chills, and drank the acorn coffee, I thought to myself that the hot sun was the only cheerful thing to look forward to that day. A short while later I realized that I was becoming accustomed and hardened to this place when I hardly noticed the dead carted off to the crematorium. So far we had lost no one, but how long could this last?

During the morning, as I sat talking with Tom, my hand brushed a tender spot on one of my legs. I saw that I had a scratch on my left shin which was red and irritated. Many of my companions also had sore spots here and there. Some of the inflamed places around the waistline were extremely itchy. Even now many of us seemed to be scratching, although there were no signs of mosquitoes or black flies. Then one of the more knowledgeable of our group said not to be so bloody naive, it could only be fleas. I was shocked. I had thought it was only tramps and beggars who picked up fleas. It dawned on me that the men I had seen outside their huts the first day working at the seams of their clothing must have been flea picking.

When our leaders came back at noon from their daily expedition, there was no longer any rush to hear what they had to say. As we had come to expect, they had nothing to offer that would boost our morale. There was still very little food. I didn't believe I could be hungrier each day, but I was. There seemed to be a lot of bickering among ourselves now. I thought that it was an indication that the hopelessness of our situation was beginning to get to us.

It had never occurred to me that there might be English civilians interned in Buchenwald. However, there must have been thousands of English nationals captured in the countries overrun by the German blitzkrieg, so I shouldn't have been so surprised to learn that there were some of them here. I was with Tom and a couple of others when an older man who was passing by stopped, looked us over, then approached us. To our astonishment, he proceeded to tell us his story in perfect English. He was an

Englishman whose home was on Guernsey, one of the Channel Islands occupied by the Germans after the fall of France. He was very worried about his wife, whom he had not heard from since arriving in Buchenwald, four years ago. He looked so elderly and frail that I wondered if he would survive the war.

Although there were clouds about, no rain fell on this god-forsaken place that day, nor that night. But, on second thought, perhaps it was not completely god-forsaken and someone was looking after us. After all, we had been in the open for three full days and had not yet been put through the torment of a chilling, soaking rain. Besides, if you could ignore the immediate sur-roundings while sitting on the slope in the hot sun, you could look out beyond the barbed wire and derive pleasure from seeing the rolling green fields, ripening harvests and, nestled in a fold, the village and church spire. I did not think I could have remained sane in this place if ugly stone walls had blocked all view of the outside world.

That night I slept reasonably well except when running to the Abort, scratching at annoying flea bites around my waist, or stamping around to get warm in the chill before dawn. The next day I hardly noticed when the Colonel and Squadron Leader slipped away after drinking their acorn coffee. I was more con-cerned about my several scratches, flea bites, and cuts that were beginning to fester. All of these were painfully tender and had yellow pus beneath the scabs, except one on the sole of my foot which was open and oozing, making walking difficult. I was worried sick about picking up more germs through it, especially when walking on the floor of the filthy Abort.

Under normal circumstances, small cuts or a bad case of summer complaint would have been of little consequence, but these were not normal circumstances. When I checked around, I found that most of our crowd also had numerous infections, most often on the soles of the feet. We discussed what we might do to help them heal. At home there were new wonder drugs, in limited supply, that were supposed to work miracles fighting bacteria, but there was no hope they would be available to prisoners here. The possibility of reporting to the *Revier*, or camp hospital, in Block (hut) 51 was quickly rejected. Several of our visitors had warned us that Block 51 was more an experimental station than a hospital and should only be used as a last resort. The staff were reputedly using patients as guinea pigs for their "research." Our informants said that they knew of many cases of men who died there after being admitted for minor ailments. We were afraid to ignore these ominous warnings.

I wondered what I would do if my infections or my diarrhea became even worse. Someone volunteered the information that a couple of Russian prisoners in the next compound were offering primitive first aid treatment. He had already been to see them and considered it better than nothing at all. So some of us decided to find out for ourselves what they could do for us. A short time later we limped into the next compound and located the two Russians, who were using the end of a barrack block as their medical room.

The Russians were cheerful, spoke no English, and acted as though they knew what they were doing. But their medical supplies seemed to consist solely of a needle, rolls of paper bandages, and a large bottle of purple disinfectant. As near as I could discover, all they did was lance infections. First they jabbed an unsterilized needle into the inflamed area, then drained it for a moment before squeezing out the last drops of pus. After that they dabbed the area with purple antiseptic before winding a crepe-like paper bandage around it. The paper dressing had no adhesive to hold it together and of course was susceptible to moisture as well as tearing. It was all very primitive, but I thought it was better to risk picking up more infection in the cure than to receive no treatment at all. I certainly had to give them credit for handling a lot of patients in a short time.

I was very discouraged, as I limped back down the hill towards my "home" area, at how quickly our health was deteriorating. We were starting our fourth full day, yet I only had to glance around to see that at least half our people were limping on sore feet or favouring festering sores. It was getting so bad that only a few were fit enough to carry the wooden food tubs from the kitchen. If this decline continued, even if we were liberated soon, many of us would have to be carried out on stretchers. Our poor state of health was also affecting our already low morale. It did not seem possible that we could endure any further shocks or deprivations.

During the afternoon, the topic of discussion was the grim thought that the ss might slaughter all the inmates before our troops could liberate Buchenwald. We hoped that by some chance they knew in England that we were here and were aware of this frightening but distinct possibility. Perhaps the Allies might already be making plans to drop paratroopers on the camp to free us before the ss could murder all witnesses to their atrocities.

There was the potential for still other disasters to strike us. Supposing the Allied armies did not realize that this was a concentration camp and shelled it while battling the retreating German armies? Or what if we were bombed because one of our own high flying reconnaissance airplanes mistook this place for a German army camp, or because it spotted the factories in the woods outside the main gate? In either case, with no shelters to protect us we would suffer heavy casualties.

Our best, and perhaps only, chance of survival had been that we would be liberated before the onslaught of winter. But after Appell we heard a rumour that the Allied armies had been stopped at the Rhine and were digging in for the winter. I doubted if, given my poor physical condition, I could survive the cold and hunger of a winter in Buchenwald. There was no prospect of shelter indoors and we were bound to get rain any day now. In a few months' time I was sure the area would get frost and snow. It didn't seem fair, I thought, after all I had been through, that each day new setbacks increased the odds against survival.

I lay down to sleep that night trying not to feel depressed. At least my runs seemed to be easing a little. My infected sores were no worse, although I had a couple of new ones. There was no indication it would rain that night. I escaped from my despair by thinking about Lyoncross, my home away from home in Scotland. How I would arrive on leave in Glasgow about midnight ... take a tram that in the blackout only went half way to Barrhead ... the trek across the lovely countryside in the moonlight, first along the roads, then shortcutting through the fields up the hill to Lyoncross ... the warmth and comfort of the old stone house ... the hot snack of tea, scones, and all kinds of good things laid out for me with a welcoming note from my aunts who would have already retired ... then up to bed, sinking deep into the down-filled mattress to feel the hot water bottle at my feet ... drifting off to sleep with thoughts of tomorrow and whether any of the girls I knew would be coming by the next day. Then I was back with reality, lying on the damp ground, looking up at the heavens above.

Finally I drifted into broken sleep, wondering why I had seen no activity on the part of our bombers and long-range fighters. It was very discouraging to say the least, almost as though the Allies had done so well this summer they planned to take a holiday while we rotted away here. It would be a great morale booster to see some of our planes fly across unchecked by the Luftwaffe.

CHAPTER EIGHT

August Twenty-fourth

August 24, 1944, started as though it was going to be like any other day. The dead were carted off up the hill to the crematorium, marked by the ever-smoking chimney. A couple of reasonably fit men from our group were delegated to fetch the acorn coffee. I examined my cuts and sores and satisfied myself that none was dangerously inflamed, not even the latest ones. However, I was angry that the infected cuts on the sole of my foot were so tender that I could hardly put any weight on it and had to hop around on one foot, so I decided that during the morning I should go and see the Russians again. After "breakfast" several of us limped up to the first aid post. As usual, there was a steady stream of patients of all nationalities coming and going for treatment.

While I waited outside for my turn, I looked down the slope to the distant green fields, rolling meadows, and partly hidden village, already shimmering in the heat of the new day. As I gazed in that direction, somehow the nearby ugly electrified wire fence and guard towers seemed to fade from view. I raised my head to study the sky around. Not a cloud in sight! No doubt about it, we were in for a scorching hot day. I wondered if it was just as beautiful back in England and whether our heavy bombers had been out last night over other parts of Germany. Perhaps today the Americans, who preferred to bomb in daylight at high altitudes, would be coming over.

When I arrived back at our "home ground," I saw that the Colonel and Squadron Leader had already departed on their daily venture. Some of the more energetic of our crowd had wandered off into the nearby compounds. Studying our group of airmen, I chuckled to myself at how ludicrous we looked. Not just because of the shaven heads, the stubble of growing beards, and the bare feet, but because of the clothes we were wearing. Some were in business suits, others dressed as labourers, and many more as farmers. I particularly remember one tall, well-built man who was wearing a pair of farmer's overalls that completely covered the lower part of his body, leaving most of his chest and muscular arms bare. It was a great outfit for hot weather but didn't cover enough of him for the cold weather which was bound to come. For some idiotic reason I was quite intrigued as to whether or not he was wearing underwear. I was ready to bet that he wasn't.

I knew it was getting near time for the noon food issue when our people started drifting back. The Colonel and Squadron Leader returned in plenty of time to send our delegation of carriers off to the kitchen. No one would risk missing this meal because it was the only real nourishment we received all day. While waiting for the rations, the sun beat down mercilessly. Glancing around I could not help but note that we had lost our prison pallor – as was to be expected since there were no trees to offer shade. In no time the wooden tubs arrived and we hungrily waited in line for our portions. After we had devoured every morsel, the empty tubs were carted back to the kitchens.

Our tub carriers had hardly returned when we were alerted by the distant sound of air raid sirens to the south of the camp. I wondered if fast RAF fighter-bombers or reconnaissance planes had set off the alarms, or if the USAF was mounting a large attack. Whoever it was, it would be great if they passed near enough for us to get a glimpse of them on their way in or out. On the other hand, it could be a false alarm and we would see nothing to boost our morale. Close to the camp, more sirens took up the nerve-wracking wail. I scanned the sky to the south and east before my eyes focused on a long white streak high in the clear blue sky. Then I saw another, and still another, until there were so many I could not count all the vapour trails from airplanes flying in perfect formation at great height. From the very precise arrangement of "Vs" at different levels, I knew it was the Americans because only they flew this boldly. The scene reminded me of movies I had seen of rank upon rank of infantry entering ancient battles and marching invincibly shoulder to shoulder toward their enemy.

As yet I could not hear the drone of engines nor could I make out the type of aircraft, but I knew they must be "Forts" or Liberators. Watching the stream of bombers carefully, I guessed they were about thirty miles south of us, flying in a northeasterly direction. I estimated that there must be several hundred, and wherever they were headed it was going to be a fairly big raid. They seemed headed for Weimar, the railway junction through which we had passed last week. As they closed in on Weimar, I could see the sun flashing off the silver fuselages and single tails of Flying Fortresses. Unwavering, they flew at a precisely spaced distance from each other, like performers in a well-trained corps de ballet. I was mesmerized by the sight. It looked more as though our Allies were giving a demonstration of formation flying at an air show than going into battle. However, the dreamlike quality of the scene quickly evaporated.

Although I was too far away to hear the noise, I could see that there was deadly combat taking place. Bright orange flashes followed by black puffs of smoke showed that the Americans were encountering heavy ack-ack fire. I was quite sure that they were also being attacked by German fighters. It did not seem possible that these bombers flying so neatly across the sky could suddenly burst into flames or break into pieces and plummet to earth. Nevertheless, I saw several of them go down. While I watched, fascinated, one of the big four-engined planes broke apart and large sections of the wings and tail fluttered lazily downward like autumn leaves from a tree. I had thought they would go straight down, trailing a long plume of smoke. Perhaps only the small fighters crashed like that. In any event, I hoped that the poor buggers flying this one were able to parachute to safety. At least they would have much more time to get out than I had had when my plane was shot down.

When a formation of fifty or sixty bombers broke away from the main stream and headed northwest, directly towards us, our impersonal involvement came to an end. I had a sick feeling in the pit of my stomach when I realized that Buchenwald was probably their target. I had an urge to jump to my feet on the impossible chance that they would see me, wave my arms at them and yell, "No! No! No! Can't you see that we are fellow airmen! Stay away you fools, you'll kill us by mistake!" I felt utterly helpless – they were approaching so fast and there was absolutely no way of stopping them. I cursed and raved at the stupidity of the bloody Americans who were about to bomb and kill us. Couldn't they see that this was a concentration camp, not a German army camp? Those bloody idiots flew so damn high they never knew what they were bombing!

There were no bomb shelters in Buchenwald for the inmates. And without even looking around I knew there were no ditches or depressions in the ground where we could shelter from the blast and fragments of a near miss. Nor could we try and run from the target area. We were sitting ducks. All we could do was lie flat on the open ground and pray for the best. I knew that bombs always fell in a long curve and would be released some distance away if they were to hit their objective. Also that on the American system the leading bomber in a formation was in charge of the attack. When the bombardier in this plane had the target in his sights, he pressed the button that simultaneously released his bomb load and the smoke flare that was the signal for the other planes to drop their explosives.

I lay flat in the open with the rest of our crowd as we watched with horror the relentless approach of the attackers. Bits of steel from spent ack-ack shells spattered around us. I estimated where the release point would be if we were to be hit and, sure enough, at that point the white smoke flare blossomed under the lead aircraft. I knew then that the bombs were streaking down towards us and that perhaps I had only a few seconds to live. I heard a loud rushing noise like an express train, then the explosions, and felt the ground shake. I sat up, thankful to be alive. The bombs had missed us, landing only a short distance away near the entrance gate.

I looked at the sky to the south and saw the main force, still heading northeast with the ack-ack bursting around it. But even as I watched, another large group broke away, banked ninety degrees to port in precise formation, and also flew northwest towards us. Again I suffered agonies of fear and despair, fully expecting that this time we would surely be killed.

I studied the flight path of the fast approaching aircraft. I convinced myself that this second wave was on a slightly different tack which would allow them a direct hit on the undamaged section of the camp where we were cowering. Sure enough, I saw the white smoke flare appear at exactly the right moment. Again I crouched down as the second load of high explosives hurtled down towards us. Again the rushing noise like an express train and the ground shaking.

We sat up and took stock. One Englishman was bleeding from a shrapnel wound in his shoulder but otherwise no one was hurt. We were fortunate; again the target had been somewhere in the direction of the main gate. Above us the last of the Fortresses to attack Buchenwald had already swung westward, and with the sun flashing on their silver bodies they headed home, still in perfect formation, condensation trails streaming far behind.

From the area beyond the main gate black smoke billowed upward, which made me realize part of the load had been incendiaries. I was afraid that if the ss had suffered casualties they would take revenge on us airmen prisoners. There was absolutely nothing that we could do except try and keep out of their way as much as possible. In the upper part of the camp the black smoke thickened and I thought I heard the crackle of flames as the fires gained hold. An excited messenger from one of the Kapos arrived with orders that we were to send men to fight the outbreaks. The required help was sent from the few most mobile of our men. I wondered how much good they would do running around barefooted and in such poor condition. If they did not understand orders shouted in German would they be shot when they were slow to respond, or even just because they were enemy fliers? I wondered if we would ever see them alive again.

By late afternoon the smoke lessened as the fires were brought under control. Anxiously we waited for the safe return of our fire fighters, who gradually filtered back until by nightfall all had returned. From them, we learned details of the havoc wrought by the raid. The primary target had been the munition factories just outside the main gate. It had been largely flattened, killing hundreds of the slave workers. Nearby, many of the ss barrack buildings, housing more than a thousand men, had been destroyed with heavy loss of life. Also within this area was the German Kommandantur, or centralized administration section, that had been badly hit. However, the fire damage caused by the incendiary bombs was confined only to several buildings in the Big Lager.

Of prime concern to us was whether or not the kitchen or food supplies had been destroyed. Fortunately, they had not. Nevertheless, there was no evening meal of acorn coffee, but as compensation, there was also no evening Appell.

An unbelievably nauseating story came from some of our reluctant helpers who, while fighting a fire in one of the buildings, found themselves in a room set up as a museum. They were horrified when they realized that among the gruesome items on display were lamp shades and book covers made from human skin. Each of these grisly objects was set up to display an unusual or intriguing sample of the art of tattooing. I suspected that the owners of these tattoos had been murdered just for the sake of obtaining rare examples, dying just to satisfy the whim of some evil person.

We had been very lucky that none of us had been killed or even seriously injured. And fortune was still favouring us with another rainless night. However, it did seem most unfair that in addition to being maltreated by the Germans, we could also be attacked by our own side. I could not help but wonder if perhaps we had been very fortunate that our cattle train had not been mistakenly attacked by our fighter bombers. Maybe our forces, not knowing who we were, would attack us many more times before the war ended. With the terrible thought that I could now be killed by my own people, I drifted off into a broken sleep. The night passed with the usual parade of men back and forth to the Abort.

CHAPTER NINE

Buchenwald – The Final Days

After the air raid of the previous day, the camp routine, at least for Appells and food rations, was back to normal. Of course the raid was the main topic of conversation. I wondered if the Americans would be back to complete their devastation of the ss barracks and munition factories. I had heard a rumour that one of the factories made V-2 flying bombs that were wreaking havoc on London. If true, it would be important to the Allied cause to destroy it.

After what I had heard yesterday about the museum of horrors, I found that I was involuntarily scanning the inmates who chanced near me for unusual tattoos. My morbid curiosity drew my attention to some magnificent art work on backs and chests that I might otherwise not have noticed. Obviously the owner of an outstanding piece of work should keep it well concealed, since he ran the risk of having it forcibly removed for public display while the rest of him went up the crematorium chimney in smoke.

In the days following the American raid, we airmen prisoners suffered no reprisals at the hands of the Germans. The fear of that possibility faded and general lethargy seemed to settle over us, perhaps due to the daytime heat and the lack of sufficient food. We were content to stay put in our small area, talking less about the present and more about our pasts.

We were in the prime of our lives, and in normal circumstances would have found the days far too short for all the living that we wanted to do. At first there had been so much to learn about Buchenwald. But now, as the terrible novelty of our situation wore off, time was becoming a burden to us. We seemed to be losing all interest in our surroundings and sat around aimlessly. Soon we started bickering among ourselves. Before long "we" and "they" groups began to form, each unjustifiably criticizing the others along national lines. Finally we were falling in for roll calls and rations in two separate groups – the Americans under their Colonel with their system of parade drill and the British and Commonwealth airmen under Squadron Leader Lamason with the British system of commands and movements. Fortunately, each group continued to maintain its own unified military discipline, so that as a whole we kept a united front against our common enemy. Our leaders still worked together, presumably on ways to improve our lot.

During one of the periods of enforced idleness, a number of us were chatting with Harry Bastable, a Canadian whom I had first met during training days in England. It seemed like yesterday, yet it was exactly a year ago that I had first met him. He and I, with a number of RCAF navigators, were participating in an army battlecourse in Devon. I particularly recalled a sunny afternoon when a small group of us were enjoying a short break. There we were, lying on a grassy hill looking down at the tiny village of Sidmouth, while to our left the cliffs dropped steeply to the English Channel. Harry was explaining his personal theories on army field-tactics. Knowing little about them myself, I was quite impressed. Shortly after that we were separated when posted to different advanced navigation training units. When we parted, I never dreamed that the next time we would meet would be in an SS concentration camp. This afternoon, although the setting was vastly changed, I was again part of a group listening intently to Harry as he held forth. This time, instead of army tactics, he regaled us with amusing stories of prewar days when he worked for Canadian National Railway Express in Winnipeg.

On the afternoon of August 29, I was squatting on the ground among a group comprised mostly of Americans who were involved in a heated discussion. I listened with interest as Whitey

Mclaughlin, from Florida, expressed his opinions on the race problems in his part of the country. I had never before realized how greatly feelings differed in the United States between southerners and those from the north when it concerned American blacks. During the argument my attention shifted to dark, threatening clouds that were forming slowly along the western horizon. It was obvious to me that the spell of summer weather, which had blessed us for ten days, was ending, and that our eleventh night in the open would be cold and wet. During the day the Colonel and Squadron Leader had been, as usual, absent from our area except for mealtimes. I hoped that today they were working on some last-minute miracle to get us under cover for the night.

When we assembled for the evening ration of ersatz coffee, our two leaders announced that – just after Appell we were to move into Block 58 where some space had been found for us. We greeted this exciting news with cheers. A new feeling of hope surged through me. The incredible news of shelter effectively dispelled my despair, which had been increasing rapidly as the storm clouds approached. Perhaps, I thought, we would now have a reasonable chance of survival.

I found it hard to curb my impatience for our move to new quarters, so I was relieved when Appell took only a short time. Quickly we formed up, then marched to the best of our ability through the nearby gate into the compound west of us. Block 58 proved to be close by, and it took us only a few minutes to get there. While the heavens threatened to drench us at any moment, we hurriedly filed into our new quarters, a long, low, windowless building of wood frame construction. Inside, my first reaction was mainly disappointment. I thought that I might have to sleep on the dirty floor because the place was already packed with men who were wearing the ugly striped suits.

I sized up my new surroundings. Immediately to the left on entering was a small room which I later learned was the private quarters of the block Kapo. Across from it was a circular, industrial-type wash basin at which six to eight persons could wash simultaneously. Along the remainder of the left-hand side of the building were tiers of deep wooden shelves, on some of which men were lying. In the open area to the right, opposite the shelves, were a few wooden tables and benches. Midway down the hut was the only other fixture of significance, a medium-sized cast iron stove. I assumed it was used for heating because of its design and because there were no cooking utensils nearby. At the far end was the only other door.

Through gaps in the crowd I was able to get a good look at the shelves that were used as bunks for sleeping. They extended out from the wall about six feet and, starting with the bottom one at floor level, were about two and one-half feet apart in height and four tiers high. On some of them were scattered a few palliasses. I imagined that one must sleep with one's head out towards the centre of the room and feet against the wall, otherwise in such close quarters the stench of unwashed bodies would be overpowering. I assumed that we had been allowed in temporarily because of the rain, now beating down on the roof, and would be thrown out in the morning. It was almost too much to hope, given the overcrowding, that this might be a permanent arrangement.

As we stood there wondering what to do next, the other occupants looked us over carefully, and I in turn had a good look at them. Some appeared quite friendly, whereas others seemed hostile, possibly because our presence left so little free space to move around. The silent scrutiny ended when the Kapo in charge of the block appeared from his room. Working through an interpreter, he told us that for the time being we were to share this hut with the other occupants who, as workers, would be away all day. A short length of sleeping shelves had been set aside for our use. We were not to remain in the hut during the day except to receive and eat our food rations. Finally, he said, we were to continue reporting at the Small Lager for Appells.

Outside, darkness had long since fallen. From the shelter of their machine-gun towers the ss soldiers sporadically swept the rain-drenched grounds with their searchlights. They were alert and ready to shoot without warning at any who thought the downpour provided cover for an escape attempt. Inside Block 58 we were tired, but there were few places to sit. None of us was in the mood to try and strike up conversation with the other occupants, many of whom were already settled in for the night. We, too, decided to bunk down, not just because of fatigue but because we knew we would be scrambling hopelessly in the dark if the hut lights were suddenly turned off from outside.

How we were to climb into the allotted sleeping space remained to be determined. Those in the higher tiers tackled it by one at a time reaching up and taking a firm grasp on one of the upper bunks. Each person then pulled himself up to a shelf and swung his feet in towards the wall. When my turn came, I managed to swing up and in between three others in a third level without kicking any of them in the face. I wiggled down until my head was no longer sticking out, then rolled on my side to await the arrival of the last ones in my section. In a few minutes it was filled. Around us the rest of the airmen settled into their places as best they could so that soon we were all stretched out on the shelves assigned to us.

In my section we were all lying on our right sides with only a few inches between the man in front and the man behind. No one could lie on his back or stomach because there was not enough room. We had all decided to lie on the same side at the same time rather than breathe directly into our neighbor's face. There was a real problem if one of us wanted to turn over during the night. First he had to convince the rest that they should also turn. If all agreed, then one man, acting as the unlocking key, would work his way out and down to the floor so that the others had space in which to roll over. Only then could he get back in. If someone had to go to the Abort his space might be filled by the time he returned and he would have to disturb those who now occupied it before he climbed back. I found that getting in and out of the upper bunks when they were crowded required considerable physical strength in the upper arms and torso. This proved to be no mean feat in my weakened condition.

As I lay there, sheltered from the rain beating on the roof overhead and with the warmth of the bodies next to me, I felt as though I was in heaven. Around me there was little chatter as each man seemed lost in his own thoughts. Drifting off to sleep I wondered to myself how many men this hut was built to accommodate; perhaps two hundred or so. I could not count how many were in it now, but I guessed at least three times that number.

After morning coffee the following day I watched the other occupants of Block 58 leave for their work assignments. One of our people came back from a trip to the Abort with depressing news. He told us that the group of Frenchmen who had arrived with us from Fresnes had spent the night out in the rain and cold. Two of their number, no longer able to endure these conditions, had tried to end it all by slashing their wrists. I was shocked. We had established a sort of comradeship with this large group on the terrible train journey from Fresnes together, so I felt a certain guilt that we were safely under cover. We were lucky. The fortunes of war being what they are, our positions could just as easily have been reversed.

Contrary to what we had expected, no one ordered us out of the hut. But most of us left, preferring the outdoors to the stale smell inside. Inhaling deeply, I delighted in the fresh air which to me always seemed to smell so much cleaner following rain. As a flyer, I instinctively followed my training and looked at the sky. The thick clouds of the previous night were already thinning and I forecast that the sun would break through by noon. My guess was that the rain had been caused by a cold front passing through because now it was considerably cooler. The bare ground was still too wet to sit on, so I joined the others who were standing propped against the walls of the hut. As I leaned back, idly scratching myself, I glanced around at my companions and observed that they were also scratching. No doubt our new quarters were flea infested.

My itchiness was driving me crazy; I had never felt like this before, certainly not when we were living outside nor even in Fresnes. "Enough is enough," I said to myself, as I pulled off my filthy trousers so that I could drive the pests away better. Surprisingly there were none to be seen on the lower part of my body … nothing but a number of minute black cinders from the dirt of Buchenwald. "Ah ha!" I thought, "the beggars must be hiding in the seams of my clothing." I turned my attention to this potential refuge and, very, very carefully, checked every square inch of material. Again, nothing to be seen, only more of the cinders. I could not believe my eyes! As I wondered whether I was going around the bend, I realized I was again scratching something biting my leg. I looked at the itchy area and saw one of the black particles. I touched it with the tip of my finger, whereupon, to my utter surprise, it shot up in the air and disappeared. What a fool I had been! The black cinders must be the fleas. Spotting another of the black cinders on my leg I made a quick stab at it with my finger, carefully pinning it against my skin. Then I pushed on it as hard as I could until I was sure it was squashed flat. I removed my finger, gloating at how easy it had been to kill. As I looked at the dead insect, it too suddenly shot into the air and away! "Damn it," I thought, "these bloody pests are hard to kill!"

I learned with time and experimentation that to kill a flea I had to squeeze it very hard between my fingernail and thumb until I felt it crunch. I found them easy to catch if I moved my fingers quickly enough. They preferred to bite where my trousers covered me, never on my shaven head, armpits, or pubic areas. At night, when we were packed into our bunk, it was nearly impossible to catch one, let alone scratch a bite. No matter how much time we spent catching them, fleas remained a constant plague.

Ever since moving under cover, I had been afraid that one of us would fall while trying to climb in or out of our crowded bunks. My fears were well founded for one day, on return from a visit to the Abort, I joined a concerned crowd gathered around one of the Americans. He had tumbled from an upper tier and sat wracked with pain on the edge of a lower bunk. His arm appeared to be broken. The accident had to be attributed to his poor state of health, otherwise how could it have happened at a time when the shelves were not even crowded? In my mind, there was real doubt as to whether the authorities would make a sincere effort to set his arm. The ss put little value on the lives of inmates. Given the rumour that prisoners were commonly used for experiments at the Revier (camp hospital), our man had to make the deadly decision of whether to risk asking them for competent medical help or trust that the break would heal with only primitive help from the Russians. A few minutes later his close friends took him off.

Five days after moving into Block 58, it was September 3. My twenty-first birthday almost slipped by without my realizing it. I told no one this was the day I legally came of age – with all the misery and suffering around me, I didn't think anyone would really care. I reflected bitterly that while my country had welcomed me with open arms to fight and die for it, I had not been considered sufficiently mature to vote. And although I could travel and live far from my parental home, I had to get my parents' prior consent if I wished to get married. Nor was I permitted to drink alcohol other than when I was asked to toast my king and country. Only yesterday, it seemed, I had awakened in my comfortable bed to be greeted by my mother wishing me a happy sixteenth birthday, and then telling me the war had started. So much had happened to me since that day. My thoughts drifted back to where I had been on each of the succeeding birthdays ... 1940, working as a clerk in a war plant in Montreal, my first job ... 1941, still at the same plant but then as a junior draftsman ... 1942, RCAF Manning Depot in Lachine with the Precision Drill Squad ... 1943, a full-fledged airman sporting navigator wings on a battlecourse in Sidmouth. Never in my wildest imagination had I ever dreamed I would be celebrating my twenty-first birthday in an ss concentration camp. I wondered where I would be on my next birthday ... still here? ... dead? at home?

Before the war, I considered that Labour Day, which often fell on September 3, marked the end of the summer. Suddenly the joyous days were over and it was back to work. Clothes smelling of moth balls were readied for cooler days ahead. With these memories running through my head, I sat with my back against the wall of our hut, then noticed that the ever-lengthening daily parade of dead for the crematorium had long since ended. Now only the living dead were around. There were no mirrors to reflect whether or not I looked as thin and sick as they did. Again I asked myself, "Is the army coming that will free us from this living hell? What is happening in the outside world? Does anyone know we are here?" I came out of my reverie, realizing it was time to limp off for my daily visit to the first-aid post.

More than half of our men were still making visits to the Russians for primitive first aid. No longer did we look like fit young airmen, although we were in far better shape than many other inmates receiving treatment. Looking at their festering, running sores wrapped under dirty paper bandages, I doubted if some of these others would last through the day. Frequently the sights I saw made me feel like vomiting. I thought I would never become hardened. I will always remember the day I was standing next to one of my fellow Canadians when the Russians lanced an inflamed swelling on his arm. Thick greenish-yellow pus spurted out, enough to completely fill a large cup. I was revolted at how much infection a boil could contain.

One morning in early September our Kapo ordered us to wait in the hut after morning coffee. We wondered what this was all about. After a while, we were told to go outside, line up beside the hut, and strip naked. This order sounded ominous to me. My thoughts flashed back to the similar command given to us by the ss while on our boxcar ride from Fresnes. As I left the hut I was afraid the ss were going to collect our clothes for slave workers, then mow us down with machine guns. Although we had not been overly harassed by the Germans for nearly two weeks, I never knew what to expect. Fortunately my fears were quickly put to rest; outside, an NCO armed with only a pistol on his belt arrived accompanied by several Russians. Under the supervision of this soldier and our Kapo, the Russians carefully inspected us for lice. Although none were found, before we were allowed to dress we were sprayed with disinfectant, as was all our clothing. Then we were dismissed. Later I learned that the authorities, who seemed so indifferent to dysentery and other life threatening sicknesses that we might have, were terrified that lice carried by the inmates would spread contagious disease to them.

As the days grew colder the small stove in our hut was kept going with coal briquettes. Soon someone in the group discovered that the slice of raw German bread, which was the essential part of our daily ration, would stick to the warm stove. When the slice dried out it fell off in a slightly toasted state that made it decidedly easier to eat. In spite of this improvement, I never did get used to the raw flavour of the coarse-grained bread, although it was supposedly packed with nourishment.

One mealtime, squatting on the floor with the others, someone passing by handed us several small vegetable buds with paper-like skin. "Here, try this," he said, "an outside worker from our hut gave them to me." He told me our slice of bread would taste better if we rubbed it with one of these. I bit tentatively into the end of a bud. Immediately I experienced a strong burning taste and pungent smell. For the first time in my life I experienced the flavour of garlic. Even after the initial shock wore off its bite was strong in my mouth. I had nothing to lose, so I rubbed my slice of bread with the remainder. Amazingly, it did improve the taste. After that I used garlic on my bread whenever the cloves were available, which was quite often.

During the course of the day the door to our Kapo's room was often ajar, giving me many opportunities to look in as I passed. Along one side was a small single bed with bedding. At the far end a writing table and chair were placed in front of the window.

A side chair completed the furniture. Books and magazines lay about. I was surprised at the comfort of this room in the corner of our overcrowded, shabby, vermin-infested hut. I could not help contrasting the life style of this man with that of the thousands of starving men who were living nearby exposed to the elements like forgotten livestock.

Gossip had it that our Kapo came from Holland and even received mail and food parcels from home. As I remember it, his contact with us was mainly with our leaders, and even then through an interpreter. He seldom spoke with others from our group, and never ate with us. Perhaps his superior status allowed him to eat better food elsewhere. Nevertheless we considered him a "good Kapo," – although it was hard for me to see how anyone who cooperated in running this place could be "good." I had heard that "bad" Kapos were often sadistic and would beat or otherwise mistreat those in their charge.

Since our arrival in Buchenwald I had found long Appells increasingly exhausting. Some nights I thought it seemed to take forever before the stupid Germans finished counting the prisoners. Now I learned it was not necessarily the head count that caused the delays. It was not that at all – the ss needed the extra time to hang prisoners in front of the thousands assembled in the Big Lager. Permanent gallows had been erected there for this purpose. I was horrified. Thank goodness we never had to witness this inhuman practice of public execution, very often for only minor offenses.

Gradually the current occupants of Block 58 accepted us. Soon they were offering us cigarettes. These were of the Russian type, without filters, very strong, with the tube only half-filled with tobacco. For the addicted smoker they were a godsend. I liked an occasional pipe but was not in the least interested in these foul-smelling things. They could be bought at a canteen for prisoners that used a special currency earned by only certain categories of inmate workers. In addition there was a thriving black market in the camp. We had no money for purchases or goods for bartering, so for anything extra we depended solely on the generosity of others.

One evening I was surprised when our leaders announced that they had arranged for us to visit the camp cinema. I don't know how they did it. Perhaps the Germans had seized the opportunity to feed us propaganda. With the longer September evenings, we welcomed the idea of a diversion. The cinema, which sat about five hundred, easily accommodated our group. When the lights went down, first we saw a long propaganda film showing German armed forces slaughtering our invading armies on the Normandy beachheads and later in France. There were many unpleasant close-ups of the thousands of dead Allied soldiers and captured prisoners. If I had not known better I might have thought Germany was winning the war. The main attraction, a romantic film set in peacetime, was unfortunately all in German, which made it difficult for me to appreciate the plot. Still, for a few hours I was almost able to forget that I was confined in Buchenwald.

To while away the time in camp we discussed almost every imaginable topic. However there was little talk about sex. Everyone seemed to keep his thoughts on this subject to himself. Perhaps it was that we were in no physical condition to have strong sexual urges. I saw no signs of homosexuality, in spite of our close physical contact. A story made the rounds about someone in another hut who masturbated over a hundred times in one day, but I thought this too impossible to warrant any credence.

A brothel staffed by female prisoners was available for camp inmates. I didn't know where they came from but I presumed they weren't volunteers. Anyone wishing to use this service had to pay for it, just as in the outside world. Given the lack of proper medical care, I assumed that the risk of contracting venereal disease was very high. As far as I knew, none of our crowd ever visited the place. One day I saw a woman, presumably a prostitute, standing at the window of a nearby building, which I guessed was the brothel. She was the only female I ever saw in Buchenwald.

A few days after the movie we heard that the American with the broken arm was dead. I was outraged. Even in medieval times man knew how to apply splints to help a broken arm mend. The result might be a crooked limb but the patient would still survive. Perhaps our man would still have been alive had he been tended by Russians at the first aid post instead of by the German doctors in the Revier. Death had struck in our midst, making me wonder who would be next. Nothing was said about what had happened to his remains. Then it hit me, my God, probably his body was now in the crematorium!

I had always been curious about Soviet Russia and its people. Few westerners had met the ordinary citizens of this vast country, whose millions lived in a completely different social system. Certainly I had not. We had been led to believe by our propaganda that theirs was a police state and their leaders were out to conquer the world. But now they were on our side in the war and the tune had changed from hatred to praise. Now it was Germany who went to great lengths to defame Russia.

The thousands of Russians imprisoned in Buchenwald were treated like dirt, like the lowest form of life, regardless of whether they were civilians or soldiers. They were assigned to the worst jobs. They were beaten, kicked, abused, and underfed. They were considered to be ignorant savages, best used as slaves. This may have been in part because Russia had never signed the Geneva Convention governing the humane treatment of prisoners of war. Most of the soldier prisoners still wore their dark green uniforms rather than the striped blue prison suits. They often told us that should they live long enough to be liberated, they dared not return to the motherland because they would be shot by their own troops for having surrendered. These unlucky men were definitely in a no-win situation. Those I met seemed very friendly. If they were fortunate enough to have a crust of bread or a cigarette, they were ready to share it, always with a quick smile and laugh, seemingly without a care in the world.

In late September the weather reminded me of home. Stretches of warm, but never very hot, sunny days were interrupted by a day of chilling rain. The hours of daylight decreased. Nights became cooler and the difference between day and night temperatures greater. At home this type of weather would soon transform the rural landscape into a spectacular blaze of colour as the leaves turned to scarlet, orange, and gold. I hoped that beyond the forbidding watch towers and ugly barbed wire the German countryside would give me a similar treat. The thought of this annual phenomenon of change in the vast hardwood forests of Canada made me ache with homesickness. I had experienced enough of war and its violence, ugliness, death, and destruction.

I just wanted to go home. I did not want to ever again be hungry and cold.

At home, the display of autumn colour also warned that the hard frosts would soon begin, followed by the first snowfall. My bare feet had toughened, but I knew I would never be able to endure walking on frozen ground, let alone standing in snow on long Appells. I still wore the thin summer clothing that I had been wearing that hot July day, seemingly so long ago, when I had been captured by the Gestapo. My one blessing was a shelter in which to sleep and eat. I shivered involuntarily at the thought that we might still be outdoors, left there by the ss bastards to die of exposure.

One early October day we were summoned to the building in the Big Lager where we had first showered and been deloused. Without any explanation we were given back our footwear, the same we had worn on arrival. It was such a wonderful, civilized feeling to wear shoes again! What a break! And just when snow could be expected any day! As a matter of course, before I slipped them on, I checked under the inner sole of each shoe. Under one, to my utter disbelief, I found my crumpled piece of "lucky" parachute.

The most unlikely things happened in Buchenwald. We were surprised when one day the whole of the Danish police force showed up. Their overt sympathy for the Allied cause had finally become too much for the Germans to ignore and they had suddenly been arrested and sent under guard to be interned. They arrived, all 1,900 of them, in excellent physical condition and good spirits, carrying suitcases and parcels as though for an extended vacation. They brought a good supply of food which they generously shared around. Their high morale was like a tonic for us.

Hunger, caused by weeks of a starvation diet, resulted in the first minor break in our discipline. This incident happened after we had finished our midday soup and, with stomachs still aching for more, were waiting to be dismissed. Before the command could be given, one of our men, who could no longer endure his pangs, suddenly broke ranks and ran to the food tubs which were about to be carted back to the kitchen. Sticking his head into one of the barrels, he ran his hands around inside to scrape up any morsels still stuck there. Regrettably there was little left to ease his hunger. This incident brought up a question which we discussed daily: Given a choice, was it better to be hungry but warm, or well-fed but cold? Having for the first time in my life experienced hunger but not as yet extreme cold, I said it was better to be well-fed. At that time my reasoning was that if I was well fed at least I could run around to keep warm.

Our morale suffered a severe blow the day our senior officers announced in hushed voices that the Allied civilians who had been convicted of spying were dead. Their status as spies had rated special attention and they had been hanged singly over a period of several days in a fortified bunker near the main parade ground. We stood stunned at this shocking news – fellow countrymen had been deliberately killed. At least they had not been executed as ordinary criminals on the gallows in the Big Lager. They were extremely brave men. I envied their courage for fighting the war for us in a different way, alone, always surrounded by the enemy. They should not have died by hanging, like criminals. I vented my feelings the only way I could, by cursing the Germans and the stupid war.

The first snow fell and the beautiful fresh mantle of white hid some of the ugliness of Buchenwald. Fortunately for those still living outdoors, it was only a few inches thick, so it quickly melted. Thank God I was under cover and now had shoes to wear. With the arrival of cold weather our Kapo did not object to our spending more time indoors. One time a large group of us were again having an after-the-war-when-we-are-back-in-civies discussion, when someone suggested that we should form a club. Its objective would be to help us keep in touch with one another in the future. This idea was greeted with enthusiasm. Others were quick to join the lively argument which developed concerning its constitution, headquarters, branch offices, meetings, officers, insignias and so on. Someone even produced pencil and paper and drew sketches of possible crests. Finally it was pretty well agreed that we would have British, Canadian, American, and Australian-New Zealand sections. Each branch would have its own executive and yearly meetings. Every few years all one hundred and sixty some members would gather in a different part of the world, for a grand reunion. The club badge favored by most featured an airman's flying boot chained to a heavy iron ball. It used the letters KLB for Kriegsgefangenlager Buchenwald, which meant War Prisoner Camp Buchenwald. I thought we might have trouble keeping in contact after the war since our homes were so widely scattered around the world. But even if nothing ever came of it, at least we could pass more of the long boring hours with something new to talk about.

By the middle of October my spirits were at their lowest point yet. I could think of nothing positive to bring them back up. I was hungry, I was cold, I was homesick. To cheer myself up I started thinking about my time in England. I wondered if Stevenson, after he disappeared through the floor of the boxcar, got back to enjoy the life of a hero in his squadron. What had Barbara, the WAAF stationed at nearby Linton-on-Ouse with whom I spent all my off duty hours, thought when I did not show up as usual after my last flight? Did she imagine I was dead? Did she know my home address should she wish to write to my folks? What would Joan, the first WAAF I ever dated, stationed in Bournemouth, think when my letters stopped coming? Or Iris at RCAF headquarters in London? And those girls in Glasgow and Barrhead with whom I went out when on leave. So many evenings dancing, or at the movies, or days walking in the countryside. So many fun times away from flying. If I ever got out of here, would I ask one of them to marry me?

These thoughts didn't sustain my spirits for long – the reality of my situation was all too present. Again, as always, I asked myself the inevitable questions: Did the Germans recognize us as POWs? Would we be moved to a proper camp? How long would the war last? If it was going to last a long time was it worth trying to stay alive in all this misery? I realized this last thought was not a good one. Too much negative thinking and I would let myself go down the drain. No, I always had to think positively to try and survive.

Sleeping at night should have been a joy, but was the opposite. No matter which side was chosen to sleep on was the wrong one for me. There was never room to lie on my back or stomach. The unshielded light bulbs burned continuously overhead. The hut was never quiet because we all groaned or talked in our sleep or yelled out with the torment of nightmares. We all had diarrhea so there was the continual disturbance of men struggling in and out of their bunks two or three times a night. There was always the sound of feet shuffling to and from the Abort. The nights seemed endless. Sometimes after one of my outings I found it was more restful to sit on a bench near the bunks, elbows on knees with head cupped in my hands. If lucky, I could shut out all the thoughts streaming through my head and the noises of the packed humanity, sometimes even doze fitfully.

I was not alone with my increasing sense of hopelessness and despair of ever getting away. We were all wasting away and looking more and more like the wretches around us. Dysentery was rampant. All of us had festering sores, cuts, or fleabites. Should we be liberated, most of us would be immediately hospitalized. Everything seemed so futile, with our armies apparently still far away and the weather getting colder.

Then one day we received our first glimmer of hope. Some officials arrived from Berlin to investigate the story that there were Allied airmen interned in Buchenwald. The Germans, who were in civilian clothes, spoke fluent English. Our senior officers told us that we would be interrogated individually and that we must of course give them our name, rank, and serial number. Our leaders gave us permission, if asked, to let the interrogators know when we were shot down and the name of our squadron. I hoped they would not ask more than this because I feared they might be Gestapo and did not think I could stand up to any more bullying such as I had experienced in their Paris headquarters. My fears proved groundless. They only asked me a few questions which I was able to answer without divulging any military secrets. They left without giving us any indication that our status would change. Now the wait began to see if our proper status would be recognized. Would we be moved to a Prisoner of War camp or left here to die?

The answer came on October 18. Our Colonel and Squadron Leader were advised by the camp authorities that we were to leave for a POW camp the next day. Seemingly our prayers had been answered. It was hard to believe that this was really going to happen. Perhaps some official would cancel the move at the last moment. All we could do was wait and see. We would only be sure when we walked across the Big Lager through the forbidding gate and departed aboard a POW train.

The good news was tempered by the fact that about a dozen of our men were too sick to come with us. We were told that when they were in better health they would join us. To me, this seemed like a death sentence for them, because they couldn't hope to get better here. I found it terrible to see the despair in their eyes, knowing that I might never see them alive again. One of those staying behind was Harry Bastable, so recently with answers to everything, tall, strong and full of life. Now he watched us, a piece of dirty blanket around his shoulders, with sunken haggard eyes, a thin wasted body, and the spark of life and vitality gone.

I was one of the fortunate 150 or so who stumbled and limped up to the parade ground in the Big Lager the following morning. We were counted and recounted as our names were checked against various lists. A cold October rain started beating down on us. No one dared break rank for fear of being told to stay behind. We waited for the next move by the Germans. An hour went by as the cold rain soaked through our thin summer clothing. From the comfort of the nearby watchtowers the sentries stood close to their machine-guns and watched us. Another hour went by as we shivered, swung our arms, and stamped our feet to keep warm. Perhaps we wouldn't leave at all. We waited, and waited, and waited, standing in the cold and wet for over six hours. Finally ss troops in greatcoats, armed with their all-too-familiar machine-guns and handgrenades, surrounded us. The massive gate in the electrified barbed wire swung open. Threatened by the menacing guns of the ss, soaked to the skin, and freezing cold, we moved off to a string of boxcars waiting to take us away from this infamous place.

CHAPTER TEN

Departure

The cold rain was easing by the time we passed through the main gate of Buchenwald and headed for the railway sidings. There was no snow on the ground, but I was so cold I was sure the temperature must be close to the freezing point. The material of my summer suit had long ago been soaked through and my shoes squelched with water. At least the walking helped stop some of my shivering.

Shouted commands brought our long column to a halt beside a string of boxcars. Here a new group of sentries who wore the blue uniform of the Luftwaffe waited to escort us. They were older than the murderous young ss troops who had accompanied us from Fresnes. Somehow they seemed to me to be less threatening – perhaps because they didn't yell and wave their machine-guns so much and didn't have police dogs straining on short leashes and handgrenades hanging from their belts. My spirits rose at the possibility we might have seen the last of the ss and be destined for a better trip this time.

I was quite surprised when only a dozen of us, instead of ninety plus, were assigned to each of the now-familiar cattle cars. The area from the centre doors forward was for prisoners, the remainder for guards. Following a shouted order, a dozen of us struggled aboard the nearest car and moved to the front. Here we had plenty of room to walk around and, even better, there was sufficient space for all of us to stretch out comfortably on the floor at the same time. Behind us, two Luftwaffe soldiers tossed their kit bags up, climbed in, and moved to the back, leaving the door rolled open.

We were far too cold to sit, so we stamped up and down and swung our arms to try and stop our uncontrolled shivering. Even if my ragged clothing and shoes had been dry, I am sure they would have been too thin to keep me warm. I don't remember ever being so cold in my life. I envied both of our guards, each of whom wore two greatcoats, one over the other. I was sure their uniforms underneath must be dry and their feet comfortable inside their heavy German jackboots. Nevertheless they, too, also stamped up and down.

At moments like this, when I was so uncomfortable that life hardly seemed worth living, I remembered how when we changed trains in France I had considered a dash for freedom down the river bank under the noses of the ss. Perhaps I might have made it to safety. And if not, wouldn't I be better off dead than suffering like this? I steered my mind away from these morbid thoughts by telling myself I must be on my way to a POW camp; if I could endure the next few days, then life should be worth living again.

Outside the boxcar I heard the commotion and shouts of our train being readied for departure. Our two Germans, who had piled their gear in a corner, decided to make more floor space by hanging some of it from the wall. One of them used the butt end of his machine gun to bang in a long nail for a hook. As he hammered away, the muzzle pointed directly at his companion, who stood watching. I was so surprised when the second man remained directly in the line of fire that I stopped shivering for a moment. I waited expectantly for the safety catch of the gun to slip off and for him to be cut down in a hail of bullets. But nothing happened. Perhaps it was just as well. I had no feeling of hatred towards these two men who were only performing their duties as soldiers.

Late in the afternoon, whistles and shouts warned everyone of our departure. Our cattle truck jerked forward, the car bumpers banging and clanging as our train pulled slowly out from the siding. I felt the sway when it clattered through switches onto the main branch line back to Weimar. As it gained speed, cold air blew in through the open door, which our guards quickly pushed shut. But wind still whistled in through the high "window" apertures. Fortunately we were partially sheltered and had dry floor-boards underfoot instead of wet mud. But, my God, I was freezing and miserable!

Desperate with the cold, we decided to use the heat of each others' bodies as our best means of survival. Quickly we peeled off our clothes and lay down on our sides tight against each other, spoon fashion. None of us acted the least bit prudish as, naked, we hugged each other for warmth. Soon I felt the body heat from the man in front and behind filtering through me. As long as we kept tight against each other, the violence of our shivering abated.

The train covered the short distance to Weimar in no time. A brief pause in the freight yards and it was off again. The rain had stopped but dark clouds still lingered. As darkness set in, my pervasive feeling of despair lifted for the first time in months. I drifted easily into a sleep broken only from time to time by the sound of boxcar wheels clickety-clacking on the rails. When I did awaken for a moment I was conscious of eerie shadows cast by a flickering lantern that the sentries had lit. I was unaware of whether or not we made frequent stops during the night, as we had on the trip from Fresnes.

I awoke, cramped and stiff, to the sunlight of a new day filtering into the car. By the position of the sun, I had no question that we were headed in an easterly direction. I thought the weather seemed a little warmer, but we still huddled naked to maintain body heat. At the back, our two guards had the collars of their coats up and their hands shoved deep in their pockets.

Sometime during the early morning the train made a prolonged halt in the railway yards of a large city. The day was warmer now and with the train stopped the wind no longer blew in through the "window" gaps. Our sentries seized the opportunity to roll back the door and have a look outside. I stood up, stretched, and peered out the slotted apertures.

Around us were many strings of empty cattle cars similar to ours. Most of them had barbed wire over the small slotted windows, but some had stove pipes poking out. The first were obviously for transporting human cattle while the others must be heated and used for troop transport. Noticing this, one of our guards jumped down onto the track, returning a few minutes later lugging a stove. Then he made a second successful foray for fuel. By the time the train pulled out, the stove was assembled and a fire started in it. Once the door was shut again and heat rising from the stove, we began to feel warm again. We no longer had to huddle together. Our wet clothes, which we had draped around the car the previous night, were still damp. Nevertheless we put them on and moved about in our end of the car. I was now less despairing and hopeless – at least I wouldn't die of pneumonia.

Much of the day I spent at the high "window" studying the countryside. Its bleakness was in sharp contrast to the summer beauty of the Rhine valley along which we had passed on our way to Buchenwald. The area through which we now travelled going away from it was generally flat, with the brown, faded look of a land touched by heavy frosts and now awaiting a protective blanket of snow. Sometimes I could read the names of cities on the stations through which we passed, but without a map they meant nothing to me. I saw working parties of stripe-suited slave workers guarded by armed sentries and, nearby, the barbed-wire compounds in which these prisoners lived. I watched occasional troop trains pass always defended by ack-ack guns mounted on flatcars. Another time we seemed to take hours to go by an extensive petrochemical complex that, no doubt, was vital to the enemy war effort. I was glad to see that it had been heavily damaged by our long-range bombers, perhaps flying up from bases in northern Italy. Or maybe they came from England, then continued on to Russia for refueling. I hoped our side had not lost too many planes.

All that day and night our journey continued without incident. Markedly absent was the fear and tension we had felt when the ss had been in charge. On this trip we completely ignored the Luftwaffe guards who, in any case, appeared oblivious to our presence. There seemed to be an undeclared truce between prisoners and sentries; it was as though we were fellow travellers on a common journey instead of enemies. We should have been giving some thought to trying to escape when the guards were so relaxed, but it was far from our minds. None of us was in shape to walk more than a short distance. We had neither adequate clothing nor a supply of food, both of which were essential for a successful attempt. We had no idea where we were nor which was the best route to take for the long journey home through enemy-occupied territory.

About noon on October 21 our train ground to a noisy stop on a siding in a busy railway junction. Somewhere I saw the name Sagan. I could not remember having seen that name on any of my navigation maps when flying from England, probably because it was beyond the normal range of our Halifax bombers. I was sure we were in eastern Germany, perhaps even in Poland. Perhaps this was the rail stop for Stalag Luft III, the camp which was rumoured to be our destination.

Our guards had already rolled open the centre door on one side and were now busy packing their gear. Somewhere down the line I heard orders shouted. A moment later they were repeated outside our car. Our two soldiers gathered up their equipment and jumped down onto the track. We followed them outside, where we joined the rest of our men already lining up under the watchful eyes of armed Luftwaffe sentries. When all had fallen in, we were carefully counted. So far, no one had escaped along the way.

On this cool but sunny day we were in countryside which seemed to be generally flat with many wooded areas. Facing us was a pine wood. Railway tracks stretched out to either side. An officer shouted the order for us to move off. Our long column of ragged prisoners, with armed guards every few yards, started down a narrow track leading into the nearest stand of trees.

Our spirits were improving and we chattered quietly among ourselves. The guards didn't seem to mind this because we were not yelled at or threatened with machine-guns. In less than a kilometer the trees thinned and we came out of the wood. Ahead was a high, double barbed-wire fence beyond which were the single storey wooden buildings of a large prison compound. Watchtowers, simply constructed on high wooden posts, squatted above the fence like huge spiders. On an outer platform, each had a fixed machine-gun and searchlight pointed inward. Sentries, armed with rifles, stared down at us.

Our column swung left onto a sandy cart-track that followed the outside perimeter of the camp. A short distance to the left we halted in front of the entrance. Here an opening in the fence was closed by a gate made from a simple wood frame laced with barbed wire. To one side was a sentry-box with the inevitable guard. From the head of our column the information filtered back to us that this was indeed Stalag Luft III.

Again we were counted, recounted, and our numbers checked against various lists. Finally we and our escorts were waved inside and the gate closed behind us. There was no ominous clang as it shut, like the many steel doors in Fresnes. Nor did the gate seem as threatening as the huge one at Buchenwald. Yet I had the feeling that this simple gate was intended to be just as effective and permanent as those at either of the two previous places. It took only one quick look at the two barbed perimeter fences and the tangled mess of barbed wire separating them to see that it was even more heavily guarded than at Buchenwald. Escape from here would be a difficult proposition.

After more than three months in the hands of the Gestapo and the ss, I had finally arrived at a POW camp. If the Luftwaffe observed the rules of the Geneva Convention, I could look forward to the same food rations as those of the German garrison. When available, I would be issued Red Cross parcels. I could receive mail and parcels from home and send letters in return. I would be allowed showers, books to read, games to play. I would live in a heated hut and wear clean clothes. In short, I would finally live and be treated like a human being rather than a caged animal.

CHAPTER ELEVEN

Kriegsgefangener Nr. 8049

Inside the main gate our column swung to the right, then marched about a hundred yards to a group of unpainted wooden buildings. We were now in an outer compound, or *Vorlager*, enclosed on all sides by heavily guarded fences. The 150 of us from Buchenwald listened to a German officer tell us we would now have to go through an admitting process. In due course, with about fifteen others, I entered the first building. Inside I was told to strip naked, keep my shoes and throw away the rest of my stinking clothes. I was deloused. I enjoyed the pleasure of my first hot shower in months. Then I was given a clean towel and a set of new military garments. My "lucky" piece of parachute, hidden in my shoe, was not found when I was searched. By the time I was interrogated by an English-speaking German officer who only asked a minimum of questions, I was in good spirits for a change. In spite of the stubble of hair on my head and still festering body sores, I felt like a new person. Now that I was in a Luftwaffe POW camp, life appeared less threatening. It seemed that at last I was in the hands of civilized people.

It was especially great to be back in British military attire, even though it was a mixture of army and air force uniforms. I wore an airman's blue tunic, khaki army battle dress trousers, and socks. On my feet were my cut down flying boots, which would be replaced by regular boots when they became available in a few days' time. I was missing underwear, shirt, and greatcoat, all of which were in short supply at the time. To my surprise, I was even issued my own personal towel and toothbrush.

It took several hours to process us, but I did not mind. When it had been completed, those of us who had been together through Fresnes, Buchenwald, and the boxcars were split into groups for assignment to the six different prison compounds comprising Stalag Luft III. I was one of six British and Canadian airmen destined for the east camp, which was the oldest. We had arrived in the Vorlager soon after midday. Now, late in the afternoon, an NCO and two privates marched the six of us the fifty yards to the inner, East Compound, gate. Through the strands of barbed wire I studied what would be my new home as we waited to be admitted.

From where I stood, I looked down a wide central passage that separated two rows of four unpainted, single storey structures built end to end. These long narrow buildings, which were raised above the ground on short posts, dominated the scene. I guessed they must be the living quarters. They were grouped as far as possible from the camp boundaries on the left and far end. Throughout the compound were POWs dressed in assorted Allied military clothing. In the large open area at the left, two teams were engaged in a game of football. Other men, either alone or in twos and threes, circled the perimeter of the compound at a brisk pace. Those nearest stopped to watch as we entered.

Once inside we were quickly surrounded by seasoned POWs. None seemed to suffer from malnutrition. All wore proper footwear, and appeared to be warmly dressed. None had shaven heads, visible sores, or tattooed numbers. As a matter of fact, many sported luxurious mustaches or long beards. Some were smoking cigarettes while others puffed on pipes. All of them seemed to be in good humour. I was surprised when they ignored the German orders to keep clear. I felt greatly reassured by these obvious signs that life as a POW could be reasonably stress free. The men who greeted us looked quizzically at our haggard and shorn appearance. But there was little doubt we were also German prisoners, so they were soon cracking jokes and bombarding us with questions such as, "Where the hell have you come from?" or "When did you get the chop?"

The German NCO in charge allowed us little time to chat or answer questions. He hurried us down the central passageway until we came to a barrack which had a blanket pinned against its wall. Here we halted. Each in turn stood against this backdrop while a German with a small camera on a stand photographed us for their records. During the "portrait" session another small crowd of prisoners quickly gathered around us. Anxious to hear firsthand the latest about the outside world, they too plied us with questions. Having already been prisoners for more than three months, we had no current news to offer about home. I thought it terrible that these men, who may have been prisoners for years, should be so cut off from all that was near and dear to them. To think that after only three months of isolation I had felt sorry for myself!

I was still thinking about this when someone called out, "Which one of you blokes is John Harvie?"

I replied, "Here I am!" upon which a man in an air force greatcoat came towards me.

Shaking hands, he said "My name is Kenneth Tutton, but around here everyone calls me 'Tut.'"

He went on to tell me I had been assigned to his mess in Block 67, and that he would take me there as soon as the "goons," or Germans, had finished with me. He was about my height, of medium build, and had slightly wavy brown hair. I judged him to be a year or two older than I. His infectious smile made it easy to take an immediate liking to him.

Anxious to see my new quarters, I set off with Tut for Block 67, which was the next one in the row. To get there we had to skirt around the fire-water pool, which not only lay in the centre of the passageway but also marked the mid-point of the barrack area. Over to our left, beyond the line of huts, Tut pointed out the lengthy single-storey structure that housed the compound kitchen, music rooms, and canteen. In the opposite direction, to the right, were the watchtowers and fences of our western boundary. I asked him why there was wooden hoarding between the double wire fence along this section. Tut said that the huge American compound was on the other side and the goons did not want us to communicate with each other.

When we entered Block 67, a German dressed in belted overalls, forage hat, and jackboots was leaning against the end doorway. He had a very long screw- driver and a flashlight stuck in his belt. I wondered what he was doing there, but Tut did not even glance in his direction as we passed. We were in a long, dimly lit corridor. Spaced at regular intervals along each side were doors that presumably marked the quarters for the many prisoners living here. We walked towards the far end, passing another "kriegie" or POW, who greeted Tut and nodded a welcome to me. Near the end of the hall Tut turned to me and said, "You are prisoner number thirteen in room number thirteen. I hope you are not superstitious!"

For the most part I thought superstitions rather silly. However, just to be on the safe side, I had always observed the air force tradition that bad luck would follow if you had your photograph taken in front of your own aircraft. And more recently I believed my chances of survival would be greater if I kept my lucky piece of parachute near me. Many airmen I knew carried good luck charms or performed certain rituals before they flew. My personal one had started with my first flight as a trainee navigator. When the aircraft started thundering down the runway on take-off, I had crossed my fingers and prayed, "Please God bring me back safely."

At the last room but one, Tut opened the door and I followed him into my new home. My first impression was of a small place, dreary and cluttered. The single large window opposite the door did little to dispel the gloom of unpainted walls and ceiling. Five double-deck and one triple-deck bunks, interspersed with occasional tall narrow lockers, lined the walls. A large table and primitive homemade chairs and benches crowded the centre area, leaving little space to move about. The only object with colour in the drab place was a stove covered with pale green ceramic tiles in the corner to my right. A single naked light-bulb burned overhead.

A closer look left me with a feeling of a place which was "lived in"; a place made warm and comfortable by its occupants. Clothing was hung here and there, boots were placed neatly under bunks. Photos of loved ones or other reminders of home were pinned up beside the beds. Books were scattered about. On one table was a pack of cards, a chess board, cigarettes and a pipe. On a counter in front of the window was a washbasin, a large metal water jug, and a cake of soap. Nearby a used towel dangled from a nail. A map of Europe tacked to a wall was stuck with colored pins showing the positions of the opposing armies. Four healthy-looking individuals were reading, snoozing, or otherwise relaxing in the room.

The first to welcome me was "Ginger" Berrisford, who had been foraging in one of the lockers. He announced with a grin that he had been voted cook indefinitely, or until such time as he gave everyone food poisoning. Then Joe Twomey, a tall, thin man, left the spongy potatoes he was peeling to come over and shake hands. He was followed by Ed Beaton, who jumped down from his bunk where he had been napping. Ed, a dark shaggy bear of a man, was the only other Canadian in our mess. The fourth man was Ward Winter, an RAF pilot who made his home in London. As he rose from his chair, I noticed he seemed almost to hide the book that he had been studying.

I had hardly met these four when the door opened and two more roommates came in, "Blackie" Blackman and Tommy Harries. They had been "bashing the circuit" (walking around the inner perimeter of our compound). Both were RAF types, Tommy having left his home in the West Indies to join up. Next to show was Tom Royds, back from a visit to another hut. With his strong accent, there was no question that he hailed from Lancashire.

The room, which I had been told was only twenty-four by sixteen feet, was getting rather crowded and yet five more had still to make their appearance. The warm welcome I received made me feel very comfortable. We talked nonstop as we waited for supper to be prepared. They asked me about the world beyond the wire, while I in turn questioned them about life behind it. Those who came from London, or with relatives living in that area, were concerned about German propaganda which claimed the city had been laid waste by a rain of V-1 and V-2 rockets. I was able to reassure them that these claims were exaggerated beyond belief.

I described how during the year I had been in England I had been aware of the astounding build-up of our armies in preparation for the invasion and battle of Europe. I told them how the previous spring, when I was cycling along country lanes near my base, I had accidentally confirmed that there were huge quantities of munitions in reserve. For miles along each side of the roads I had seen long tiers of canvas-covered objects. I had dismounted to find out what was hidden beneath and, to my amazement, the canvas hid row upon row of neatly piled, unguarded, bombs and artillery shells.

My new roommates asked me to tell them about the treatment my group had received from the ss and Gestapo in Fresnes and Buchenwald. They found what I had to tell them hard to believe, but my physical condition was ample proof. They told me mail and parcels from home were still getting through but took many months to arrive. When I heard there was still enough to eat even though Red Cross parcels were temporarily in short supply, I thanked my good fortune.

I crossed the room to have a good look at the war map, updated daily according to the official German news bulletins blared from loud-speakers in our compound. At last I learned my exact location in this huge country. I studied the map closely, just in case I should have to find my own way home. I noted that Stalag Luft III was about midway between the eastern and western fronts. Sagan, the nearby city, was an important rail junction near the mid-point of the main line which ran southeasterly from Berlin to Breslau, then on into southeastern Europe. These two cities were roughly ninety miles from us to the north and to the south. Twenty miles to the east, the Bober, a major river, flowed north to the Baltic. To the west, the line of battle was stalled along the Rhine. In the east, the fighting seemed to have been frozen to a halt by the onslaught of winter. I was disappointed to see how far away our armies were from us.

Daylight began to fade. Lights were switched on along the boundary fence. In their glare, sentries paced back and forth outside the wire. From the watch-towers, searchlights intermittently probed the deepening shadows inside the grounds. Ginger, who had been busy opening canned food, closed the blackout shutters on the window. I was glad he had because I did not like these reminders that I was in a prisoner of war camp.

I asked directions to the Abort. It was housed, together with primitive washing facilities, in a separate structure between our hut and the next. It was a small, multiseat, wooden structure straddling an open pit and, with no flushing capabilities, was similar to the outdoor country toilets at home. There was no resemblance to the stinking cesspit at Buchenwald because it was a fraction of the size, spotlessly clean, almost odorless, and was pumped out every few weeks by a "honey wagon." The washing facilities consisted of one of the four cold water outlets in camp to which a tin can had been rigged as a shower head for those hardy enough to enjoy freezing cold showers. Running hot water was nonexistent in our compound.

When I returned, the room seemed colder than when I left. It did not bother me too much because at Buchenwald I had become hardened to cold. Imagine the pleasant surprise I received when I saw Tom lighting a fire in the green stove. He said that since he was the "stooge" responsible, he had decided we could spare a few coal briquettes from our meager ration to warm the room in honour of the new arrival. Soon afterwards Johnny Bircham and John Lisle came in from rehearsals, laughing about the forthcoming camp production in which they each played the part of a female. More introductions. It was getting hard for me to remember all the names and keep everyone sorted out.

At this point the question was raised as to what they would call me. I was surprised that anyone should want to change my name. Certainly I did not. I thought "John" was the very best. Unfortunately, the parents of four of my new messmates had thought the same. The result was too many Johns in one room. And now I made the fifth. Prior to my arrival, the solution had been to have one of the four answer to "John," another "Johnny," and the remaining two by nicknames. Hence "John Lisle," "Johnny Bircham," "Percy" Purnell and "Ward" Winter. Without further ado, it was decided that I would be known as "Jack."

Ginger kept glancing at his watch as he worked at the big table near the window preparing supper. I wondered how he could possibly cook a meal for thirteen on the green stove in the corner. But suddenly he said, "Righto, time for our turn on the top of the cook stove." Loaded with pots and pans of food he hurried out the door, almost colliding with someone entering. This latest arrival was "Percy" Purnell, back in time to do his chore as table-setting stooge, having spent the afternoon studying in one of our libraries. Before I could ask where Ginger had gone, I was told there was a large stove in the end room which was shared by the cooks for the eleven messes. Severe coal shortages limited its use to only a few hours each night. Working to a previously posted schedule, a meal for a dozen or more men had to be prepared on it within half an hour, using only the allotted area on either stove top or oven.

The last to arrive for the impending meal was Padre Thompson, the oldest member of our mess. He was short and slim, with sandy-coloured hair, a trim mustache, and glasses, and was neatly outfitted in army battledress. He had just finished work in his chaplain's office, a tiny room at the far end of our building. He slept there on a small cot but took his meals with us. For administrative purposes he was considered part of our mess.

Smells of food cooking in the kitchen next door were driving me crazy with hunger. Just when I thought I could stand it no longer, Ginger arrived back with our meal. I resisted a terrible urge to grab the food from him as he passed. Following close behind we squeezed in around the already laid table as he very carefully measured and handed around exactly equal portions. Again I had to control an animal urge to start wolfing down my share even before the padre had a chance to say grace.

As soon as the blessing was said, we set to with gusto. For the first time in more than three months I ate something other than watery soup. Fried bully beef, fried potatoes, and boiled kohlrabi made a wonderful feast. The meat, mixed with the soggy potatoes which had fried away to almost nothing, had a real spicy flavour. It was not just a few isolated, hard-to-find shreds, as in Buchenwald. Even the chewy kohlrabi, which I was trying for the first time, tasted great and helped fill the void in my empty belly. I was famished so I ate quickly, finishing long before anyone else.

I glanced across the table at Padre Thompson who was eating slowly, savoring each mouthful. He looked up suddenly and caught me watching him. To my surprise, with only half his meal eaten, he pushed his plate aside, saying he was no longer hungry. He offered me the remainder. I accepted with alacrity and quickly gobbled it down. The dessert which followed consisted of stewed prunes covered in a thick creamy sauce made from powdered milk. After that we moved away from the table to smoke a cigarette accompanied by genuine coffee, laced with powdered milk and real sugar.

During the dinner conversation someone addressed a topical question to Jack. During the long silence which ensued, I waited expectantly for Jack's answer. Suddenly I realized that everyone was looking at me. Only then did I remember I was now called "Jack." The supper table was quickly cleared, utensils washed, dried, and put away by the stooges responsible. Visitors dropped in to meet "Jack," the new kriegie from Buchenwald. Johnny and Ed started a game of cribbage, Tut and Tom a game of chess. Ward brought out his book and studied it. Others departed on various tasks, read, or sat around and chatted. I was too hyped up to participate in any of the board games, much preferring to talk and ask questions.

Already I was beginning to understand and even use some of the POW slang. I had figured out that "goon" meant a German, a "goon skin" was a German uniform, and a "goon-box" was a sentry-box. "Kriegie" was short for *Kriegsgefangener* or prisoner of war. A "stooge" was a job or task to be done. The man who had to do it was also called a stooge. "Ag-on!" was frequently used by Tut to express disgust, dismay, annoyance, or describe something unsuitable. It was derived from the word "agony." One of the most frequently used words was "bash", which could be used in various contexts. "Bed bashing" was sleeping, "bashing the circuit" meant walking around the inside wire of the compound and, "having a bash" meant "living it up."

Someone passing down the corridor shouted out, "Lockup in five minutes!" Percy explained to me that at ten o'clock a goon patrol locked the doors to each barrack. Until they were unlocked in the morning, armed sentries, accompanied by police dogs running free, patrolled the compound. Any kriegie who ventured out ran the risk of being shot without warning or attacked by one of the guard dogs. Soon after lockup our brew stooge fetched a jug of hot water. He proceeded to make tea for us all. A special treat was a biscuit each with a piece of cheese. I continued to be amazed at these touches which to me were beyond imagination. Shortly before midnight we started preparing for bed, brushing teeth, washing and undressing. I left to use the night chemical toilet in a small room at the far end of the hut.

Outside the door to this night Abort, used by all in our barrack, the light had been turned off, leaving this part of the hall in darkness. I was surprised to make out a shadowy figure in a greatcoat with upturned collar leaning against the wall, well back from the wide-open end window. He was staring fixedly across at the next hut. Without turning his head, the mysterious kriegie muttered a greeting and something about it being bloody cold. Although piqued with curiosity I did not ask any questions. I guessed he must be a lookout stooge for some secret activity. Back in my room, I felt exhausted by the exciting events of the day. Thankfully I climbed into my bunk at the top of the three-decker. I stretched out my tired body on a clean, straw-filled palliasse covered by a canvas sheet. I pulled a thin blanket over me. What comfort, what luxury!

Before snuggling down, I glanced around the room. All had settled in by now except for John who was finishing his ablutions. Those who had been prisoners the longest occupied the bottom bunks. I noticed that these men, as well as many of those in the second tiers, used an arrangement of cords instead of bed boards to support their palliasses. As a result, their mattresses sagged quite noticeably and did not appear at all comfortable. "Oh well," I thought to myself, "Each man to his own choice."

A few minutes later the overhead bulb flickered off, then on again, a warning from the goons that all lights would be turned off at midnight, in ten minutes' time. John was ready for bed now, so he turned off our light before opening the blackout shutters to let in the fresh night air. Every few minutes the beam of a search-light lit the room with its glare as it swept back and forth across the compound.

For awhile I lay awake thinking about all that had happened in the last few days and how I had come from the depths of despair and depression to this place that was so alive and vibrant. It might not be freedom and home, but what a difference from Fresnes and Buchenwald! Perhaps I no longer had to worry about hunger, sickness, and cold. Finally I fell asleep on something other than bare ground or boards, and with plenty of space around me to toss and turn as I wished.

Luft III – The First Days

Gradually I awakened, refreshed by sleep that had been undisturbed by fears and worries as to what the next day might bring.
Nor had I suffered from flea bites or cold. The thin bedclothes
had kept me warm. I had enjoyed the freedom of sleeping on my
back, side, or stomach as I chose, not as had been dictated by the
majority on the crowded shelves at Buchenwald. I had not been
disturbed by a steady stream of prisoners climbing in and out of
bunks on frequent trips to the night Abort. I was in no hurry to
leave my cozy nest, so I lay awhile listening to the sounds of my
roommates preparing for the new day. I watched with half-
opened eyes as they scrambled down from their bunks, dressed,
then left for the outside Abort. When they returned, they took
turns washing in the basin on the counter in front of the now
closed window.

I enjoyed the pleasure of lying undisturbed, thinking happy
thoughts about the day ahead. I remembered it was Sunday, so I
decided to attend the Protestant church service. The last time I
had been in a place of worship was on D-Day, June 6, in the small
church at Skipton-on-Swale where our squadron had prayed for
success. My thoughts drifted from church services to the possibility of the many exciting activities I could participate in at Luft III.
My meditations were rudely interrupted when someone called
out "Better shake a leg, Jack, ten minutes to Appell!" I came down

from my upper bunk in a hurry. Through the window, I saw kriegies already assembling on the football field. Dressing only took a moment. A quick dash to the Abort, back again to wash in cold water, then I was set to go.

When I left the hut to walk the short distance to the sports field, John Lisle was just ahead of me. I caught up and said, "Please clue me in about the Appells." "Normally there are two a day, at 9:30 A.M. and 4:30 P.M." he replied. "Frequently, however, the goons will enter the compound after lockup and make a surprise bed count. And periodically they make an unforeseen daytime prisoner tally or barrack search. But they are most likely to do these sudden counts and searches when they suspect we are working on tunnels or other illicit activities."

We joined the group from our hut, already gathered at the edge of the sports area next to the barbed wire. Here the ground underfoot was almost pure sand, as it was everywhere else in the compound. Nowhere could I see grass or hard-packed dirt. The approach of our group captain with his adjutant was the signal for each of our eight huts of men to assemble leisurely in files five deep.

The German Kommandant, with his aides, arrived on the parade ground. In traditional military fashion our "Groupie" (group captain) called us to attention, exchanged salutes with his German opposite number, then handed the parade over to him. The Luftwaffe now used the straight-armed Nazi salute, rather than the usual military one with bent elbow. I heard this was done on direct order from the *Oberkommando der Wehrmacht* (Army High Command) after the attempt on the life of Hitler. We were ordered to stand at ease while a German *Feldwebel* (NCO) walked slowly along our front rank counting the files of five kriegies, while at the rear a private made a duplicate tally. As this was going on, other guards went through the barracks checking the numbers of POWs who were in bed, too ill to attend. No prisoners were missing, so after an uneventful fifteen minutes we were dismissed. No one had been pushed, shoved, kicked, or cursed. I left the parade ground feeling much easier about our guards. These Luftwaffe soldiers were human, I decided, not animals like the SS.

The instant the parade was dismissed, the hot-water stooges ran to get their large metal jugs from their huts. They made it a daily race to the camp kitchen for the first hot water issue of the day. When I returned to our room I was hungry as usual and looking forward to my first breakfast in Stalag Luft III. I watched Ginger cut two very thin slices of bread for each of us from a heavy German loaf, then set out margarine and jam. The moment Tommy, our stooge, arrived back with the hot water for our "brews," the camp term for any not drink, we sat down to a breakfast of bread and jam with a cup of tea or real coffee. I was still nursing my cup of tea when there was a loud rap on our door. It opened wide enough for a bearded face to appear in the gap and call, "The new kriegie is to report to the camp security officer's room in half an hour."

Thirty minutes later, I was at my meeting. I sat comfortably ensconced in a chair made from Red Cross crates enjoying a cup of coffee and a cigarette while across from me sat our security officer. Since he was an RAF wing commander, he was privileged to have a small room to himself. He explained that his responsibility was to establish beyond doubt that I was indeed who I claimed to be. It was quite common for the enemy to have one of their men pose as one of ours to spy on our activities. It did not take long for him to note the important details of my adventures since my last flight in "W" Willie. After that he asked a few tricky questions which only a real Allied flier could answer correctly. He finished with a warning about the importance of our security precautions, then said I would hear from him in a day or two.

After this short interrogation I accompanied Johnny Bircham and two others to the camp theatre where the Protestant church service was held. This small auditorium could seat 150, but to my surprise it was less than half full. I had imagined that in a POW camp more people would have attended. Padre Thompson's sermon was either boring or my mind was elsewhere, for I do not remember much about it. Nevertheless, I welcomed this first opportunity to give thanks in a place of worship for surviving all that I had been through. But I could not understand why the god that had allowed me to survive should allow so many others to suffer and die.

At noon each day the compound kitchen, which was staffed and operated by Allied NCO prisoners, supplied each mess with a thick soup made from our German meat and vegetable rations. When Percy brought back our allotment, Ginger rationed each of us a thin slice of bread to eat with it. This was followed by the usual choice of tea or coffee made with hot water from the cook house. After lunch Ed Beaton invited me to bash the circuit with him. Everything was so new and exciting that this seemed like a great opportunity to learn more about Stalag Luft III. So I said I would give it a try but did not know if I was in shape to walk very far. I was especially interested in studying the perimeter fences which kept us prisoners, and in trying to see the "free" countryside beyond.

On our way to the nearest part of the circuit, to the west of us, we passed a tall kriegie talking in German to a goon who leaned with his back against the end wall of Block 66. The guard wore the now familiar belted coveralls with long screwdriver and flash-light stuck in his belt. Ed said he was nicknamed "Bing Crosby." I asked Ed if "Bing Crosby" was an electrician since he carried a screwdriver. Ed chuckled at my question before he replied, "No, far from it! We call these goons 'ferrets' because their job is to ferret around trying to catch us at escape or other such *verboten* activities."

He went on to explain, "The most likely place for escapers to start a tunnel is under a building, so this is where the ferrets spend considerable time, crawling around searching for traces of the bright yellow sand which is exposed by digging. If they see anything suspicious they push their long screwdrivers into the ground to try and find the buried wooden cover hiding the entrance shaft. Or they might hide in the empty space between the ceiling and the roof to try and pick up careless talk on our part, perhaps even hear us working our secret radios. The overalls protect their uniforms during these activities." "Be wary of the ferrets," Ed continued, "because most of them understand English. At any time they may be lurking in a hall doorway or outside a window listening to unguarded conversations. If you have anything private or confidential to discuss, it's best to talk outdoors, away from buildings and people."

We started around the circuit. I guessed there must have been fifteen or twenty others scattered around the loop doing likewise. Everyone walked in a clockwise direction, a tradition established the day the camp opened. I could not help but notice curious glances surreptitiously cast in my direction. With stubble instead of a luxurious growth of hair and with cuts and sores, I must have stood out like a sore thumb. I was in sharp contrast to those we saw, most of whom looked disgustingly healthy.

I had presumed circuit bashing was only for fresh air and exercise. But, I soon learned, there were even greater benefits. Here in the open a kriegie could isolate himself for a short while from the inevitable irritants of life that develop in crowded quarters. It was the only place in camp where he could stride around and around undisturbed and alone with his thoughts. In privacy he could exorcise bad memories of the war and vent to the four winds his anger and frustration at enforced idleness. Here he could voice his private thoughts with little fear of being overheard by either friend or foe.

As I trudged along beside Ed I studied the nearby barbed wire that enclosed us in our compound. There was a double wall of it, ten feet high, eight feet apart, with more in a tangled mass in between. I looked closely but saw no indications that the wire was electrified, as it had been in Buchenwald. About every hundred yards, manned sentry-boxes straddled the fence. I was surprised we were allowed to come anywhere near. In Buchenwald, we would have been struck down in a hail of bullets, and I mentioned as much to Ed. He quickly pointed to a single strand of wire strung on short posts beside us, thirty-five feet from the nearest fence. "Anyone stepping over this trip wire will be shot at without warning," he said. This sobering statement sent a chill down my spine. I continued on, but not as close to the trip wire as before.

We paused for a moment when we came abreast the outer compound adjoining the north side of our compound where we had been processed on arrival yesterday. Now Ed pointed through the wire to other features: the dentist's office, sick quarters, Red Cross parcel-stores building, and general storage area with coal dump. This whole area was off-limits to us except when accompanied by armed guards.

We made a right-hand turn to continue our circuit along the east side. Outside the perimeter fence there was a narrow sandy road, then thick pine woods. Not far away I could hear locomotive whistles and other sounds of rail traffic. Sagan, with its railway yards, lay in that direction. When we neared the now-familiar parade area, Ed slowed, then stopped. "Do you see that shallow depression in the ground slanting out through the barbed wire?" he asked. "That is where three kriegies, hidden inside a vaulting-box, slowly tunnelled their way to freedom while POW gymnasts practiced on top. Within a few weeks they made it back to England via Sweden. After the goons discovered the 'wooden-horse' tunnel, they collapsed it by pumping it full of water from fire hoses."

Our circuit took us between the edge of the football field and the warning wire. The playing area to our right was quite small, only about a quarter the size of a regulation one. Ed said that to overcome this problem the number of players on the teams was reduced proportionately. A hotly contested game of football was in progress. Ahead of us a misplaced kick sent the ball sailing over the warning wire where it came to a stop beside the main fence. One of the players called to the goons in the guard towers on either side and received permission to retrieve the ball. During the short time he was in the "Fire" zone he placed a white hand-kerchief on the trip wire. His every move was closely watched from above by the sentries.

At the southeast corner we swung right to walk along the short south side. Outside the fence the sandy road, with pine trees beyond, continued as before. So far the sentries who stared down at us from the goon-boxes, as well as those who patrolled on foot outside the boundary wire, appeared to be older men, perhaps no longer fit for front-line duties. Soon we had turned the last corner and were heading back down the west side to our starting point. East Compound, I realized, was surrounded on two sides by the American and Vorlager compounds, and on the remaining two by thick pine woods. I was disappointed that the ground was so flat, with no place where I could look down a hill and see the outside world of farms and villages, as I had at Buchenwald.

When I asked Ed the size of Stalag Luft III, he said there were six different prisoner compounds, each independent of the others. The RAF and British Empire airmen were in the oldest and small-est East Compound as well as the North Compound and just down the road in Balaria. Although the Balaria Compound was some distance from the others, it was still a component of Stalag Luft III. The Americans were in the South, West, and Centre Compounds. Ours, he said, held about a thousand men housed in eight barrack blocks.

I was feeling quite exhausted by the time we completed our first circuit. This distance, just short of half a mile, was the longest I had walked since I had been captured. After months of lethargy and a starvation diet, I had had enough for this first day, so I cut back between the buildings to our hut, leaving Ed to plod along by himself.

I appreciated the relaxed atmosphere in the warmth and comfort of our room. The few in it were either reading, studying, or sleeping. Before I stretched out on my bunk for a rest, I asked if anyone knew when I would be allowed to write home. Ward looked up from his manual long enough to say that our Red Cross representative, with whom I was scheduled to meet tomorrow after first Appell, should be able to tell me. I pulled my blanket around me and in no time was fast asleep.

I was awakened by the bustle of my roommates preparing to leave for afternoon Appell. I joined them on the roll call, which was a repeat of the one that morning. Back in our room, I sat and chatted. Twenty-four hours had not yet passed since arriving here and I was still far from talked out. Ed did not join us. Instead he climbed into his bunk, rolled himself up in his blanket, and dozed off. Among the topics of conversation was the tobacco supply. Everybody in Stalag Luft III seemed to smoke constantly. Although I was a confirmed pipe smoker, I had been offered so many cigarettes in the brief time I had been here that I found it easier to accept than to refuse. I would have thought that tobacco would be in short supply in a POW camp. The main source was the Red Cross parcels, each of which contained a carton of cigarettes. These were augmented by those included in next-of-kin packages.

I hardly noticed darkness settle over the camp, but long before supper was ready my stomach told me it was due. This time the meal featured spam, with a repeat of kohlrabi and potatoes. Dessert was biscuits and cheese. Once again I wolfed everything down, then wondered why the others took so long to eat. Tonight Tommy Harries couldn't finish all his meal. No one else seemed to be very hungry so Tommy's leftovers ended up on my plate. I found it unbelievable that anyone could not be hungry enough to finish the meagre portions which comprised his rations.

When supper was finished and the stooges had washed the dishes and put things away, I watched Ed and Tom play chess.

Both were good players, even though they did a lot of joking and kidding during the game. Ed, I thought, seemed to be the better of the two. Then and there I decided to take advantage of so much idle time to brush up on my chess skills. Perhaps if I played often enough, I might even give these two a run for their money.

As the time for "lights out" approached, I could hardly wait to see if there would be a dark shape in the shadows at the far end of the corridor when I visited the night Abort. I need not have wondered, for again a mysterious figure stood looking out the open window. As I was coming back, curiosity overtook me, so I detoured the few extra steps past our door to check the passageway at our end. Sure enough, my assumption was right. Another sentry stood there peering across to the next hut. When I climbed into my top bunk, I wondered what secret activity required these lookouts. But I was too tired by all the day's activities to think about it for long. I fell asleep quickly and slept soundly except for a short period when I was vaguely conscious of somebody talking in his sleep.

After breakfast on Monday I visited our Red Cross representative. He, too, like our security officer, made notes as I retold the story of the last flight of "W" Willie and my subsequent adventures. He said he would advise the Red Cross that I was now officially a POW. Then he gave me my ration of German letter-forms and postcards that must be used for outgoing mail. Clutching my correspondence materials, I dashed back to my room. I thought about the exciting things I could now tell the folks at home. Better still, they would be able to send me all the news of family and friends!

Before I could start on my letter writing, there was a sharp rap, the door opened, and someone called quietly, "News up!" I followed my roommates as they filed quickly into the hall and stood waiting expectantly in hushed silence. We were speedily joined by more people from the rest of the hut, who had also been summoned into the corridor. At each end of the hall, back from the window, one of our lookouts kept watch to warn of nearby goons. No ferrets were in the vicinity so they signaled "All Clear" to a third man standing midway along the corridor. He pulled a scrap of paper from his pocket and read aloud, "Here is the official BBC evening news for October 23. On the Western Front, British and American troops suffered light casualties while capturing German strong points around ..."

Reading the broadcast required only a minute or two, after which we quietly returned to our rooms. I had been so surprised at hearing the latest BBC bulletin boldly read aloud to British prisoners in a POW camp that I had paid little attention to its actual content. What a tremendous boost to kriegie morale to hear not only recent, but authentic, news! Questions raced through my mind. "How did we get it?" "How did we know there were no ferrets hidden within earshot listening to it all?" I was longing to have these questions answered, but because I had not yet received my security clearance I decided to curb my curiosity for the time being.

After the midday soup I borrowed a pencil and, full of enthusiasm, sat down to write my first letter home. I examined the form carefully. It was about six inches wide and ten inches long. I was permitted to write only on the twenty-four ruled lines. My spirits sank. Only twenty-four six-inch lines; how could I say anything? And all I could send were three of these and four much smaller postcards each month. This was most discouraging!

I thought about all the things I wanted to tell them at home. My parachute jump, wandering around the countryside, living with my French "family," and the trip to Paris. Then I realized that anything I wrote about events prior to my capture, when read by the German censors, would endanger the lives of those who had helped me in France. And anything I said about the Gestapo, Fresnes, the two boxcar rides, and the horrors of Buchenwald would certainly be censored. Besides, I did not want anyone at home worrying unnecessarily about me.

Nor could I put down anything about secret activities in Stalag Luft III. So here I was bursting to finally tell my family and friends all about my harrowing adventures, but everything had to remain secret until after the war. With these restrictions, there was actually very little I could write about. I was so discouraged that I felt like throwing the stupid forms away. Finally I wrote a letter full of half truths that implied I had sufficient to eat, was warmly clothed, and in good health and spirits among friends.

Should I drop dead tomorrow, my folks would still know little about what had happened after we took off from Skipton-on-Swale

– unless of course, my French "family" had written to them after France was liberated. I concluded my letter writing with a postcard to my second home in Scotland, where I had enjoyed so many happy leaves with my two distant aunts. I wondered how many months it would be before I received any mail in return.

Supper time came, and with it a different variation of bully beef. For vegetables, we had boiled swedes, something I had never tasted before. In texture and taste they were much like turnips, a vegetable which was no favorite of mine, but in my present circumstances everything tasted good. Tonight it was Johnny Bircham who couldn't finish his meal, so I finished it for him when no one else seemed interested.

Before drifting off to sleep that night, I lay for a while reflecting on my first two full days as a POW. They had passed quickly without a dull moment. So much so that I had little time to become homesick. Would I always be busy like this, with no time to feel lonely, until that far distant day when the war ended and we all went home?

CHAPTER THIRTEEN

October 1944

Next day, the new arrivals from Buchenwald were told they would be issued high-protein Red Cross medical parcels instead of the regular ones. I thought this was great news, especially since I was unaware that such packages even existed. I also heard I had been given full security clearance by the "Wingco" (wing commander). For me, this was similar to acceptance in an exclusive club or becoming part of a special team. I was again recognized as a trusted member of our forces, still fighting the war but in quite a different way. Sooner or later I would be participating in the camp's covert activities.

I felt self-important when, later, I stood in the corridor with the others to hear the daily BBC news. My day would have been even better if our troops had made some big advances – but it was not to be. The coloured pins on our war map remained where they had been since my arrival. After the news, Tut stopped beside me. "Come on, Jack," he said, "let's go and bash a few circuits!" This suggestion could hardly have come at a better time. I hoped that since I was no longer a security risk, he would volunteer to tell me about some of the secret activities in the camp.

We waited outside the barrack while a horse-drawn wagon loaded with coal briquettes passed us. Following behind were three kriegies carrying empty Red Cross boxes and small scoops.

As "Dobbin," or whatever the animal was called in German, plodded along, he had to answer a call of nature. As soon as the large steaming globs dropped from the horse's rear, the waiting kriegies shoveled them into their containers. This was my first view of the avid prisoner-gardeners gathering manure for their vegetable plots alongside the barracks.

We had hardly started around the circuit when Tut began explaining about wireless sets and the operations of our news team. "Incredible as it may seem," he began, "not only do we have more receiving sets than we can use, but we also have a transmitter. They are concealed in widely dispersed locations around the camp. Our first radio was kriegie built; since then they have been sent from home. As a matter of fact, so many have been smuggled in that it is difficult to hide them all. We have had to send word home, 'Thanks, but no more, thanks!'"

"Responsibility for operating and hiding the sets," he continued, "is entrusted to a small team. This group receives then relays the daily news bulletins. They need less than fifteen seconds to hide their receivers if an alarm is sounded. The BBC news is excellent for our morale. Of course the goons know we receive it, so they search constantly for our equipment. There have been numerous close calls."

We were approaching the lager gate so Tut changed the topic of conversation to a more mundane subject until we had ambled past the stony-faced *Posten* (guard). When we were beyond earshot, Tut talked about the wireless transmitter. "We can only use it to send urgent messages. Otherwise, should one of our transmissions be intercepted by the Germans, we would be accused of spying. Life could be made miserable while they tore buildings apart searching for the transmitter. The number of Appells could be increased; theatre, sports, and other privileges could be curtailed or cancelled. It's very reassuring to know that we have the capability to contact England in an emergency," Tut continued, "even if we can seldom use it."

We came to the sports field, which was fully utilized each day. At this time of year the soccer season was at its peak. Excuses for a game were endless ... English leagues, Scottish leagues, Colonial leagues, Barrack leagues, Compound leagues, and others. We paused to watch the final minutes of a match because Tut knew many of the spectators and some of the contestants. When the contest ended, we moved on and Tut explained the reason for the night lookouts in each end of our hut.

"These stooges," he said, "watch for goons when secret activities, such as the reception of the news, are in progress. If danger threatens, they call a warning to their opposite number in the next building. This alarm is then passed to the next hut, and so on down the line. In moments the radio team, or those involved in other forbidden activities, are alerted. In daytime, the 'duty pilot' keeps us informed of any Germans in the compound " When I asked what he meant by "duty pilot," he laughed and said, "Be patient, you'll soon find out when your turn comes!"

I could still complete only one circuit before tiring, so I left Tut to continue by himself. On the way back to my hut to rest, I stopped at the library and borrowed my first book. After lunch I stretched out on my bunk and enjoyed the pleasure of reading, a pastime that I had sorely missed these last few months. When I did look up from my novel, Ward was studying his manual, Blackie was engrossed in a book, Ed was bed bashing, and Ginger mucking around in the food locker. The others were off somewhere.

The novelty of the new kriegie from Buchenwald was beginning to wear off so we had fewer visitors dropping by. A frequent caller was a tall slim man from a mess down the hall. He was nicknamed "Lofty" because of his height. Since he spoke excellent German, our "X" Committee, in charge of our secret activities, had assigned him the job of translating the *Oberkommando der Wehrmacht* (okw) communiques. He also read all available German newspapers so that he was always abreast of current events from the enemy's point of view. I enjoyed his visits because they always provoked a heated discussion about the progress of the war.

That night at dinner, I relished the extra meat and other high-protein items from my medical Red Cross parcel. My messmates made do with still another variation of bully beef and vegetables. As usual, I gulped my food down. My plate was bare long before anyone else had finished. Tonight, after eating, I seemed to be minutely less hungry than after previous meals. Perhaps it was only a figment of my imagination. In any case, it was just as well, because for the first time since I arrived, no one had any leftovers that I could eat.

At lights out, I wrapped myself in my blanket for a good sleep. But something was disturbing my peace of mind enough to keep me from drifting off. I lay for a while trying to figure out what was bothering me. I was sure whatever it was had occurred at supper time. Why was it, for the first time since my arrival, that everyone had eaten all their meal? Was there a reason for it? Suddenly it dawned on me! What a fool I had been! For the past few days, my new messmates, still almost strangers to me, had been almost as ravenous as I was at mealtimes. But realizing that I was even more starved for nourishment, they had contrived, one by one, the excuse that they were not hungry in order to share their meal without embarrassing me. Tonight I had my extra rations from the Red Cross, so they had considered that this ploy was no longer necessary. I was left with a warm feeling inside at this explanation.

On Wednesday morning I was circuit bashing with Tom when a team of horses entered from the Vorlager pulling a wagon with a large cylindrical tank. Tom cursed. "Best keep up-wind of that lot!" he said. Observing my puzzled expression he explained, "That's the honey wagon coming to pump out the two Aborts. Anyone with a sensitive nose should keep well up-wind of the operation."

We ambled along in silence for a little while, before I asked Tom, "What exactly is the duty pilot, and what's his job?" "The duty pilot is one of our blokes," he replied. "His post is at a table in front of the library window in Barrack 63 where he commands a wide view of the entrance gate and the approach to it. He stations himself there and logs the time of entry and departure of every German who enters or leaves the compound during daylight hours. If he knows the person's name, nickname or rank, he records it."

At the risk of sounding näive I asked, "But what use is this information?" Tom smiled briefly. "One of the keys to keeping our activities secret is to know how many and which Germans are in our compound at any given time. For example, when the BBC crew are ready to distribute the news, they first check with the "duty pilot" to find out how many Germans are in the compound. Then they assign stooges to find and shadow each one. If a goon knowingly or otherwise ventures near the barrack where the news is to be read, our men are warned. The Germans are aware of the duty pilot and his logbook," he said, "but of course can do little about it."

Tom's ruddy face broke into a grin as he told the amusing story of how the goons put the duty pilot's log to their own use. "One morning a German officer and NCO were the first into the compound. They hurried directly to the duty pilot in the library and demanded to see his logbook. There was nothing that our man could do except let them examine it. A few tense moments ensued while the intruders studied the previous day's entries. They seemed pleased by what they read. Turning, they thanked him and strode off. We heard the sequel later. Apparently the Germans suspected one of the ferrets assigned to our compound had been AWOL the previous day. Our logbook confirmed their suspicions. On the strength of our records he was disciplined by ten days confinement to barracks!" Tom and I had a good laugh at this anecdote. We continued our walk until we had completed one circuit, then returned to our hut. In the hall we passed Lofty deep in conversation with the ferret Bing Crosby.

That evening I attended a lecture given by a kriegie who had competed in the world famous Monte Carlo motorcar race. Although he was not a professional speaker, his presentation was excellent. The following week a lecture was scheduled on English Common Law, which I thought would be interesting.

I was finishing my ablutions just before morning Appell on Thursday when two friends of Johnny's rushed in carrying cardboard boxes. Of course my curiosity was aroused when they asked Johnny to hide the cartons for the rest of the day. I wondered what this was all about, but the sound of "*Zum Appell! Zum Appell!*" called me outside. The usual goons who took Appell were accompanied by a squad of ferrets and machine-gun toting soldiers. The latter quickly surrounded Hut 68, while the ferrets disappeared inside. "Oh my God," I thought to myself, "the goons have discovered something!"

But Ward, standing next to me, said, "Don't panic, it is only one of their unannounced, random, detailed searches of a hut. They hope the element of surprise will give them a better chance of finding a tunnel under construction. Or if not a tunnel, at least radios, civilian clothing, maps, compasses, forged documents, or other illicit material. Armed guards," he explained, "are necessary to keep the kriegie residents from harassing and interfering with the searchers. Especially since more often than not, the ferrets turn the huts inside out, leaving quite a mess to be cleaned up. Fortunately we often have advance warning of a surprise search. This gives us the chance to move sensitive items to a safer place." Now it wasn't hard to guess why Johnny's friends were in such a hurry to leave their boxes in our room.

During the afternoon, when Blackie and I were trudging around the circuit engrossed in conversation, we heard someone behind us shout, "Fore!" A moment later a small ball thudded to the ground close by. "Those rotten sods," cursed Blackie, "are going to kill someone playing golf in such restricted space!"

I could hardly believe my ears. Golf in a POW camp? Turning, I saw, not far away, two men, each of whom carried a club. Incredulous, I asked Blackie, "Where do they get the equipment?" "They make it themselves," he replied. "They forge the club heads from pieces of stoves and make the balls by winding elastics and string around a hard core, over which they stitch a tight leather cover. Fortunately for us the balls don't travel well when hit, so as yet no one has been hurt. Each time the golfers wish to play they have to get permission from the Senior British Officer (SBO). It's not always given."

Today, for the first time, I managed a little more than one circuit before tiring. On our way back to the hut we passed Lofty, who was again chatting with Bing Crosby. I was beginning to feel hostile towards Lofty because he spent so much time fraternizing with this goon. Several times I had seen Bing Crosby smoking a good-quality cigarette. Probably it was one of ours, a gift from his pal Lofty.

When I entered our room, Ed was bed bashing as usual, completely oblivious to everything. It was hard to believe that anyone could sleep as much as he did. He was at his best at night, excelling at cribbage, bridge, and chess. Ed was a knowledgeable person, the only one in our room, I had been told, who had a university degree. Because of this, he was often consulted as the final authority when settling a dispute.

The next day, Friday, Johnny Bircham didn't have theatre rehearsals until after lunch. So we left together for the circuit. Outside our hut he called, "Hi," to Lofty who was nearby chatting with Bing Crosby again. "Boy," I thought to myself, "Lofty sure is great on fraternizing with the enemy!"

I asked Johnny how we managed to have space for the theatre. "Each barrack block has six rooms for living quarters on either side of the hallway. Two more small rooms face each other at each end. In one building the Germans have allowed us to join together three large adjacent rooms to provide the space required for our theatre." Johnny talked about the kriegie theatre with such enthusiasm it was obvious he enjoyed being a part of it. He said there were no shortages of talented thespians from which to draw when casting. The stage crews, he said, even with limited resources invariably came up with ingenious solutions to the problems of staging major productions.

Then Johnny explained how further recreational space was provided. "In other huts, only one of the large rooms has been sacrificed for other than living quarters. Although this makes our accommodations more cramped, it allows us three libraries (non-fiction, fiction, technical), two lecture or quiet rooms, one sickroom, and one combined educational store and administration room."

After lunch I finished my novel. Then, since those in the room seemed to be occupied with their own pursuits, I did some bed bashing. So far I had not seen anyone in our room playing chess, bridge, cribbage, or other such games during daylight hours. It seemed as though there was an unwritten rule that these were evening activities.

After supper I watched some of the chess games. Then I felt confident enough to challenge Ward to my first game in Luft III. He put down his manual long enough to wipe me off the board. That night I slept fitfully, largely because someone was talking in his sleep. At some time or other most of us mumbled in our dreams, but never this loudly and clearly. It was not the first time I had heard the voice and I was sure it was John Lisle.

Next day, while Ginger was checking through his supplies, he explained about German rations and Red Cross food parcels. "According to the Geneva Convention we are supposed to have exactly the same food as the German garrison troops, but in practice it is somewhat less. These rations consist mainly of root vegetables, bread, and occasionally a little meat. The bread, which is 90 per cent potato meal and 10 per cent sawdust, is the most important item. The Red Cross parcels are our main source of food. They come from either Canada, Britain or, the USA, and are shipped in consignments of six to eight weeks' supply via Sweden or Switzerland. When our reserves are ample, each man is allotted a whole one per week. When reserves are down it can be only half, or perhaps even none. Depending on where they come from, the content varies slightly. The parcels are distributed from one country at a time, irrespective of whether the recipient is British, Canadian, or American. The basic contents are a tin of either bully beef or Spam, a can of either powdered milk or condensed milk, a can of either margarine or butter, a package of sugar, a tin of coffee, tea, or hot chocolate, a package of dried prunes or raisins, a package of soda biscuits or tea biscuits, a package of cheese or tin of jam, a carton of cigarettes, and a package of vitamin C tablets. A highly prized item in the American parcels is a bar of American army "D" ration semisweet chocolate."

Ginger said that as cook for our mess he took charge of our parcels. Before handing them over to each individual he removed the food items needed for the following week but left such things as cigarettes, chocolate bars, vitamin C tablets, and sometimes a can of condensed milk or package of raisins.

As we prepared to turn in that night I was warned that my days of lazing around were over. Tomorrow the new schedule for room stooges would be posted and my name would be on it. After lights out I said a little prayer of thanks for the Red Cross. There was no question that their parcels made all the difference. If we had had only German rations to eat, we would have been almost as hungry as in Buchenwald.

Sunday morning I found myself musing about the two padres in our small compound of a thousand men. It was rather surprising to me that padres, who were considered noncombatants, should be POWs. Our padre, Thompson, was a Methodist who had done missionary work in China. When war came, he joined the army and was shipped to North Africa with his unit. During the desert fighting he suffered a stomach wound and was captured by the Italians. He was in Italian hospitals and army prison camps prior to his transfer here. So far I had never heard him talk about religion while in our room. This, I thought, was a good thing, because we didn't need religion pushed at us. We all had many problems and since he was always available in his study, we could go there when we were ready for help.

Today the Catholics had first use of the theatre for church services so while waiting after Appell I went with Tommy Harries to the kriegie exchange market. The "mart" was set up in a room behind the kitchen. It operated through accounts that kept track of points given for any surplus goods you brought in, such as food from Red Cross parcels, cigarettes, chocolate, gloves, socks, or books. These credits could then be used to buy other articles already in stock. The point value of an item varied with the demand for it.

Coming back from church service I passed Lofty talking to Bing Crosby. I felt a little less cheesed off with him today because Tut had cautioned, "Don't let it bother you – sometimes there are more things going on than meet the eye." Then he had grinned and winked.

After lunch, the list of weekly chores was posted. My lot for the coming week was vegetable stooge, peeling potatoes and preparing the "vegs" for supper. Anyone who didn't like his assigned duty could make a private agreement for a substitute. This arrangement might be for credits on the "mart" or an exchange of jobs. Percy was a frequent wheeler and dealer because he, like many others, was preparing for the English equivalent of Junior Matriculation. He needed extra time to attend lectures and study for the exams which were scheduled to be written early in the new year under the supervision of the Red Cross.

The Geneva Convention stipulated that only those prisoners below the rank of officer could be forced to work, and then only in nonessential war work. In our compound, our central kitchen was staffed by air crew sergeants. These men, who considered themselves lucky to be in an officers camp instead of working on farms or in factories, also swept our rooms every day.

During the night I was awakened by John talking in his sleep. It was almost worthwhile staying awake just to listen in on his fantasy situations. Tonight he was unquestionably in an English pub describing his wartime experiences. I distinctly heard him say, "Hell camp, it was!" followed by, "Don't mind if I do." then, "we were on starvation diet ... don't mind if I do." In his dream, his sympathetic audience was obviously buying him drinks as he recounted his adventures. He was treated to so many rounds it was a wonder he didn't get drunk and fall out of bed!

Another time John awakened me by loudly chiming the bells of Big Ben. Each hour was meticulously rung out, "Ding-dong-ding-dong, Dong-ding-ding-dong! ... Dong!" He seemed to take ages as he went from one o'clock to twelve without missing a chime. Some of the others must also have awakened because I heard subdued snickers from different parts of the room. John had been a fleet air-arm pilot. One moonless night early in the war he and his observer had been dropping mines from an old Fairey Swordfish biplane into the harbour of Le Havre when a defective altimeter caused them to hit the water. Before a German torpedo boat could rescue them, his observer drowned. Perhaps John's dreams stemmed from this traumatic experience.

On Monday, I sent off my second letter and postcard. The letter went to my best friend, George Cairns, the postcard to my aunts in Scotland. There was little more I could say to George than to my family. I repeated to him my cryptic comment about the possibility of mail arriving from France.

Every day I tried to get in shape with at least one circuit. On Tuesday, the last day of October, I was trudging along with Ed when the topic of conversation switched to escaping. We knew Hermann Goering had boasted that Stalag Luft III, the newest air force camp, was escape-proof. While at first glance it appeared that he was right, there had already been the completely successful Trojan Horse escape from our compound and the big one from North Compound last spring when seventy-nine men had broken out. Unfortunately, the last escape had ended tragically when, after most were recaptured, fifty were murdered by the Gestapo.

Ed explained about escaping. "Getting out is only half the battle. Once outside the wire the escaper faces the problems of language, food, shelter, clothing, and documents – this, while travelling perhaps a thousand miles through enemy territory before facing the final challenge of crossing a heavily guarded frontier into friendly territory. Although some men have escaped through the main gate, it is very difficult. A few have gotten out through or over the wire, but normally this route is next to impossible. So far most of the successful escapes have been by tunnels. This approach is time-consuming and dangerous for the diggers because of the high risk of being buried alive or suffocating due to poor tunnel ventilation.

"There are two major problems associated with a tunnel: concealing the entrance, and hiding the large quantities of excavated yellow sand. The best method of concealing the entrance is to have it under a building. The goons knew this when they built the camp, so they located most of the huts and structures well back from the perimeter wire. This means that most tunnels are as much as four hundred feet in length. The longer it takes to excavate a tunnel, the greater the chances of its discovery. The best feature of this escape route is that the breakout can be timed for important factors such as suitable weather conditions, train connections, and head start for the escapers."

Ed fell silent as we passed a party of kriegies near the main gate. They carried towels and, guarded by Postens, were headed for the hot showers in the Vorlager.

Once out of earshot he continued. "In this sandy soil tunnels have to be shored against collapse. Bed boards are ideal supports because they are the perfect size. Everyone is asked to donate them. Why do you think the long-term kriegies in our room have rope instead of wooden slats holding up their sagging palliasses? Ventilation is an absolute must in all tunnels. A hand pump made from a canvas kit bag is used to force fresh air through a pipe made from powdered milk tins to the face of the digging."

We were near the end of our planned circuit now and I was tired. "A well-executed escape requires countless helpers. There are diggers, electricians for tunnel lighting, mechanics to build tunnel railways and trolleys, disposal crews, lookouts, and forgers to prepare passports, official papers, railway tickets, and identifications. Tailors are needed to make escape clothing, others to procure maps, train schedules, and props for the escaper. The list of assistants is endless," Ed concluded.

We finished our walk and headed for our hut. Ed chose this moment, while still out of range of unwelcome ears, to pique my curiosity by asking, "Have you had a good look at the book which Ward studies surreptitiously?" and, "Has anyone confided to you about the tunnel our hut dug which is ready to 'Go'?"

For a moment I thought he was pulling my leg but his tone of voice told me he was deadly serious. I dared not question further because we were close to the barracks, where someone might overhear. I would have to wait another day to learn more. That night I made sure to catch a glimpse of Ward's book. It seemed to be written in German, with many diagrams.

Sleep was a long time coming because I was so excited about the things Ed had told me. As I finally drifted off I realized I had almost forgotten the terrible sleepless nights at Buchenwald with the constant running to the Abort, the hunger, the cold, the homesickness, and the biting fleas.

CHAPTER FOURTEEN

November 1944

By next morning my spirits, which had skyrocketed with Ed's talk about tunnels, had crashed. Perhaps it was because of the November weather: shorter hours of daylight with the threat of winter cold and snow soon to come. This climate, I imagined, must be very similar to that of Montreal. Had there been blue skies overhead at that moment instead of dark clouds, I think I would have felt more perky.

When Ed climbed back into his bunk after breakfast, I realized that this morning he preferred bed bashing to circuit bashing. I would have to wait if I was to hear more about tunnelling from him. Because I needed some time to myself for a change, I decided I would do the circuit alone. I put on my newly issued airman's greatcoat and turned up the collar against the damp air. However, it was not to be a solitary walk – when I left the hut Johnny Bircham joined me.

We initially trudged along in silence, each alone with his thoughts. I decided that although this first week as a POW had been exciting, I still needed contact with home to boost my spirits. A long letter from my family would do the trick. Four months without a word was far too long.

Soon we were walking along the east side of the compound where I hoped that, through the strands of wire, I might see something different from the POW life to which I was becoming accustomed. I would be lucky if I did, because the road between the trees and the barbed wire was so seldom used it might as well have been a lumber road in northern Quebec. All that ever passed here were occasional Luftwaffe soldiers. Just when I thought that I would be disappointed, I heard male voices raised in song. As I looked for the source, a German Youth Labor Brigade, with shovels instead of guns on their shoulders, marched out of the forest onto the perimeter road. They wheeled towards us in precise military formation, singing marching songs. When one ended, the leader called out the title for the next one. Johnny said that at one time our kriegies considered it good sport to shout rude insults at them or to drown them out with English patriotic songs. These provoking tactics were so successful that the German youths were all set to do battle with our men.

Another day passed without Ed finding time to tell me more about the tunnel that was ready to be used. Needless to say, I kept my eyes open for signs of it, but without success. I guess it was quite presumptuous for a greenhorn like me to think I could spot a tunnel dug by experts. But I did hear other escape-related stories from Tom Harries. The first one, which proved quite amusing, came as a result of my asking him how escapers obtained real photos for their forged passports.

Tommy laughed. "One time we stole the German photographer's camera while he was photographing new arrivals. This happened when he foolishly turned his back to adjust the blanket used as a backdrop. It was the perfect opportunity for one of our welcoming hecklers to snatch his camera and run into the nearest hut with it. By the time the goon caught up with the thief, the booty had been passed to another kriegie, then to another, and still another until it could no longer be traced. The German knew that even a search by armed troops would not find it. Furthermore, he would be in serious trouble should he report the theft to his superiors. He took the only course of action left to him – he appealed to our SBO for its return. Since we considered this goon a decent sort, the camera was returned in due course, but only after it was used to take passport photographs of potential escapers."

My next question for Tommy was, "Where do the escapers get maps and money?"

"In the early days they were sent from England," was his reply.

I must have looked astonished at such a surprising statement, because he quickly explained. "One time someone in England whom Ed didn't know sent him a 'games' parcel. One of the games was a glass-topped thin cardboard box with several loose metal balls sealed inside. The object of this game was to manoeuvre the small spheres into recesses in the pasteboard base. Many kriegies, as well as ferrets who frequently visited, spent countless hours testing their skill with it. One day, unfortunately, Ed accidentally trod on the toy, shattering the glass cover and breaking the cardboard backing. When he picked up the debris, something about it aroused his curiosity. He examined the pasteboard backing and found it to be tightly packed with maps and German paper currency."

After breakfast on Friday, Ed called across to me, "Hey there Jack, it looks as though we are going to see the sun for a change, care to do a few circuits?" I quickly accepted, hoping that I might hear more tunneling stories.

Ed didn't let me down. "The other day I told you about the tunnel which our hut has ready to use. It's a very short one because the entrance is on the open parade ground, a few feet from the trip wire. Its abbreviated length meant less dirt to remove and conceal, fewer bed boards for shoring, and less of a ventilation problem."

"But how on earth could you dig a tunnel in plain sight of the goon-boxes, only a few hundred feet away in either direction?" I questioned.

"We took advantage of the fact that our hut always 'falls in' for roll call at the same place each day, midway between two goon-boxes. We started the tunnel halfway between them, which was at the same time the middle of the area where we assemble. We blocked the view of the entrance from the watchtowers by having our tallest kriegies standing in the end ranks. When all was ready, the entrance trap was set into the sand during an Appell. The shaft below was dug on succeeding roll calls. Eventually the day came when the hole was deep enough to conceal one, then later, two workers between Appells.

"Once the vertical access was completed the horizontal digging started. One tunneller dug at the face, shoring the roof and walls as he progressed. The other, at the foot of the shaft, pumped fresh air to the front at the same time as he filled sausage-shaped bags with the excavated sand. The tricky bit was changing tunnel shifts and bringing up the diggings during roll calls. First the old crew came up before our barrack was counted. Then the fresh team went down while the goons were tallying the other huts. Before and after our hut was checked, the spoil bags were passed up to the disposal team. Luck was with us. Not once did the Germans spot anything amiss.

"The disposal stooges concealed a bag of sand inside each trouser leg. Then they strolled about the compound until there was a suitable opportunity to pull the drawstring that allowed the tell-tale yellow sand to trickle out over a wide area. As with all tunnels, progress was painfully slow, sometimes less than half a foot a day.

"The only major crisis occurred when one day the Germans made a surprise head count in the barracks between Appells. The result showed two men missing, but not which two. Before the goons could mount a man hunt, they had to establish the identities of the two absent bodies, always a time-consuming procedure. So the German staff returned to the Vorlager to collect their files and more help. Time passed before they returned with documents, clerks, and squads of machine-gun toting soldiers. The kriegies were herded onto the parade ground where clerks sat at portable tables with their records spread in front of them. One by one, each POW was called forward and matched against his identity card. After hours of this, everyone was reported present. The goons decided they had erred. Life in the compound returned to normal."

"But how did we cover for the two missing men down the tunnel?" I questioned.

"That wasn't too difficult," Ed explained. "While the goons were collecting their documents, an English rugby game was quickly organized. During a wild scrum above the tunnel entrance, the two tunnellers surfaced." I stopped for a moment to watch two Focke Wulfe 190 fighters practicing battle tactics overhead. When Ed saw why my attention had momentarily been diverted, he said the planes were from the nearby airfield at Soreau where there was a fighter training unit as well as a Focke Wulfe factory.

Then he continued, "If the tunnel is ever used, Ward Winter will be one of the escapers. The escape committee has approved a plan for him to steal one of these planes and fly it to Sweden. He is preparing himself by studying the German flight instruction manual for it. Don't ask me how he obtained the manual. The tunnel was ready for breakout about the time of the Great Escape from the North Compound. But when fifty escapers were murdered by the Gestapo, England sent us orders that all escape attempts were to cease for the time being. I think Allied High Command expected the war to be over by September and did not want to risk further killing by the Gestapo."

On our way back we passed "Gunga Din" carrying a large water jug. I chuckled to myself at how he had been nicknamed after the fictional water carrier in one of Rudyard Kipling's stories about the northwest frontier.

My sleep that night was disturbed by fleeting dreams of tunnels and heroic escapes in FW 190 fighters. At one time I woke to find the light on and two ferrets counting the sleeping bodies. Another time I heard the distant sound of air raid sirens. Berlin, about ninety miles northwest of us, was a frequent target for our bombers during the longer hours of darkness in winter. Some of the attacks were primarily nuisance raids by fast Mosquito bombers to disturb the sleep and lower the morale of the civilian population.

At breakfast next day Ward commented on the previous night's bed count and laughed about "missing bodies." When I asked what he meant he explained that after every escape two or three additional kriegies would hide inside the compound to deceive the Germans as to how many were actually at large. There was always the hope that these "missing bods" might have an easier chance to slip away at a later date because they had already been reported as having escaped. However, sometimes there were problems keeping them hidden. One time a missing bod was sound asleep under a bottom bunk when the goons burst in on a night body count. Although well hidden, he was snoring loudly. The secret was kept when the man in the bunk above pretended to be sleeping, with fake snores timed to those of the missing bod below.

At the beginning of the week I wrote my third letter home, mostly about the forthcoming theatre productions. I still had absolutely no news from my family. I might as well have been living on a different planet, I was so out of touch with anything concerning my prior existence.

The next day was Tuesday, November 7, 1944, when the American presidential elections were held. I had heard very little about the campaign or platforms of the various candidates. I hoped Roosevelt would be re-elected but thought it might be some time before we heard anything either way. But I had underestimated our news team who, in broad daylight, received and delivered hourly election bulletins without being caught.

Later that afternoon I watched our coal ration officer divide a pile of coal briquettes into equal portions outside our hut. Others loafed around too, including the ferret "Dopey." As usual, the kriegies puffed on cigarettes, making sure their smoke drifted past the ferret to tantalize him with the smell of good tobacco. Any hope he had of a free butt ended when, with a calculated air of nonchalance, each of us in turn ground his half-smoked cigarette into the dirt with his heel. We knew full well that if we did not do this the goons, who were desperate for good tobacco, would salvage the long butts as soon as we turned our backs.

The following week the stage show "Bubble and Squeak" opened. It was scheduled to run about a week so that everyone in camp could see it, including the German staff, who were always allotted front-row seats. The scripts often included good-natured jibes directed at the goons, who seldom failed to attend.

Our room had opening night tickets for this show. I was excited about seeing my first POW play. I wondered whether it would be any good, considering that the stage, seats, scenery, and materials for it had to be improvised from whatever was available. Tools that were needed were supplied on parole from the Red Cross. I remembered the time when I had been assistant electrician for the high school play and many things had gone wrong, even though anything we needed was easily obtainable. I came back enthralled. In spite of limited resources the producers were able to stage a near-professional production. The bright lights, the costumes, the colourful sets, the acting were impeccable. Even our two Johns played convincing female roles. For a whole evening I was able to forget the reality of POW life.

Later in the week, when I was pounding the circuit with Tut, I brought up the topic of fraternizing with the enemy. I told him this had been disturbing me for a long time, especially when I saw Lofty spending so much time with Bing Crosby. "Perhaps,"

I said, "you can explain your recent remark about there being more to it than meets the eye."

After thinking for a moment, Tut said, "The X committee coordinates all escape activities to ensure maximum success. All schemes for breakouts have to have its approval. Each plan is assessed not only on its chances of success but on such other critical factors as resources required, risk of injury to escapers or helpers, and whether there might be reprisals against those left behind. A good scheme receives the backing and help of the whole camp, which often means the difference between success or failure. The committee is also in charge of activities which indirectly affect escaping or other clandestine activities and our well-being. Thus, as part of an overall plan it has issued an order that only designated kriegies are to fraternize with the Germans.

"For example, Jack, you are wrong about Lofty. He is only one of our many fluent goon speakers who have been selected to cultivate a close friendship with a specific, unsuspecting ferret to learn as much as possible about his private life. Frequently the goon is invited into the kriegie's room for a cup of genuine coffee, real chocolate, or a good cigarette. Once the target's confidence is obtained he might return our kindness with 'harmless' information such as advance warning of a surprise barrack search. Little does he know how invaluable this information can be to us.

"When we urgently require some information or forbidden item, we resort to serious deceit. For example, our contact might offer his German 'friend' coffee, chocolate, cigarettes, or other scarce items to take home on leave. For most guards, it is hard not to accept these innocent gifts for his wife or children. But if he does accept, he is wide open to blackmail by his English 'friends.' Then, under threat of being reported to the Gestapo, he is asked to smuggle in such items as materials for forging passports, travel documents, film for taking passport pictures, parts for making radios ... the list is endless."

This explanation of the dirty side of fraternization gave me food for thought. Somehow it did not seem to be a decent way of waging war, especially against these Luftwaffe soldiers. But against the Gestapo or ss, anything went.

On Friday night at ten o'clock I did my first stint of sentry duty. Well-bundled against the cold night air, I stood motionless in the shadows at the end of our hut, peering out the open window.

Somewhere in our compound fellow kriegies were relying on my alertness and sharp eyes to warn them of any danger as they dug tunnels, listened to radios, sewed civilian clothes, or forged passports. At long last I felt I was again doing something to fight the war. Searchlights in the goon-boxes periodically glared into life, swept back and forth, then went out. With no moon the night was too dark for me to see the sentries behind their machine-guns. Occasionally I glimpsed a guard patrolling among the barracks, but none came near my post. More frequently I glimpsed a shadow and heard a police-dog pad by. Far off, in the direction of Berlin, air raid sirens wailed. To my relief, and disappointment, nothing really exciting happened during this watch.

My initial stint at guard duty was a one-night effort, so after supper the following night I sat on the edge of one of the lower bunks to enjoy my coffee. As soon as the table was clear, Ed and Tut produced the cribbage board for their ritual round. The two contestants were the most frequent players in our room. Each time they played, it was with great enthusiasm, loud talk, and friendly arguments as to who was the better player. Their chatter was a continual source of amusement for the rest of us. Tonight they decided to play a series of games that would settle once and for all who was the best. The championship series would comprise one hundred games played over the next few weeks. The series seemed to continue forever. It was decisively settled when one of them (I have forgotten who) won fifty-one games to the other's forty-nine.

The following week, when I was returning to my room from the technical library, I passed several kriegies gathered around the bulletin board in our hut. I stopped to read the recently posted notice which they were discussing. I was astonished to read that someone was offering to teach ballroom dancing. Surely the offer couldn't be serious. Dancing in a POW camp! It must be just another subtle British joke. After all, how could anyone teach ballroom dancing without female partners, music, qualified instructors, and a large floor on which to practice? But then again, why not learn ballroom dancing in preparation for return to civilian life? Others were already preparing for going home by upgrading their formal education.

On entering my room I joined Ward, Tut, John, Johnny, and Tom, who were also discussing the offer of dance instruction. When I expressed my opinion about a qualified instructor, I was told in no uncertain terms that the kriegie offering the lessons was from the family which operated the largest chain of dance studios in England. This seemed to clinch the argument that he must know what he was doing, so several of us, just for a lark of course, signed up for instructions. I was sure there would be little response to the offer so promptly forgot about it. To everyone's surprise, the entry lists were over-subscribed. The dance studio was to be the quiet room next to ours. Because of its small size only ten pupils at a time could be accommodated, so the schedule called for two sessions each night, four times a week. This way, eighty different pupils could receive instruction in a given week. Even then there were waiting lists for the next set of courses starting in six-weeks' time. Johnny, Tut, Ed, and I were booked for Thursday evenings at eight o'clock, starting in ten days.

The week before I was to start my dancing lessons marked the middle of November. It was almost four weeks since I had arrived from Buchenwald and I was beginning to feel stronger each day. It so happened that in the middle of the week our room was scheduled to play soccer against another room in our hut. Our team was short a man, so I was asked to fill in. I felt confident I was fit enough to play, so accepted. Moreover, I was promised an easy position since it was the first time I had ever played English football. I started at one of the defense positions but lacked the stamina to run more than a few feet before becoming exhausted. Thereupon I was charitably switched to goaltender, where less exertion was required. But even there I fared little better. When the final whistle blew I was completely played out.

There was another air raid alert that night. The wailing of the sirens gave me an exhilarating feeling. It was positive proof our Allies were not far away keeping up the fight.

Towards the end of the week I was pacing the circuit with Johnny when we caught up with a kriegie who was the centre of attention of the large group accompanying him. He was both cheered and heckled as he strode purposefully along. Johnny knew right away what the commotion was about because he said, "Oh, another of those wagers about eating Red Cross parcels. I bet he doesn't win." Right away I knew he was referring to the recent discussion in our mess about whether any of us could eat a complete food parcel in one day, something a starving person may have thought easy to accomplish. But many a kriegie had tried and failed, I was told.

The hardest part of the bet was digesting the rich items, such as a pound of margarine, without being sick. The best chance of success was to mix everything, margarine, powdered milk, chocolate, cheese, raisins and so forth into a goulash, and then, over the twenty-four hour time period, eat small portions interspersed with a lot of physical activity. Ahead of us someone who was trying to win one of these bets was attempting to burn off calories. His chums walked with him offering encouragement while those betting against him watched that he did not cheat by throwing away food or vomiting.

Indoor activities increased as the days became shorter and colder. One which caught my interest was the forthcoming Block 67 chess tournament. I didn't expect that all the competitors would be experts – and it should be fun competing, even if I did lose in the first or second round. So on Saturday morning both Percy, who was our room champ, and I signed up. My disastrous chess game with Ward Winter had shocked me into playing several times a week to hone my skills and regain my confidence. Of late I could even challenge Ed or Tom to a contest and win my fair share.

On Sunday I wrote my fourth letter home. It was a "nothing" letter because there was really nothing to write about that would pass the censors. I did say that if I was sent a parcel, to put in lots of chocolate, a highly prized item here and one which I loved.

On Monday night Ginger served "fried biscuit." This was my first taste of the much-talked about dessert. As with all kriegie delicacies, it was served infrequently because weeks of hoarding were required to accumulate the basic ingredients. The prime component was a large round soda wafer that came from Canadian Red Cross parcels. Ginger selected thirteen of the soundest and soaked them in water over night. Next day the biscuits had swollen to about six inches in diameter by half an inch thick without splitting or cracking. Perfect! Then he set them aside until he was ready to continue at supper time. That evening Ginger used his allotted time on the stove top to fry the biscuits until they were a light brown on each side. Then he placed them on a plate and smothered each in a thick sauce of heavily sweetened powdered milk. The final touch was a topping of strawberry jam. Sickening, but so delicious!

Every few weeks a film, supplied through the Red Cross, was shown in the theatre. Tonight, as a finale to a good day, I saw *The Spoilers*, my first English film in more than six months. Next day the draw was posted for the chess tournament. I was horrified when I saw that in the first round I had drawn the hut champion (and erstwhile camp champion) as my opponent.

The first from our room to compete in the tournament was Percy Purnell. Reputedly he was the best of our group, although I had never seen him play because he was always busy studying. Consequently when this initial match was played a few days later I made a point of watching, on the chance of learning some tricky moves. Unfortunately, Percy lost in a relatively straightforward game. If our best chess man could lose that easily, I could foresee disaster when my turn came against the hut champion!

On Thursday night I reported for my first-ever dance lesson. I felt very self-conscious and a little foolish. I wondered if my three roommates did too. Our instructor first explained a basic step on a blackboard, then demonstrated it to music from an old windup record player as we watched and took notes. Then, one or two of us at a time, we tried repeating it. Sometimes our teacher danced as the female partner. After we had mastered the basic steps we were shown how to blend them smoothly into routines.

I really enjoyed the lessons. I fantasized about returning home, inviting a girl to a dance at the Ritz Carleton, and astounding her with my ballroom expertise. I would hold her in my arms as I effortlessly led her through the most intricate of steps and routines. The other dancers would stop to watch, and when we finished would show their appreciation with a round of applause. We would retire to a candle-lit table in the corner where, holding hands, she would easily persuade me to talk about my heroic wartime adventures. I didn't think I was alone with my dancing daydreams, for I often saw, in a quiet corner of the compound, a kriegie with a faraway look on his face humming to himself while taking odd little steps and turns.

I must have been worried about my forthcoming chess game against the hut champion on Saturday because I didn't sleep well the night before. Nor did it help to hear John talking in his sleep or hear the wail of air raid sirens as RAF bombers paid their nightly visit to Berlin. Next afternoon, watched by some of my roommates, I played my big chess match. I will never forget how, after about two moves, my opponent's queen was left completely unguarded for my taking. Knowing his reputation as a chess player, I suspected his queen was bait for a game-ending trap. I thought long and hard as to whether I should take it. No matter how carefully I studied the board I could not spot his ambush so, taking my courage in my hands, I took his vital queen off the board. With his most important piece gone I was able, after a few minutes, to remove more of his key players without significant losses to my own forces. I allowed myself a slight feeling of optimism.

But then disaster struck. My opponent settled down and proceeded to methodically demolish me, piece by piece, until finally I was checkmated. Afterwards, I asked him to explain the trap at the start of the game when he left his queen exposed. "Oh," he said, "there was no trap at all. I knew you were a beginner and I expected you to leave my queen alone because you thought it was bait for a trap. You did not fall for my ruse but took my queen and several other good men. For a while you had me on the ropes!"

The next day I skipped church service for the first time since my arrival. I did not always find it inspiring. The familiar hymns and music made me very homesick and I did not need any more emotional stress.

So far, in five weeks as a POW I had not tried my skills at any handicrafts. But now I had the urge to do something with my hands, to make something useful that was typically kriegie. I decided on a tin coffee mug. Tin bashing served a dual purpose; it was an excellent way of passing time, while making both useful and fun items not otherwise available. Useful articles were communal cooking pots, pans, and utensils, and tin mugs. Someone had passed many long hours building a grandfather clock that kept perfect time. Another had constructed a toy submarine, powered by rubber bands, which sailed on the fire-water pool and which supposedly could even submerge.

Among the countless examples of kriegie ingenuity was the condenser used in the first illicit radio. This was constructed with tin foil substituted for the usual metal plates. The sheets of foil were placed between the pages of a book to achieve the precise spacing, then the book was dipped in wax to seal it. All the air pumps and ventilation ducts for escape tunnels were built from limited resources, as were the trolleys and railways for carrying muck from the tunnel face to the exit shaft.

Of course we were not allowed even the simple hand tools of a home workshop. However, over the years the kriegies had secretly acquired pieces of steel for hammering and banging and made primitive implements by sharpening scissors for cutting tin and honing and serrating the edges of kitchen knives for sawing wood. Wires and small metal pieces were soldered together with the lead which sealed the bully beef tins. All that was needed to melt the lead was a pinpoint of heat. This was created by blowing at a candle flame through a small tube.

There were many excellent examples of tin bashing in our room from which I could learn the technique. I started my project with a Canadian butter tin, which didn't rust easily. First I worked hard scraping off the outside red, yellow, and blue paint until the metal underneath shone a bright silver. I didn't touch the inside, which was a dull yellow. The one-piece handle was made from a long piece of tin bent into a hollow square that turned ninety degrees near each end to connect with the mug. At top and bottom a narrow strip of metal secured the handle to the mug.

Towards the end of November, in my fifth letter home, I tried to explain the long delay between the day I went missing and when I was recognized as a POW by saying, "I had slept in many strange places." A few days later, in a postcard to my friend George Cairns, I made another cryptic comment. I wrote, "Too bad I was not here on my birthday." This I hoped would let them know I had been in other places before Stalag Luft III. I hoped these comments would get by the censor so that my family would know that a few unusual adventures had befallen me.

At the end of the month, all but two of those who had been too sick to travel when we left Buchenwald arrived at Stalag Luft III and were assigned to various compounds. They still looked barely alive. One was Harry Bastable, whom I had never expected to see again.

One day when I returned to our room there were some of our fellows intently watching Joe Twomey, who sat at a table in front of the window peering at some small object. When I went over to see what was going on, I was surprised to see that he had taken a wrist watch apart, placing the tiny screws, levers, and springs into little boxes made from folded paper. His tools were minute screwdrivers made from slivers of tin, and tweezers made from another tin scrap bent double. I watched fascinated as he cleaned and repaired the watch. No one had told me that Joe was a self-taught watch repair expert, one of the best in East Compound.

Joe was a quiet, retiring individual, well over six feet tall and extremely slim. He had been a fighter pilot, flying Spitfires from a base in Italy. During daylight hours his squadron often flew from a forward base in Yugoslavia to help Marshall Tito's Partisans. During one of these Yugoslavian expeditions Joe was shot down and captured. He was put in the local jail pending transfer to Germany. Shortly after locking him in a cell, the jailer was surprised when he returned with blankets to find Joe had already escaped. Joe had made his getaway after he examined the bars on his window, which seemed to be widely spaced. He had stripped naked, squeezed through, and departed. Unfortunately the alarm was quickly raised and his freedom was short-lived. After short stays in various jails and camps, Joe ended up in Stalag Luft III.

The month of November drew to an end. The weather was much colder now. Coal shortages did not permit a fire in the stove after lights-out. At night we slept fully clothed with our greatcoats piled on top because our blankets were so thin. Some lined their covers with newspapers for additional warmth. Many of the English wore woolen balaclavas in bed, with only their eyes, nose, and mouth showing. More frequently now, when the window was left open for fresh air, the first man to wash in the morning had to break a thin layer of ice which had formed in the washbasin.

I wondered how long I could keep my spirits up without becoming depressed. How did the men in my room do it? None was over thirty, all were in the prime of life, and most had been in various camps in Germany and Poland for long periods of time. Yet, at least outwardly, they remained cheerful and full of energy. Did some hide their fears, frustrations, and boredom with bed bashing and endless pacing of the circuit?

CHAPTER FIFTEEN

December 1944

With the start of December, my dreams of being back with my family for Christmas quickly faded. Pangs of homesickness, which had occurred all too frequently of late, worsened with the realization that I would have to celebrate this special day behind barbed wire. What would it be like? Would there be special Red Cross parcels with turkey and all the trimmings? Would the kriegies make decorations, sing carols, play Christmas music, and exchange gifts?

Nowadays, I told myself, I had much for which to be thankful. I had food, shelter, and clothing. Even more important, my health had improved to the extent that I could "bash" several circuits each day without becoming exhausted. I was most fortunate to be here. I could just as easily be slowly going mad in solitary confinement in a Gestapo prison such as Fresnes. There I would have a roof overhead but barely enough to eat. I would suffer the deprivation of no contact with other humans or the outside world. I would have absolutely nothing to stimulate me mentally during the long hours of loneliness. Alternatively, I could still be in Buchenwald, where in addition to death from starvation, disease, or cold there was the more-than-likely possibility of being murdered by the ss. I remembered that even there I at least had the company of comrades with whom to talk and share experiences, fears, and expectations, all of which were important to me. A bonus was being able to see the beauty of the sky overhead and the real world beyond the deadly electrified wire.

As a POW, I soon realized that the bane of life was the monotony of the unchanging routines and the complete lack of uncensored contact with the outside world. This regimented existence was compounded by communal living that allowed no privacy. Typically, thirteen kriegies ate, slept, and passed most of their day in a twelve-by-sixteen-foot room. Such close quarters inevitably led to individual conflicts. Often trivial things, such as the way a person held his cigarette, cleared his throat, or sat at a table, became extremely irritating, almost to the point of blows. When it became this serious, the only way to resolve the situation was for one of those involved to swap living quarters with someone from another room. This was a frequent occurrence. In fact, I heard there was one room that had accumulated all the "eccentrics."

Fortunately mental illness, as well as physical disability, was recognized by the Geneva Convention as justification for repatriation. Anyone in these categories could apply to be sent home on medical grounds. Each case was assessed by neutral Swiss or Swedish Red Cross doctors who periodically visited the many POW camps. One of the candidates for repatriation was Lt Gregory, a charming naval flying officer who was a frequent visitor to our room. He was a member of the crew rescued from a British aircraft carrier torpedoed in the Mediterranean early in the war. When I first met Greg at the beginning of December, he was expecting to hear momentarily whether his application had been approved. He appeared so normal to me that I did not think he stood a chance of going home.

Each prisoner was affected differently by continual confinement. The majority adapted to it in their own way, while others made primitive escape attempts, just to be free of the prison compound for a few days. There was the sad instance some time ago of a kriegie who could no longer endure the POW life. No one realized his suicidal intentions until he suddenly jumped over the trip wire and rushed the main fence. He ignored the shouted commands to halt and died in a hail of bullets from the nearest goon box.

The only safe way of getting beyond the wire for a few hours was on parole. This privilege, which occurred about twice a month, was granted to ten long-term kriegies at a time. Those selected were treated to a walk in the country in the company of a couple of German officers. The Germans were usually decent types who would stop at a pub and treat the fellows to a beer. On these special occasions our men took great pains to be immaculately attired in dress blue uniforms. Few had them, because most often they had been shot down while wearing battledress, so the dress outfit had to be borrowed from various sources throughout the compound. In our mess, Ward Winter was already preparing for his upcoming first walk. My turn, I calculated, would come in about four years!

One day, about two weeks before Christmas, it was our room's turn for the communal hair clippers. This happened infrequently, so Ed and I decided to spruce up for the festive season. For me it would be the first time in many months that I had had enough hair to clip, whereas Ed, who was a bushy character, had no such problem. The fact that neither of us had ever cut hair did not deter us. First, Ed cut my hair, then I cut his. During the process we were the target of rude comments from fellow roommates. But after we had surveyed each other's handiwork, we decided the insults were justified, so we asked Ginger, a neutral and reputed expert, to repair the damage.

As Christmas approached, my spirits sank proportionately. With no news from home, I developed a feeling of loneliness, even when among so many fellow airmen. Perhaps it was because those around me were comrades by circumstance rather than friends by choice, much like the "togetherness" of our bomber crews. When I thought about it, I decided Ed Beaton was probably the closest to being a friend in the true sense. Possibly it was because we shared the common ground of being the only Canadians in our mess. We had trained and flown with the RCAF, who had different methods of training and operation than the RAF. We were less stuffy than the British because we did not consider military rank and social status to be all-important.

As the days grew shorter, the weather turned even colder. Temperatures dipped below freezing and remained there. Snow covered the ground with a mantle of white. But these frigid conditions did not discourage indomitable kriegie spirits. This was the season for skating and hockey. Enthusiastic volunteers started a small rink next to Hut 63. After days of carrying jugs of water from the nearby washhouse, the ice was pronounced ready.

The limited supply of skates and hockey equipment came from the Red Cross and other service organizations such as the YMCA, Toc H (British service organization similar to the YMCA), and Salvation Army. Everyone shared in what was available.

Skating was so popular that schedules were drawn up in order to distribute the ice-time fairly. I skated every opportunity I was allotted, even though it was for only a few minutes each day. Our seldom-seen RAF group captain caught the enthusiasm, and ventured from the seclusion of his private room to participate. He enjoyed it so much that on one occasion he overstayed his ice time. Our carefully prepared rosters were disrupted and we had a hard time concealing our anger.

The colder weather did not stop most of us from doing daily circuits. No longer were they a struggle for me. I could do four or five without tiring. Ten days before Christmas, American Red Cross parcels were delivered to the Vorlager warehouse. These were to be in addition to our weekly issue, but had to be shared one parcel to every two men. Our morale took a tremendous boost. Forgotten for the moment were the frequent German propaganda claims that the war was far from over.

But, unfortunately, the enemy was right. Late in the afternoon of December 16 Lofty dashed into our room. "I have just heard the German OKW news broadcast. According to it, something big is happening on the western front. The Wehrmacht claim to have started a major offensive into Belgium and have broken through the American lines." My spirits sank. We all knew the enemy made exaggerated claims, but apparently not without some basis in fact. I despaired because if this proved to be a major offensive it would mean months, perhaps even a year longer as a POW.

The shocking news of a major attack by the supposedly beaten German army spread like wild fire. Our war maps were studied. Armchair military strategists had a heyday expounding their theories to all who would listen. Saner heads suggested we wait for the BBC news for an honest appraisal of the situation. Next day our bulletins confirmed that the Wehrmacht had indeed attacked, broken through Allied lines, and made deep penetrations towards the English Channel.

We tried not to let this dampen our spirits as we continued with Christmas preparations. For my part, I helped Tom prepare the cake. The ingredients for it had been hoarded for many weeks.

The kriegie recipe called for prunes, raisins, powdered milk, and ground biscuits to be mixed into a stiff batter. As a substitute for baking powder, which was not available, a dash of German tooth-powder was substituted. This concoction was baked until the cook decided it was done. If the tooth-powder worked as intended, we would have a cake. Otherwise we would have a heavy, flat Christmas pudding.

We were lucky; our creation was a cake. We iced it with a mixture of cocoa and undiluted, condensed milk. Our final touches were decorations made with melted D-bars and a sprinkle of "nuts," kernels laboriously extracted from prune pits. To avoid the chance of anyone feeling short-changed when the cake was served, it was very carefully divided into equal shares. Even then, each of us drew from a pack of cards to establish the rotation for selecting his piece. Sometimes I thought a pack of playing cards was the most useful item in camp, not just for games, but to ensure a fair distribution of food, clothing, chores, privileges, coal, and so forth. We absolutely could not risk someone feeling he had been cheated, even when all portions appeared equal.

The fact that alcohol was not available induced some kriegies to build stills and produce all manner of brews from hoarded prunes, raisins, potatoes, and so forth. The week before Christmas, the sbo banned the use of intoxicating beverages during the festive season. I wondered why he would do this, especially when I had heard that on Christmas day security was relaxed and increased fraternization took place between the British and the Germans. I thought the drinkers in camp would be really upset with this order. But Johnny explained the reason for it.

"Obviously the sbo does not want a recurrence of the near-disastrous happenings of last year. Then, the gates into the Vorlager from the American and British compounds were opened so that we could visit back and forth. The kriegie amateur distillers took the opportunity to generously share their potent homemade liquor with both fellow kriegies and goons. In no time at all the powerful brews were undiscriminatingly felling both friend and foe. The German drunks were rolled under a bunk while the RAF bodies were dumped on top to sleep it off. Outside, drunken kriegies staggered around. Many tried to climb the barbed wire fences separating the compounds, only to fall into the tangled mesh in between. Fortunately, because it was Christmas, they did not draw the fire of the Posten. We were lucky no kriegies or goons were injured. It was a proper bloody shambles!"

The week before Christmas, the pantomime "Robin Hood," a lighthearted farce satirizing life in a POW camp, was staged in the camp theatre. I enjoyed it so much and laughed so hard that I scrounged an extra ticket to see it a second time.

The news from the western battlefront cast a pall over our festive spirit. The significant progress of the German army as it advanced into Belgium and towards the Channel was tracked with coloured pins on our war maps. We paid little attention to the eastern front, where we anticipated no fighting before the end of the long, cold winter.

No decorations brightened our quarters. How could the drab life of a prisoner of war have room for frivolous things which might have lifted our spirits? Life continued its normal routine with two Appells a day. Skaters filled the ice rink at every opportunity. Kriegies trudged the circuit. Only occasionally did I hear someone whistling or singing Christmas music.

On Christmas Eve we opened our special Red Cross parcels which featured tinned turkey, plum pudding, cranberry sauce, nuts, and gifts for each of us. I was lucky enough to end up with a pipe. After supper I attended communion service in the theatre. Tonight the place was packed. The polished silver chalice holding the wine seemed to shine brighter tonight, and the linen napkin with which Padre Thompson held it seemed whiter than usual. The traditional carols triggered a flood of homesickness and depression in me. I was sure I was not alone with these feelings.

On Christmas Day the BBC brought us better war news: the German advances on the western front had been halted. Supposedly we were now pushing the enemy back. My spirits lifted. Perhaps this would be my last Christmas here.

The same morning, the kriegies staged a "Fun Fair" in the canteen. Our room won a prize of fifty cigarettes each in a simulated horse race. In the afternoon there was an exhibition hockey game, England vs Scotland. It seemed strange that these two countries, unknown in the world of hockey, should supply the players. Probably it was because they did the most work preparing and maintaining the rink. No matter, it was all in good fun, although I found it rather chilly standing in the snow watching.

We sat down to our special dinner in the evening. Unfortunately, our stomachs were not in shape for the unaccustomed rich fare, so Ginger's mince pies had to be saved for later in the week. Everyone tried to be gay and festive. After dinner, when I sat and puffed on my new pipe, my thoughts were of home, thousands of miles away. I was sure the others were feeling the same way.

When I climbed into my bunk for the night, I decided that today had been better than average, although it had not been a real Christmas. Yes, there had been some special fare to eat and lots of good companionship. But Christmas should be celebrated with one's immediate family, not behind barbed wire under the nozzles of machine guns. I lay awake for some time, my mind churning with thoughts, both good and bad. Would the war be over next summer? If not, where would I be next year at this time? Since I had received no mail, did my family know I was alive? Had any letters arrived from France? Was David at flying school yet? Were Jean and Bert married? Was Bert even now flying with Bomber Command?

After Christmas I wrote my last letter home for the month, and sent a postcard to Scotland. There was still no mail for me.

When I had arrived at Stalag Luft III, I had been issued an airman's jacket. I had been surprised to find, in the pocket of it, a note from a girl in Birmingham, whom I assumed worked in the factory where it was made. The slip of paper had her name and address on it and a request that the recipient of the garment drop her a line. I assumed that she did this quite often and was rewarded with letters from airmen based in interesting places. I had saved the note, thinking that someday it would be amusing to surprise her with a letter. So I used one of my four postcards and, in the minuscule space allowed, scribbled a few words to her. I had fun doing this. I doubt she ever dreamed an answer would come from someone in a German POW camp.

During the last week of the old year, new bets were placed as to when the war would end and previous bets that the war be over in 1944 were paid off. I watched one loser pay off his debt by dashing stark naked through the snow to the fire-water pond. Amidst the cheers of a small crowd, he broke the ice, jumped in, and splashed around in the frigid water. At no time during the festive season did I see anyone drunk. I presumed that the sbo's edict had been observed.

Most of us thought the war would end in 1945. The Allies had retaken France, Belgium, parts of Holland, and Italy. The Russians had recaptured most of the vast tracts of land lost to the enemy. An often discussed topic during these last days of 1944 was whether we would be liberated by the western Allies or the Russians. No matter who it was, most thought Germany would fight to the bitter end rather than capitulate. None of us ever voiced the thought, but I suspected many of us wondered if Nazi fanatics would shoot all their prisoners of war at the final collapse of Germany.

New Year's Eve was very ordinary, much like any other day in a pow camp. I could not help but feel a little bitter when I thought of all those back home, safe in cushy war jobs, who I imagined would be out all night getting drunk. What right did they have to celebrate? Canada had no conscription for overseas service so they would never know what it was like to face enemy fire, or to be hungry, or cold, or without shelter.

CHAPTER SIXTEEN

Luft III – The Last Days

New Year's Day 1945 was cold. Temperatures were below freezing. Beneath the leaden skies a mantle of snow covered the frozen ground. Such weather was still with us, cold, damp and miserable, a few days later when I stood on morning Appell. I was chilled to the bone by the time the count was finished so, as I often did, I raced with others for the warmth of the huts. A sharp stab of pain in my right knee brought me up short. It was so excruciating that I could hardly put any weight on that leg. In fact, I was barely able to limp to my room.

My roommates summoned "Timmie" Timmims, who had interrupted his medical studies to join the RAF. His educated opinion was that I had probably torn a knee cartilage and the best cure was lots of rest. He did not think it warranted asking the Germans for professional medical assistance. His diagnosis seemed to be correct because the following day my knee was slightly better. I was able to limp about and not miss any Appells. But I realized it would be some time before I could skate again or do serious circuit bashing.

I was quite concerned about this unfortunate curtailment of my mobility. There was little doubt that there would be Allied spring offensives on both western and eastern fronts that might affect our stay in Stalag Luft III. I had long since learned that to survive I had to be ready for the unexpected. I must be in good physical condition should we be required to walk long distances. Already the wise kriegies were circuit bashing more frequently, each time increasing the number of laps. We were quietly hoarding canned food, chocolate, and cigarettes. This year, apparently, more than ever before, we had to be prepared.

One who no longer had to scrimp, save, and prepare was F/L Gregory. We were all happy for and envious of him when his application for repatriation was approved. Greg was ecstatic when he came to say good-bye to us. He noted all our home addresses so that he could write each of our next of kin an uncensored letter from England. He departed for home on January 5.

Gregory's departure revived the often-expressed concern of many kriegies that years of confinement would adversely affect a man's sexual prowess. However a former POW had already written specifically to tell us that on his return home he had definitely proved this to be a myth!

One night during that first week of January, for no apparent reason I awakened from a sound sleep. I lay in my top bunk with my blanket wrapped tightly around me for warmth, listening to the sound of trains shunting in the nearby railway yards. Something seemed different. There seemed to be a great deal more activity than usual tonight. I wondered if it was military traffic heading for the eastern front. Maybe the Germans were preparing to initiate a winter assault.

A few days later, on January 12, the BBC announced that the Russians had launched an extensive winter offensive into Poland. I realized then that this must be the reason for the sharp increase in rail traffic. If true, a major Red Army attack was great news, but I was skeptical as to whether it would amount to much when the weather was so cold and the ground blanketed with snow. However, Lofty insisted that it must be a serious campaign because even the OKW communiques were conceding major Russian advances.

Once again our hopes were raised that we might soon be liberated. Our war maps became the focus of attention and one of our military strategists calculated that if the Russians kept up their rate of advance they would reach Stalag Luft III by the end of January.

The noise of railway traffic through Sagan continued and intensified with each passing day. It was no longer restricted to the protective cover of darkness, positive proof that the Germans were in urgent need of troops and munitions on the eastern front. The possibility that our POW compound might be overrun by rapidly advancing Russians was a reality.

We debated endlessly whether the goons would transfer us westward or abandon us when the advancing Red Army neared Stalag Luft III. Because I had already been moved once by the Germans at the approach of Allied armies, I thought we would be evacuated. Perhaps it might be better for us to remain in German hands and then be liberated by our western Allies in the early summer. If the Germans retreated without us, I thought we ran the risk of being caught in the cross fire between the advancing and retreating armies.

We airmen knew little about infantry fighting. Should the Russians free us, many thought they would hand us rifles and expect us to fight side by side with them against our common enemy. It might be too much to expect them to simply feed and shelter us until we were shipped home. I had mixed feelings about our Russian partners. To me they were an unknown entity in spite of all the western Allies had done to help them. I believed they set even less value on human life than the Germans and therefore should not be trusted. Talking it over I learned I was not alone in my fear that we might be attacked in error by the Soviet air force. Fortunately for us they had only a small bomber fleet, which was primarily employed against the most vital targets, usually not far behind the German lines.

We still attended lectures, rehearsed plays, completed chores, and continued daily routines. Yet there was always an undercurrent of both anxiety and excitement, a feeling that we were caught up in momentous events. Our camp became a hotbed of rumours and life no longer seemed monotonous and dull.

As the active war zone rapidly engulfed us, we checked and rechecked the supply of food we had hoarded in case the Red Cross parcels were interrupted and the Germans had nothing for us. This time, should we be moved, I had to be fit to endure any extended travel. My general physical condition had greatly improved but I worried about my knee, which still bothered me. It seemed as though it was never going to heal. Each time I thought it was back to normal, I would accidentally strain it and end up limping. I had experienced enough of the enemy's mentality to know that those not fit enough to keep up could possibly be shot. Perhaps not by the Luftwaffe, but I couldn't be sure we would always be in their hands.

The pace quickened. In mid-January, we began hearing muffled "whoomps" to the east, the frequency and intensity of which increased each day. These sounds were similar to those I had heard from my cell window in Fresnes, seemingly so long ago. I knew it was artillery fire as the battle moved closer. I thought it incredible that the Russians could advance so rapidly in the dead of winter and was surprised that I saw no air action, German or Russian.

Of all the various possibilities which might happen to us, a forced march was the only one we could try to be ready for. Our activities, no longer kept hidden from the goons, now concentrated on preparations for evacuation. We didn't know where we might be going. We didn't know how much food, clothing, cigarettes, and personal effects we could each take with us. We didn't know what to anticipate about shelter at night, cooking, or transporting our belongings. Every spare moment became a frenzy of activity as we prepared for the worst.

We made compact slabs of high-protein nourishment from our hoarded food. We patched and sewed clothes and waterproofed boots with cooking fat. We packed cigarettes and matches in waterproof cans. We separated personal belonging into piles to be carried or left behind and exchanged home addresses. We made backpacks and smokeless burners. As time went on, more and more worked in groups to build sleds and carts.

By far the most popular choice for carrying supplies was a backpack. My roommates and I chose this option and made crude rucksacks by stitching a pair of suspenders to a kit bag. Although mine was somewhat uncomfortable on my back, I considered it the best solution because I was sure the sleds and carts would not survive rough travel.

Those who gambled on wooden sleds built them from Red Cross crates, bed boards, or whatever was available. As an added refinement they increased the durability of the runners by covering them with tin. Others worked in teams of two or more to build two-wheeled carts that could be either pushed or pulled. They used pieces of iron from stoves to make the axles and other metal parts. The rims of the handmade, round, wooden wheels were fitted with tin, again for increased durability. Several groups even built spare wheels.

The smokeless burners, which many of the kriegies planned to include in their gear, fascinated me with their simplicity and usefulness. The design was quite simple and materials for it readily available. A Canadian butter tin with the top removed was suspended by wires inside a larger tin that had once held Klim powdered milk. The bottoms of each tin were left intact. The inner can, which had small holes punched around its lower perimeter, hung about an inch above the bottom of the outer one. The fuel – small twigs, shavings, bits of wood, or whatever was available – was burned in the centre compartment. Whatever was to be cooked rested on top of the Klim tin. In a matter of minutes this tiny stove could boil a tin of water or heat a can of food. The design was such that the draft feeding the fuel caused any smoke generated to be consumed. This was an important feature because it meant they could be used indoors without smoking up the surroundings. Ingenious as they were, I didn't intend to make myself one because I thought, with snow on the ground, it might be difficult to find fuel.

Activity on the circuit increased tenfold as everyone worked to get in shape. Some bashed the circuit to check the durability of their homemade packs and the weight they could carry. Others walked with loads on their backs simply to improve their stamina. By January 25, although the noise of artillery fire had increased, it did not sound any nearer. We guessed the Russians were twenty miles east of us, preparing to cross the Bober River. Any day now they would swarm across and quickly overrun us. The betting was that we would wake up one morning to find the German guards gone. No one doubted that zero hour was at hand.

Last minute decisions were taken as still more favourite chairs, pots, pans, and furniture were butchered to build sleds and carts. Cigarette hoards were checked and counted to see if even more could be carried in packs. Personal mementos and other items were lovingly handled as the difficult individual decision was made as to whether they could be carried or had to be left behind. Being a recent arrival, I had few disposables. In fact, when at the last moment Padre Thompson asked if anyone had room for one of his bottles of communion wine, I volunteered to carry it. Again I stowed my "lucky" piece of parachute in my boot.

January 26 came and went with no word from the Germans about their intentions and no sign of the Russians. I thought that if the goons waited any longer to move us, it would be too late to evacuate the thousands of POWs in the Stalag III complex. I saw no reason why we couldn't stay here without any more hassles. I wished we knew what the Red Army was doing – we had heard nothing on the BBC news about whether it had yet crossed the Bober.

January 27 started as a cold, bleak day. Intuitively I felt this had to be it. The guards, like zombies, stared down at us from the goon boxes. Morning Appell was held as usual but activity in the nearby railway yards ceased. The sudden quiet sounded ominous after all the noise of the previous few weeks. Some thought this meant the Russians were just down the road. Rumours flew, each one seemingly contrary to the previous one. Yesterday we were going to be abandoned to the Russians. Today we should prepare to be evacuated, but no details as to how. None of the hearsay mentioned provision for those too sick to travel on foot.

With regret, we started incinerating everything we couldn't carry with us. For the first time since I had arrived, our stove was kept burning continuously. It was depressing having to destroy cherished mementos and personal effects. Cigarettes and food, which we had hoarded so carefully but could not take with us, were tossed into the flames or ground into the floor. We did not want to leave anything behind for German soldiers or civilians to scavenge. One of the countless rumours that flew around was that to get his men in shape the American SBO in the Centre Compound had spent the day marching them around and around the circuit.

About seven P.M., January 27, orders came from the German commandant that Stalag Luft III was to be evacuated that night. The Americans would leave first and East Compound would follow. Even though we had been expecting it momentarily, the news came as a shock. Nothing was said about how we would travel, whether we would get food rations, or what was our ultimate destination. I shivered at the thought of starting off in the dead of night, in the middle of winter, in a hostile land.

Final packing took place and superfluous food was eaten. The room stove continued to be fed with pieces of furniture. The quarters had never before seemed so comfortably warm. We sat, each immersed in his own thoughts, waiting quietly for the order to quit the hut, the atmosphere tense and the laughter forced. The winter night dragged on. The Americans seemed to be taking forever to clear their compound. Perhaps the goons had changed their minds and fled without us! Maybe the Russians were even now at the gates!

Finally the first of the East Compound huts was ordered into the Vorlager. Our turn came after midnight. We pulled on our outdoor clothing and hoisted our uncomfortably heavy packs to our backs. Then, before filing out into the cold and snow, we looked for the last time at what had been our cozy little room. It made no sense to me that we should start in the middle of the night when we could easily have waited the few hours until daylight.

After straggling through the gate into the Vorlager, we halted near the Red Cross parcel building. We were surprised to hear that we were each to be given two parcels. We were not prepared for this so had to reorganize and repack our kits to accommodate them. The wiser of us threw away tinned butter, margarine, powdered milk, and most of the cigarettes, keeping only high-calorie nourishment. No one wanted to waste food, so tins were stuffed into pockets and packsacks, or placed in Red Cross boxes and slung with cords over the shoulder. The much larger American group had left the camp. The food that they had discarded littered the snow. I was shocked by the amount.

The sky was overcast, so the night was black. The circuit lights above the barbed wire were still lit, but no searchlights swept the area. I couldn't make out if the goon boxes were manned. In hushed silence, we stamped our feet to keep warm while we waited for orders. Fellow companions were shadowy figures in the darkness; guards were not obviously present. There was little conversation among us.

Orders were quietly passed from our SBO: "Keep together for mutual safety. No escaping for now." A red glow, increasing in intensity, became apparent in the East Compound. Soon flames were leaping skyward as one of our barracks went up in smoke. Either the fire had been deliberately set or one of the little-used stoves had overheated. There was an eerie, unbelievable atmosphere to the whole scene.

A figure materialized out of the shadows. I knew by the cut of his clothing that he was a fellow kriegie. He checked quickly to make sure we were POWs before he whispered, "England knows we are being moved out." He was gone as quickly and as quietly as he had come. I tried to take comfort in the fact that our wireless transmitter had been used for a good purpose.

The trancelike spell was broken when the last parcel was issued and the last man counted. The eastern sky was streaked with the first light of dawn. Cold and sleepy, we passed through the main gate of Stalag Luft III for the last time.

CHAPTER SEVENTEEN

Forced March

For the first time in three months I was outside Stalag Luft III. I felt a fleeting sense of freedom, perhaps because I was now on the other side of the barbed wire and sentry boxes that had confronted me every day for such a long time. This surprising impression lingered for several minutes despite the ever-present armed guards. In the first light of the new day, I paused for one last look. The mantle of white that hid the monotonous, sandy ground failed to brighten the dreary view. The dull, unpainted buildings, lifeless now, looked cold and depressing. The burning hut, with flames shooting high in the air, did little to dispel a sense of gloom. An involuntary shudder passed through me. I turned my back and quickened my pace to join my comrades.

I silently cursed the stupidity of the arrangements for our move. With no sleep in more than twenty-four hours, we were starting off in freezing temperatures before eating a hot meal. This might not have been so bad if we were to travel by train, but we were now heading southwest, away from the city of Sagan and its rail connections. I consoled myself with the knowledge that we might have more chance of survival on the open road. There we could dive into the ditches for shelter should we be mistakenly attacked by the air force or artillery of the nearby Russian army. On the other hand, if we were locked in boxcars or trucks we would be sitting ducks. I tried to convince myself that the hardships of a long journey on foot would prove to be the lesser of two evils.

The dawn became full daylight. A gray overcast sky hid the sun and the snow crunched underfoot with each step. We continued along the forest road bordering the Stalag Luft III complex. Soon it was behind us. We saw no one other than those from our contingent.

We kriegies, in assorted air force and army clothing, walked near the centre of the road. Our guards, in blue-gray field uniforms, kept to the shoulders. We ambled along at our own pace, either singly, in pairs, or in groups. As usual we tried to hinder and delay the Germans by making no attempt to keep in rank and file. This would have been difficult in any case since we were loaded with packs and bundles or pulling carts and sleds. We were dead tired from lack of sleep; I suspected the goons were too. With each kilometer the long column stretched out further.

The Luftwaffe soldiers were burdened with weighty army field-gear. They carried rifles slung over their backs, not ready in their hands as alert sentries would have done. None that I saw carried machine guns. They were older men who seemed somewhat bewildered by all that was happening and were so few in number, and so widely spaced, that anyone of us could have slipped away without being noticed.

The first diversion occurred when, not far from Stalag Luft III, we passed an army prisoner of war compound on our left. A large number of khaki-clad kriegies wearing red berets left their huts to watch us. They shouted to us across the barbed wire that they were British paratroopers captured last fall at Arnhem. These elite troops, who had been in summer battle dress when caught, had not been given winter gear. Now they stood wrapped in blankets to keep warm. We exchanged words of encouragement. No doubt they too would soon be evacuated and, without suitable clothing, would fare badly.

At the end of the first hour, while still within the pine woods, we made our first stop. Before I sat down on my pack to rest I looked back in the direction of Stalag Luft III. Although the barbed wire compounds were hidden by a bend in the road, their position was marked by a wisp of smoke that rose from the still-burning hut in East Compound.

Towards the end of the ten minute stop I was chilled through and began to shiver. Otherwise I would have fully enjoyed the rest. When the guards shouted, *"Raus! Raus!"* I was quite happy to sling my packs on my back and set off. Many of those up ahead had already found their packs heavy to carry, even after such a short distance. During this first stop they had tossed surplus gear aside to lighten their loads. A few broken sleds and carts joined the litter. I thought it was a bad omen that so many were already finding it hard going when even worse could be ahead.

The sky remained overcast, the day windless. After a few miles the thick forest on either side thinned, then ended. We were now in open country with scattered farms and only a few wooded areas. The gently rolling landscape looked cold and forbidding. At the intersection of a major artery we turned west along it.

This new road, as far as the eye could see in either direction, was jammed with farm vehicles fleeing westward. The tightly packed, horse-drawn open wagons moved haltingly, a few feet at a time. Their pace was so slow that I doubted they travelled a kilometer in an hour. Each four-wheeled cart groaned under the load it carried. Crates, trunks, suitcases, cardboard boxes, chairs, tables, mattresses, baby carriages – everything to be found in a farmhouse. Piled on top or secured to the sides of each wagon were white sheets tied at the corners that held still more belongings. All carried sacks of feed for their hard-working horses.

Weather-beaten elderly men, too old for military service, sat bent over on the high driver's bench gripping the reins. They waited hunched against the cold, caps pulled down over their ears, coat collars up. Beside them sat women, scarves wound tightly around their heads. At the back of some carts, children peered out from between the bundles and packages. These people, I assumed, were refugees – the German "home front" who, suddenly uprooted from their homesteads, were seeking safety within the rapidly shrinking boundaries of their country. They were bringing with them all they could carry of their worldly possessions.

We kept to the right of this massive throng and walked steadily past them. We stared at these enemy civilians and they at us, but exchanged no words. I wondered if they knew where they were going, and whether they really thought they would find food and shelter farther west. They had little hope, I thought, of outdistancing the rapidly advancing, mechanized Red Army. I was very disturbed by this pathetic sight of helpless refugees fleeing the relentless advance of an invading army. It was the first time I had ever witnessed this other side of war; I hoped it would be the last. It was a sight I shall never forget.

Sometime later we turned onto still another road, which we apparently had to ourselves. At long last the sun broke through the overcast clouds to add a little warmth to the day. Each hour we stopped for a rest, and each time I became chilled before we were ready to move on. Each time we saw more abandoned kriegie carts and sleds that had failed to live up to expectations, more cans of food, which had become too heavy to carry, thrown in the ditch. It seemed a crime to me that food should be cast aside.

At one point during this unforgettable day we passed a few unguarded Russian POWs on the outskirts of a farm. They wore only the vertical blue and white striped cotton jackets and pants of slave labour workers, with bare feet in loose wooden clogs. I imagined they must be frozen stiff. However, they sounded quite cheerful and called to us in their own language, which unfortunately no one near me understood.

We maintained our slow but steady pace and the goons made no attempt to speed us up. At the end of the hourly breaks it required no gun waving and shouting to get us moving again. So far I didn't think of it as a forced march. In fact, guards and prisoners seemed for once to have a common goal, that of reaching some unknown destination as best they could. There was even fraternization. Many of our people shared their plentiful cigarettes with Germans, although they expected nothing in return. Had the Germans not carried rifles, one might have wondered who in fact was in charge.

We continued through the monotonous countryside. Whether by accident or design, our route passed through few villages. Scattered farmhouses, well back from the road, appeared lifeless. Perhaps the inhabitants watched from behind curtained windows. Perhaps they had already fled. We neither heard nor saw any signs of military activity. The land seemed ominously hushed, much like the calm before the storm. It was hard to believe that desperate fighting was taking place only a few miles to the east. None of us sang, yelled, or showed any outward sign of emotion. We simply trudged resignedly onward. I regretted that we had exchanged the comparative comfort of our POW camp for this uncertain future.

Watches were scarce, so we had no way of keeping track of how long we walked or rested. We only knew the approximate time of day by the sun, when it was visible. Not that time was any longer of great interest to us. Earlier in the day we had chattered among ourselves, but now we had tired of it. At first I had been interested in the countryside through which we passed. I thought the others had been too, especially those who had been behind the barbed wire of Stalag Luft III for a long time. But we soon became bored with looking at endless fields and seemingly empty farmhouses. Instead we concentrated our flagging efforts on keeping going.

The brief halts each hour continued. Not once did the Germans offer us food or drink, as required by the Geneva Convention. The few kriegies who had brought smokeless burners, if lucky had time to find twigs and heat a brew. For the rest there was no means to heat anything. Sometimes we munched on a slab of bread or biscuit with cheese, or perhaps some cold tinned meat. We were reluctant to dig too deeply into our supplies because we did not know how many days or weeks they had to last. At least we ate better than our guards, whose standard fare was a slice of German bread spread with lard.

I stayed in the familiar company of my roommates. We were with the others from our hut, near the middle of the long column. Within our mess we soon realized we should work in pairs, each helping the other. This way, if one tired for a while the other would help with his pack for a short distance. Or if one was feeling down then the other tried to boost his waning morale. Ed and I worked together like this. The majority of us had been air crew and, as such, were in our twenties, and in good physical condition. But months or even years of inactivity and poor food had taken their toll. Our packs seemed to grow heavier with each step.

I felt sorry for the older men, such as Padre Thompson. He was a small man and didn't appear very sturdy. The fellows from our mess, as well as from others, frequently offered to carry his pack for short distances, but he refused to be spelled. I was pleased that in a small way I was helping with his good work by carrying one of his bottles of communion wine carefully stowed in my pack.

As usual, rumours abounded. They were all plausible: the Germans are going to abandon us after dark tonight, the Red Army have encircled us; or the sick are being picked up by German transport. These stories only raised false hopes or new fears. Although difficult, it was better to try and ignore them. During the day I saw no signs of the American POWs from Centre Compound who had left Stalag Luft III a few hours before us. Presumably they were well ahead on the same road. They must have been exhausted from their long practice march the day before.

Throughout that interminably long day we continued the never-ending plodding. We just walked and walked, kilometer after kilometer. We didn't know where we were going, nor how far. If we had known our target for that day, I think it would have been easier for us to keep on.

By midafternoon waves of fatigue swept over me. My boots were not waterproof and my wet feet soon became numb with cold. The pain in my bad knee increased. I limped with each step and could hardly wait for the next stop to rest. The farther I went, the more tired I became, and the quicker the cold bothered me when we did stop. Each time when I sat down on my pack I was soon shivering with cold. For the first time I had doubts as to how much farther I could walk.

Others must have felt the same way, because many spent part of a rest pause stamping their feet and swinging their arms to keep warm. And during the walking we frequently passed kriegies whose pace had slowed so much they had fallen behind their original group.

Late in the afternoon winter darkness set in, but this did not stop us. No one knew how much further we had to go, or if there would be a warm shelter and food awaiting us when we reached our destination. Eventually, we halted on the outskirts of what appeared to be a small village. We waited for the shouts of, "*Los! Los! Fertig machen!*" that would signal the end of the rest. But the hated shouts were not heard. Time slipped by. I was sure twenty minutes must have passed without the order to press on or an explanation for the delay. I allowed myself a glimmer of hope that this hamlet might be our haven for the night.

More time passed. Dead tired, we waited and waited. We sat shivering on our packs. Then we stamped up and down. Finally, after what seemed like an eternity, word came down the column that we would stop here for the night. I was afraid this might be just another cruel rumour. In the darkness ahead I could make out kriegies stirring, picking up their gear. My group followed suit, then started edging forward. We moved into the village by fits and starts until we were in front of a small church which proved to be our billet for the night. We left the snow and cold behind and filed through the front door into the dry, brightly lit interior.

The house of worship, which was supposed to seat perhaps five hundred, now swarmed with some one thousand or so unkempt kriegies. The chilly interior soon warmed up from the body heat of so many men jammed into the closed space. In no time each of us had picked his place for the night and cluttered it with his gear. There were bodies on and under the pews, in the aisles, in the choir stalls, in the organ loft, in the pulpit, and even on the communion table. I chose a spot on a pew a few rows from the front on the left-hand side.

After establishing our territory, the next priority was food. As we had learned to expect, the Germans had none to offer, not even a hot drink. Nor had they made any provision for heating our Red Cross supplies. After a long march, with no sleep in two days, our cold bully beef, German bread, slice of cheese, and perhaps dried prunes didn't seem like much.

When I saw kriegies eating and sleeping on the communion table and using the power outlet in the nearby pulpit to receive the latest BBC news, I felt uncomfortable. I thought they might be committing a sacrilege, but reassured myself with the thought that churches were supposed to offer comfort and shelter to the needy. Surely we were in desperate need!

Before I settled down for the night, I hung my wet socks and boots over the back of the pew, where, if I was lucky, they would dry overnight. In the meantime I put on dry socks from my pack. Thankful to be indoors, I stretched out fully dressed on my pew. Over me I had my blanket, which I had carried, and my greatcoat. Warm for the first time that day, I slept like a log. Next morning I learned that not everyone had enjoyed an undisturbed sleep. For the majority the cold, the diet, and other changed living conditions had afflicted them with the "runs." All night long there had been a never-ending procession to and from the temporary Abort outside a barn behind the church. The unlucky had made more than one trip.

Surprisingly, we were not rousted out at the crack of dawn. We had time to eat a cold breakfast from Red Cross food, readjust backpacks for comfort, and scrap more nonessential items. Those with sleds and carts had time for hurried maintenance. When we set off, it was full daylight on another cold, cheerless day. I guessed it must have been after eight o'clock before we were clear of the village. I was not as sleepy. I had food in my belly, my knee didn't ache, I wore dry socks inside my still-damp boots. I felt I was in better shape for today's march.

Again we seemed to be the only humans foolish enough to be using the roads on this wintry day. Our pace, I thought, was a little faster, and the rests shorter. Possibly the Russians were getting closer. The novelty of being outside the wire and away from the normal daily routine of POW life seemed to wear off even more quickly than yesterday. In no time I had lost interest in all that went on around me. I rapidly lost my pep and energy. From the actions of those around me, I decided I was not the only one feeling this way.

We walked and walked, and then walked some more before we rested. Then we plodded and plodded, and plodded still further before we took a break. We moved like automatons through the bleak countryside. We saw no refugees. We saw no sign of either German or Russian troops preparing to do battle. Again we knew neither our next destination nor how many days we might be on the road. Exhaustion from lack of exercise and heavy packs contributed to the growing mood of depression. Morale sank to new lows. Padre Thompson retrieved his bottle of communion wine from my pack. He moved up and down the line offering a sip to anyone who seemed to be in trouble. The bottle was soon depleted.

Tom Royds was the first to break in our group. We had just shouldered our packs after a midmorning stop when we realized that Tom was still sitting hunched over on his pack. His buddy, encouraged him, "Come on, Tom, time to shove off!" but Tom sat there unmoving. Again he was urged to get going. This time he muttered, "I have had it up to here and I am bloody well not going anywhere." Concern swept through us as we saw that Tom had reached the end of his rope. Without a word, two of us pulled him to his feet while others added the weight of his belongings to their backs. Padre Thompson gave him a sip of wine. He started stumbling along, helped by two of us. Gradually he worked himself out of his hopelessness. We shared his packs between us until the next stop. After that Tom carried them himself.

That afternoon, as I sat on my pack during one of the rest stops, I despaired of ever again being warm, eating real food, or being with loved ones. My knee ached, my feet were numb, I was dead tired. I was cold. No one knew how far or where we were going. Everything was so bloody useless, stupid, futile, and insane. With no thought as to what might happen to me, I felt it was pointless to continue this senseless, never-ending walking to nowhere. I just sat there, not caring if it was forever.

The time came to move on. Before I knew what was happening I was pulled to my feet. My gear was on other shoulders. I was given a sip of wine. On each side of me someone took one of my arms and helped me along while offering words of encouragement. My despair left me. In no time I, too, was trudging along with my friends, carrying my own load. I realized that this was the first time since parachuting into France that I had been on the point of giving up the fight for survival.

We continued to stumble along until after nightfall, when we entered a small town. Tonight, thank God, we did not have to shiver and wait while he Luftwaffe searched for billets. Instead we were quickly herded into a glass factory. As on the previous night, the German guards remained outside while we were left to do as we pleased in this heated, brightly lit building.

Glass containers produced by the factory were everywhere. There were jugs of all shapes and sizes and rectangular containers ranging from large aquarium size to small kitchen ones. The plant workers must have only recently left leaving the furnaces unattended. There were boilers on which to heat food and dry wet clothing. There were countless taps which, on demand, spewed forth limitless hot water. There were warm floors on which to walk or sleep.

The surprise of being assigned spacious billets in this heavenly place temporarily revived us. For a short time we forgot our tiredness, our fatigue, our aches and pains. We cooked ourselves hot meals and steaming brews. We showered and shaved. We washed the sweat and grime from our clothing. We quickly dried our wet gear in front of the hot furnaces.

We put the glass vessels to use carrying water, heating brews, or as basins in which to soak aching feet. Not all could hold the boiling water and often they shattered, much to the laughter of those filling them. We invented a game to see which of the glass containers would and which would not hold boiling water. We explored every nook and cranny of the place.

We behaved like schoolboys let loose after final exams. We shouted, yelled, and sang. We stripped naked and stood in front of the furnaces revelling in the abundant heat. For a short time we forgot about tomorrow; we came alive again. Then exhaustion set in. The majority of us abandoned the high jinks and settled down for the night. The factory was so warm that, for the first time in months, I slept without covers. I had long since learned to sleep anywhere, so the hard floor did not bother me. I slept soundly, except for getting up for the unavoidable "runs" that now affected all of us. We knew of no cure, other than regular diet and civilized living.

Next morning we were up and about by daybreak. Each made himself a hot meal from his Red Cross food before readying himself for an expected early departure. Before starting this third day on the road, we sacrificed even more useless items. Again the packs, sleds, and carts were adjusted, repaired, or patched. It seemed such a pity to leave this warm haven for the frigid roads of eastern Germany. We still did not know where we were going nor how far we had to walk.

We waited for the shouts of, "*Los! Los! Weiter!*" but they were not forthcoming. The minutes passed and became hours. It became apparent there had been a change in routine. Finally we heard that the "official gen" was we would not be setting out before nightfall. Inevitably rumours circulated: at some point our trip would be continued by train; the Americans, whom we had not seen the last few days, would be sent to a different camp; the British would be split into smaller contingents for other places; the Russians have cut us off.

So far I had heard little of what had happened with the other compounds from Stalag Luft III. We heard only that anyone who had been too sick to walk or who had fallen by the wayside had been picked up by German motor transport, but I saw no proof of this. Our radio team received the BBC news each day, but could still not pinpoint the exact position of the Russian armies. Although we saw no massive preparations by the Germans to defend against them, we were sure they were not too far behind us.

The day passed as we rested and relaxed in preparation for the late start. After dark, we had hardly finished our evening meal of Red Cross food when we heard the hated shouts of, *"Raus! Raus!"* Reluctantly we laced on our boots and bundled ourselves into outside gear. We hoisted packs to our backs and left the warmth and brightness of the glass factory for the frosty darkness of night and another forced march of unknown distance and duration.

We first made sure we were with our buddies and with our usual groups before, urged on by the guards, we set off westward in a long, straggling column. Before long we learned that during the rest at the glass factory the kriegies from East Compound had been combined with the ones from North Compound. This group was destined for one camp while the Americans and other compounds were to go to a different one. Those unable to walk were being moved by German motor transport.

Once more we greatly outnumbered our spreadout, older guards. So far I had not heard of anyone taking advantage of this to make good an escape. I was sure that the chances of survival would be slim in the middle of winter. An escaper's chances of finding food and shelter would be next to nonexistant. Moreover, any one seeking shelter in the woods could easily stumble into German army deserters who would shoot first and ask questions later. Far better, at least for the time being, to stick with our main body for mutual safety.

The moonless night was clear. For a change it did not feel quite as cold as the previous days. Judging by the consistency of the snow, I thought the temperature had risen, perhaps even above freezing. We tramped through partly wooded, gently rolling hills which were white with snow. Nowhere did a light shine, not even in the few villages through which we passed. The blackout was complete. The only sounds to be heard were the sounds of our passage. We saw so few signs of other humans we could have been hiking through the wastes of Siberia or across the barrens of the moon.

I thought we walked at a faster pace than the two previous days. The stops seemed to be less frequent, the rests shorter. Tonight, for a change, the guards worked hard at keeping us moving. They continually hounded the loiterers and laggards to keep moving and not to slow the column. Other than tiredness, there was scant reason for us to dawdle – it was too easy to get chilled when stopped. Besides, most of us believed there was truth to the rumour that tonight's hike would end at a town where we would board trains for our final destination. The possibility that this could be our last stretch of walking was sufficient motivation to spur us on.

Nevertheless, the journey seemed endless. When we thought we could not struggle beyond the next rest stop we somehow would. When we thought we had gone ten kilometers and the next stop would be for good, we would still continue on, and on, and on. We plodded mechanically, step by weary step, throughout the long night. There was little chatter. The usual kriegie humour was missing. We fought to boost our morale with the hope that tonight would be the last of the long marches. If we had not, I am sure many would have quit in despair.

For the most part we were too tired, the rest stops too short, and the night too dark to forage in our packs for food. After the countless lightenings of packs during the last few days, I thought we would have nothing more to throw away. But I was wrong. Some found the going so tough they were now tossing aside, without apparent thought or care, items which were formerly considered absolutely indispensable.

The first glimmer of a winter dawn in the eastern sky marked the end of that terrible night. The sun rose in the cloudless sky of a new day. But still we walked. My spirits sank. I was sure we had already covered a much greater distance than any of the previous days. About midmorning we struggled into a small town. Numbed with fatigue, we were herded to the railway station and a waiting string of wooden boxcars. At long last we were about to continue our journey by rail.

Guards checked and counted us before dividing us into groups of forty-five to a wagon. We needed no urging to climb aboard. The doors were slid shut and locked. We were not too crowded for space and, even if we had been, I don't think anyone would have cared, such was the state of our exhaustion. I must have fallen asleep as soon as I stretched out. I don't remember when the train pulled out or whether I was hungry or cold during the next two days. I don't remember looking out the window slots to watch the country go by or whether the sun shone or the clouds poured rain. I don't remember if we stopped along the way.

Late in the afternoon of February 5, 1945, the train came to a halt. The doors were pulled open and we were ordered out into pouring rain. There was no sign of snow anywhere; we must have been in a warmer part of Germany. The guards fell in around us and we set off through the rain and darkness. Soon we saw the perimeter lights of a prison camp. When we arrived at the gates we had to wait and wait before they were opened to allow us in. We were counted, recorded and searched and finally let in to our new prisoner of war compound.

CHAPTER EIGHTEEN

Marlag and Milag Nord

The raucous shouts of, *"Raus! Raus! Zum Appell!"* woke me with a jolt next morning. I opened my eyes. In the feeble light of a solitary window, half-awake kriegies lay in wooden bunks huddled under greatcoats and blankets, their gear scattered everywhere in the unfamiliar large, cold room. I wondered where I was.

More yelling. A fist pounded on the door, then on the interior wall as some noisy bastard in jackboots thumped along the corridor, bellowing his raucous summons every few yards until the crash of a door closing signaled his departure. Slowly at first, then with a rush, I came back to reality. I remembered arriving late last night at the gates of this camp with the other kriegies from Stalag Luft III. Then standing for ages in the rain, cursing the delay at not getting in. And how once inside and assigned to a room with my own group from Stalag Luft III, I had tumbled into the first available bunk, almost too tired to first eat a snack of Red Cross food.

Fully awake, I struggled out from under my greatcoat and blanket and stepped down to the cold red-brick floor. I stretched and yawned. I pulled on my worn boots and greatcoat before shuffling out to my first Appell at Marlag and Milag Nord. The day was gray, cold and damp. Thankfully, the ground was bare of snow. After a seemingly interminable amount of counting and recounting, we were dismissed.

Back in the room, Ed and I made ourselves breakfast. My spirits began to return to normal and I took stock of my new quarters. The dreary, unpainted room was larger than that at Sagan. In one corner stood a small cast-iron stove for heating and cooking, but there was no sign of fuel for it. There was little in the way of furniture other than sleeping accommodation for sixteen men in eight two-decker wooden bunks spaced regularly around the walls. The lack of furnishings made the place seem quite spacious.

All of those assigned to this room were in it at that moment, so we seized the opportunity to set up our new mess. We sat on bunks or squatted on the floor while we discussed and established rules, rosters, schedules, and so forth. Our old group, which was still intact, had increased in size with the addition of three new bodies from Luft III, Timmie Timmins, Dick Armstrong, and Peter Strutt.

Once this attempt at normality had been concluded, I could hardly wait to explore our new camp, so I set off with Ed and Tut. We had a look at the layout, circuit, location of goon boxes, other huts, recreation facilities, Aborts, and all the items important in the restricted life of a kriegie. It was very apparent that this place lacked most of the material comforts that made everyday living easier to bear. Such things as libraries, lecture halls, theatres, and recreation equipment were nonexistent. On the positive side, we were nearer to the western front and probably would eventually be freed by our western Allies rather than the "unknown" Russians. The climate seemed to be more temperate. And, since it was an older camp, I imagined it lacked many elementary security arrangements to make it escape proof.

Marlag & Milag Nord was situated about a kilometer south of the village of Tarmstedt, through which passed the Bremen-Hamburg highway. Bremen was twenty-five kilometers to the southeast and Hamburg sixty kilometers in the other direction. The camp consisted of two separate compounds for captured seamen. We were in the Milag section, previously occupied by Merchant Navy sailors. A small number of Allied navy kriegies were still held in the nearby Marlag compound.

Outside the perimeter wire the ground rose slightly towards the north and northeast where scattered farms and houses skirted the main highway. In the opposite direction the terrain was flatter, with numerous small wooded areas and fewer cultivated fields.

No mysterious, forbidding forest closed us in, as it had at Sagan. When I paced the circuit, I was thrilled to find that I could look through the threatening barbed wire and past the menacing machine-guns to see farms and people living a normal civilian life.

Another welcome change was that there was black earth under-foot instead of the cursed yellow sand. I was sure our perennial tunnellers would appreciate this, since earth was easier to shore when digging. Still another difference was that the hut floors were at ground level with no crawl space underneath for snooping ferrets. Even more surprising was that we were allowed outside after dark to use the main washrooms because there were no inside night Aborts. It seemed to me that a determined escaper would have less trouble getting out, and when he did, would have to travel only a few hundred miles west to reach the nearest Allied lines. Our SBO still forbid escaping, otherwise I was sure the veterans would soon be on their way, even at the risk of being murdered by the Gestapo if caught.

A few days after we arrived there was a flurry of excitement when one of our gardening enthusiasts, while checking the gardens for spring planting, discovered an escape tunnel dug by previous occupants. Our X committee concealed the entrance again for future exploration and possible use. I wondered if anyone had yet discovered the tunnel dug by our hut, and never used, back in East Compound of Stalag Luft III.

We spent the first weeks trying to make the place more livable. We needed furniture, cooking and eating utensils, and items for leisure activities. None of these were provided by the goons so we made our own. I had learned the elements of tin bashing when I produced my own coffee mug at Sagan, so it was not too difficult for me to help make, among other things, baking pans and kitchen utensils.

An early problem was that we had a good supply of tea, coffee, and cocoa for our frequent brews but no quick method of heating the water for them. The room stove was not usually available because coal could only be spared for brief periods at night. Then someone in our mess, I do not remember who, came up with the brilliant idea of building an electric immersion heater. He did this by covering two pieces of wood with tin and connecting them by wires to a wall socket. Then he carefully immersed these two electrodes in a container of water, trying to space them so they would not short circuit. If everything was done right, the water heated quickly.

Unfortunately the device short circuited easily and blew the main circuit breaker at the hut entrance. When this happened the whole barrack was plunged into darkness. We didn't want the other rooms to know that we were the cause of the frequent power failures, so one of us always stood by to reset the breaker each time it popped out. The situation became somewhat "hairy" when other messes discovered what we were up to and tried it themselves. As a result the hut lacked electricity more frequently than it had it, and the SBO banned the use of our brilliant idea.

During the first weeks no Red Cross parcels got through to us. We lived on the last of the food carried from Sagan and the meager German rations. When our food was exhausted, we were left with only the goon supplies, which were of terrible quality. There was no meat and the vegetables were often rotten. One time, when I was vegetable stooge, I peeled our daily sixteen-man ration of twenty-four golf-ball-sized potatoes and had to throw away thirteen because they were bad.

The poor food played havoc with our bowels. All night long, in pitch darkness, a stream of kriegies stumbled back and forth to the outside Abort. You were lucky if you didn't have to get up more than three times during the night. At such times I often despaired of ever again enjoying an undisturbed sleep in a warm bed.

Although the snow and cold of winter were gone, during the first weeks of February the weather remained damp, foggy, and cheerless. I thought of it as typical weather near a sea coast. Occasionally there would be a cloudless night. When I struggled out into the cold and darkness to the Abort, the silent night sky would be a mass of twinkling stars. At such times I would force myself to ignore the lighted compound so that I could look up and admire the beauty of the night sky. Momentarily I would have a feeling of peace and quietude. My worries and doubts of returning home alive would briefly be forgotten.

Our spirits reached new peaks when, after many weeks of anxious waiting, a shipment of Red Cross parcels was delivered to the compound warehouse. The first of our weekly issues was made the following day. Then, unexpectedly, the bloody goons decided we should not be allowed to keep the canned food containers. They claimed that the tins were a serious security threat because they could be fashioned into all manner of escape devices and would issue no further Red Cross parcels until we provided receptacles into which they could dump the contents. Since we had few containers, we envisaged the idiots opening our cans of perishable rations and mixing them all into one huge, easily spoiled, inedible mess.

Rather than have our food go bad before it could be eaten, we refused to accept our parcels and threatened to lodge a protest with the International Red Cross. Such a complaint to the protecting powers often caused the Germans to see things in a different light. We suffered increasing pangs of hunger during the long stalemate which followed. However, we won the battle of wills and at the end of the week the goons relented and issued our parcels untouched.

Even though no mail got through, I had little trouble keeping my spirits up. Spring was fast approaching and I was sure that I had seen my last damp, cold, German winter. No longer was it a question of how many more years. Now it was how many months, perhaps even weeks. Everyone seemed more lively and full of pep. There was an undercurrent of excitement and optimism amongst us.

From the moment we had first arrived, it had been common practice to barter cigarettes for food with the Germans. One of our goon-speakers would stand behind the warning wire and negotiate a relatively simple transaction with a posten outside the perimeter fence. As soon as an agreement was reached, the sentry would warn his fellow guards not to shoot. The kriegie would step over the warning wire and approach the main fence, where they would exchange the bartered items. Many such transactions were completed without incident until one night, when I was enjoying my after-supper coffee with my roommates, the stillness was rudely shattered by the crack of nearby gunshots. I sat stunned. The last time I had heard this feared sound close at hand was when the ss murdered the young French boy on the way to Buchenwald.

There was dead silence in the room as each of us considered the possible significance of the gunfire. Then, with the same dreaded thought in mind, we jumped to our feet and rushed out into the cold night to join a rapidly assembling crowd of prisoners. Searchlights from nearby goon boxes lit the area where a group of kriegies stood at the warning wire shaking their fists and shouting obscenities at a small group of Germans outside the main fence. Inside, close to it, a kriegie lay crumpled on the ground.

In minutes I learned the apparent reason for the shooting. One of our veteran kriegies had negotiated a deal with a sentry. When he stepped over the warning wire to make the exchange at the main fence his luck ran out. Without any warning, he was shot and mortally wounded by a goon officer who happened to come along.

As I watched horror-struck, the bastard stood waving his revolver, threatening to shoot anyone who crossed the trip wire to attend to the dying man. It was some time before tempers cooled and the kriegie was removed to the German hospital. We were incensed by this cowardly, senseless deed. The guards realized this, and later some of the decent ones privately apologized. When our fellow POW died a few days later, a German military funeral service was held for him. A few of his friends in dress RAF uniforms participated. This useless, callous bloodshed seemed even more tragic because, after surviving four years as a POW, he had been murdered so near the end.

One day I decided it would be fun to play chess again. I remembered the many hours of pleasure that Ed, Ginger, Tom, Tut, Ward, and I had derived from it at Sagan. None of us had taken the game too seriously, so no one felt bad if he lost. Unfortunately, we had not brought a set here. If we were to play again I would have to make one. I scrounged some bits of wood and carved my own chessmen. My results were crude but the pieces were recognizable. The white ones became somewhat grubby from use and the black were an odd pale blue because the ink used to dye them faded quickly. But this did not deter us from playing again with great enthusiasm.

I well remember a series of games I had with Percy, our reputed room-champion who never participated at Sagan because he was always too busy taking courses. When he challenged me to a match, I accepted with trepidation but, much to my surprise, I won. In the return match I also beat him, as well as in the other dozen or so games which we played. I suspected that his intensive studying at Sagan had dulled his chess skills. I wondered how he would have fared against Ed Beaton, whom I considered to be the best in our mess.

February became March. The constant running to the Abort slowed. Each day the sun climbed higher in the sky. We watched and listened with enthusiasm to our planes flying overhead. We listened avidly to the news from our secret radios, which remained our only contact with the outside world. Their bulletins continued to announce astounding advances on the Eastern Front by the Russians, who were now fighting on German soil. We were disappointed that, a scant hundred and fifty miles west of us, the Allies had not yet crossed the Rhine. I felt that I was living in extraordinary times and that momentous events were soon to take place.

Surprisingly, the lack of equipment and facilities for recreational activities did not seem to bother us too much. We could spend many a long hour relating our POW experiences or discussing plans for after the war. We could kill time bed bashing. We could talk about our homes and our lives before the war.

I was one of many who spent longer hours circuit bashing, especially as the weather became warmer. On the good days I enjoyed sitting outside in the sun listening to the adventures of others. I heard some great stories. One concerned a few kriegies who, on the exhausting last night of our forced march, decided to slip away for a rest and a beer. They found a pub in the next small village but, on entering from the cold and snow, were dismayed to find it crowded with German panzer troops. Before the kriegies could beat a hasty retreat they were spotted and recognized as POWs. Much to their surprise, they were invited to join the Germans. Hostilities were forgotten as the kriegies were plied with drinks. When the party finally broke up, our men caught up with our weary column, courtesy of their "enemy" drinking companions and their panzer motor transport.

Another time I had a long talk with one of the survivors of the Great Escape from North Compound. As with most of those recaptured, he was returned to the jail in nearby Gorlitz and locked in a cell with three other escapers. A few days later the Gestapo took the other three away. My friend cursed his bad luck in not returning with them that day to Stalag Luft III. Later, when he was brought back to Sagan, he learned that his three cellmates were among the fifty recaptured escapers who had been murdered in cold blood.

Except for our brief radio bulletins we were completely out of touch with home. We were not allowed to send mail and we received none. It had been eight months since I had received any family news and I often thought about how everything was back there. The majority of us were sure that all we had to do was to wait another month or two and then be overrun by our advancing western Allies. A few pessimists still thought we might be shot rather than liberated. Except for this small minority, the betting was we would be home by next Christmas.

Exciting events occurred more frequently. One dreary morning I heard the sound of an airplane flying low overhead. I was part of the crowd who ran out to have a look before it flew away. When we spotted the red, white, and blue roundels on a twin-engined Mosquito fighter-bomber circling beneath the low clouds, we cheered and waved excitedly. This thrilling moment was the first time in months that most of us had seen one of our aircraft so close at hand. It was something we could relate to.

The cheers and waving ceased abruptly when a German single-engined fighter dived from a cloud onto its tail. I was sure the "Mossie" had not seen its attacker closing in astern. But I need not have worried, because it suddenly banked sharply to the left just as the German closed to within firing range. The attacker, which was flying too fast to follow, shot past without firing, climbed back into the clouds, and disappeared. Our plane resumed circling the camp at low level. The grand finale, again to our wild cheering, came when it dived and shot up a goon truck on the nearby entrance road. The drama that day was a great morale booster. Moreover, we were certain the Mosquito had identified us as a prisoner of war camp and must be keeping a protective eye on us.

More excitement followed a few nights later when a kriegie returning from the outside Abort shouted down the corridor to come outside quickly. I dashed out to see what the excitement was about. A crowd of kriegies watched searchlights, flares, and bursting ack-ack illuminate the cloudless sky north of Hamburg. We heard no sound because the aerial battle was some sixty-five kilometers from us.

I realized I was witnessing, from the German side, the first phase of a typical Bomber Command raid. At that moment our pathfinders were trying to penetrate the outer defenses of Hamburg. Then brilliant target indicator flares floated down on the city. As I watched, spellbound, the sky above it became a kaleidoscope of flashing lights and thousands of exploding artillery shells as some seven thousand of our airmen in a thousand bombers bore down on their target. I could not believe that any of our closely packed, slow-moving bombers could survive the death and destruction directed at them. I shivered with fear and excitement.

Even at this distance, I could feel the ground shake as tons of high explosives rained down. A red glow lit the sky as the target began to burn. All were silent around me. I shuddered at the thought of the terrible ordeal to which Hamburg and its inhabitants were being subjected. After a few minutes the anti-aircraft fire died down when the attackers turned for home, but the ominous glare increased in intensity. Now I heard the roar of nearby German night fighters taking off to intercept our bombers.

Our excitement reached new peaks when we heard the familiar sound of British aircraft engines and realized that our home-ward bound airmen would pass directly overhead. We could not see them but knew they were overhead by the steady roar of their engines. But we could also hear the different sound of fighters moving in to attack. I witnessed the exchanges of tracer fire and watched a bomber successfully repel an attacker. More often I saw a bomber, hopelessly outgunned, hit by cannon and machine-gun fire, followed by the increasing glow of flames as it curved ever more steeply downwards in a fatal plunge. I watched with horror when, each time before it hit the ground, it exploded in a blinding flash. Nine times I watched fellow airmen die.

On March 8 we cheered when our radio brought the long-awaited news that the Allies had crossed the Rhine at Remagen. They secured the bridge head and poured tanks and troops across. In the east, the Russians were at the outskirts of Berlin. As the month wore on there was never a day without air raid alerts or the distant "crump" of explosions. This happened even when we could see no signs of bombers and I could only assume that these were localized, low-level Allied attacks beyond sight of the camp.

The pins on our war maps marked the progress of the ground war as it moved ever closer to us. We began to worry that the Germans might move us again as they retreated. I found it hard to believe that this would happen when there seemed so little left of Nazi Germany, but we reluctantly prepared for the worst. Once again high-calorie food was hoarded and compacted. Backpacks were retrieved from hiding places, repaired, and, based on actual experience, modified. This time a larger number of two-wheeled carts, with spare wheels, were constructed. I elected to use my proven backpack. I also made myself a smokeless burner, as did most of the others. We were quite sure we would be sleeping outdoors with no roof overhead. We had learned on the previous march that we managed best with the buddy system and I again joined forces with Ed Beaton.

March came to an end. Fighting desperately, the German armies retreated on all fronts. We expected the Allies at the camp gates within a few days. We knew the Germans would shortly decide our fate. Rumours abounded and once again we thrashed out the familiar arguments as to whether we would be left behind to be overrun by our forces or evacuated.

My hopes of an early return home were dashed when, during the day of April 9, we were ordered to prepare to leave on foot that night. A pall of gloom descended on the camp. Frustrated and angry, I cursed the stupid Germans. I consoled myself with the thought that this time we were better prepared and would not be walking through snow in freezing temperatures.

This time we did little agonizing about what to leave behind or destroy because our ten-week stay had given us little time to accumulate surplus food and personal effects. We anticipated a long walk that night, so prepared and ate a substantial hot meal late in the day. Early in the evening the goons started the slow process of issuing each of us extra Red Cross parcels and checking everyone against his identity card.

The group from our hut was well back in line, so it must have been after nine o'clock when I passed through the gate. The evening was beautiful. The stars shone brightly from cloudless skies. Temperatures were well above freezing.

CHAPTER NINETEEN

The Last March

In the darkness, I could make out hundreds of kriegies standing around the gate and on the road leading away from Marlag Nord. My mess became part of the crowd. Impatiently we waited and waited, seemingly forever, for those still inside to join us. Now that departure was about to become a reality, we were too stunned and angry to do much talking.

It was too cool and damp to sit so I stood, shuffling from one foot to the other. My greatcoat and worn army boots seemed to be of little help as the chill night air began to penetrate to the bone. I swung my arms and stamped my feet to keep warm. My spirits were low at the prospect of another march away from our rapidly advancing Allies. It was damned stupid of the goons to wait until the middle of the night to set off on what might prove to be a long walk. It was a waste of their rapidly dwindling manpower and resources to take us with them as they retreated. They must have some ulterior motive for it. An ugly thought occurred to me; perhaps we were to be used as hostages.

The sound of an approaching, low-flying airplane interrupted my mood of despair and frustration. I could not see it when it passed nearby, but I was fairly certain it was twin-engined. Although it drew no ack-ack fire, I guessed it was one of our night intruders, probably a Mosquito fighter-bomber. My assumption was confirmed when a moment later I heard it diving, followed by a burst of machine-gun fire. It was comforting to know that our air force was close at hand, but at the same time I wondered if they knew that down below were fellow airmen.

The long wait finally ended about midnight when the last of the kriegies were cleared from the camp. We began moving off in a northeasterly direction, our few possessions in backpacks or on flimsy homemade carts. Again I heard the prowling Mosquito somewhere up ahead. It must have found another target because a few minutes later I heard the "crump" of an exploding bomb. Although these marauders were ours, they set my nerves on edge because I doubted they could distinguish friend from foe in the blackout. Our low-flying aircraft must have worried the goons, because before we were out of sight of Marlag Nord we were abruptly ordered back to it. For a short while I hoped the march might be canceled for good, but these hopes were dashed when we were ordered to be prepared to leave again at daybreak.

The following morning, April 10, the tedious departure procedures were repeated. This time there was no turning back. Our long column of air force kriegies, with a few navy POWs in dark-blue uniforms at the rear, walked up the road to nearby Tarmstedt and turned right along the main road to Hamburg. I hoped last night's delay had brought our rapidly advancing Western armies half a day nearer.

This second march started on a different note when our SBO, Group Captain Wray, a Canadian, issued orders that we were to hinder progress by every conceivable means short of being shot. If we covered as little ground as possible each day, the Allied armies behind us might overtake us. With so many experienced goon baiters in our ranks I realized this should prove quite exciting and we required no urging to comply. We ambled along slowly, either singly or in groups scattered all over the road. We paused frequently to adjust our gear. We stopped to barter with civilians. We halted early for our hourly breaks. We remained sprawled on our packs when it was time to continue, studiously ignoring the postens' shouts of, "*Raus! Raus!*" until we had finished our coffee and cigarettes. We made sure that ten-minute stops lengthened into twenty minutes.

For the most part our guards, who were older men, tried their best. First they would shout at us to get going but we would pay no attention. Next they would rattle the bolts of their rifles and make warning gestures of shooting. This was the ticklish stage, when we had to decide whether or not they meant business ... if we thought they did, we would slowly struggle to our feet, collect our gear, and leisurely set off. Otherwise we would let them continue the begging, pleading, and threatening until we decided it was time to move.

I do not think I was alone in feeling a certain amount of sympathy for these sentries, most of whom were old enough to be our fathers. They were Luftwaffe, not treacherous Nazis. They were ordinary people, unwillingly caught up in this frightful war. As time wore on it was common to see a kriegie offer one a cigarette or a cup of real coffee. Frequently one of our goon-speakers walked beside a Posten, chatting with him in German. Reportedly one of our men was even seen carrying a Posten's rifle for him.

The early spring day warmed us as we sauntered slowly through farmland interspersed with woods and small towns. Our morale improved. This march was so different from the one last winter ... the absence of snow, the sunny spring weather, the easy pace and the thought that we would soon be going home. If only we knew where we were headed! At any time we could easily have escaped but did not risk it for fear of meeting hostile ss or Nazis.

Our food supply was adequate, and as usual consisted mainly of Red Cross rations. At each rest stop we were able to find enough twigs to fire our smokeless burners and make a cup of coffee. At noon these tiny stoves heated Red Cross canned meat in a matter of minutes. Overhead the RAF fighters, which enjoyed air superiority, were a constant threat to German vehicle traffic. The goon staff-cars and trucks that passed invariably carried lookouts, either clinging to the car fenders or, in the case of trucks, standing in the open back. These spotters were supposed to warn the drivers in advance of attacking aircraft. If a plane was spotted in time, the vehicle would skid to a halt and the occupants would dive for cover in the ditches or foxholes dug along the shoulders of the roads.

That first day our "go slow" tactics were moderately successful. I estimated we walked about fifteen kilometers before we set up camp in an open field, just short of a small village straddling a crossroad. Ed Beaton and I chose a spot for our bivouac near the middle of the area. From our pooled Red Cross rations, we prepared and ate our evening meal. We chatted with others nearby and did not bed down for the night until the sun had sunk below the horizon. High in the cloudless sky the moon shone brightly.

My solitary blanket was too small to wrap completely around me, so I lay on top of it with my greatcoat over me. The damp of the bare ground soon penetrated from below, chilling me. I tried different arrangements to get warm so I could sleep. None were successful. Eventually I drifted into fitful sleep from which I was awakened with a start when one of our intruders roared low overhead. I was sure that in the bright moonlight he had spotted us and mistaken our dark shapes for enemy troops.

I thought my fears had become a reality when, a few minutes later, it returned and circled in the blackness above. A parachute flare floated down, turning night into day. Although it was centred further away towards the village, it clearly revealed our sleeping forms. I heard the frightening scream of the airplane diving towards us. I was about to run for cover at the edge of the field, when there was a loud "crump" and a bomb exploded near the crossroads. The flare flickered and burned out. The intruder flew off in search of other targets. I started breathing again. Fortunately we were not bothered again that night. Once again I had experienced the terrifying feeling that I was the sole target among the many around me.

Next morning we walked for some distance along an open road that was built well above the low-lying flat meadows on either side. Our column of kriegies was clearly visible for miles as we shuffled along in the sunshine, dressed in a mixture of khaki, air force, and navy uniforms.

We had been walking only a few hours when I heard the sound of approaching aircraft engines. From somewhere a flight of patrolling RAF Typhoon fighters appeared and crossed overhead from left to right. We knew that the pilots did not have a clear view beneath them, so when they tipped their wings as they flew over we realized they were not signaling us but trying to see whether we were friend or foe. They continued on at right angles to the road until they were about half a mile from us. Here they banked sharply in a hundred and eighty degree turn and came diving back at us. We knew then that we had been mistaken for enemy targets. We hurled ourselves off the exposed road into the ditch away from the attacking planes. The Typhoons screamed down, guns blazing, then climbed back up and disappeared. We breathed a sigh of relief and scrambled back onto the road.

Unfortunately a few navy kriegies thought our pilots had recognized them as POWs when they first flew over. These unfortunate men had remained on the road waving a welcome when the fighters attacked. Several of them were killed. This erroneous attack by our own forces was a demoralizing experience. After that any sound of aircraft engines set my nerves on edge, and I could not rest easy until the source had been identified as no threat to me. Whenever possible I made sure I knew the location of the nearest ditch, foxhole, or other shelter. I was never comfortable inside a building for fear I might be trapped by a sudden attack from the air.

The harrowing events of the day slowed our progress so that we only managed about eleven kilometers, slightly more than half of that allowed by the Geneva Convention. Next day our SBO somehow persuaded the goons that we were too tired to move. This break was badly needed, not for resting but because many of us already had to readjust backpacks, repair carts, and redistribute loads.

Because we were in frequent contact with German civilians we had quickly learned that our better-quality cigarettes were highly valued. So it was easy to exchange a handful of them for a large baby carriage or a child's wagon in which to pull or push our gear. Either one was considered superior to a backpack or kriegie cart. Our cigarettes would also buy potatoes, vegetables, and, on rare occasions, a cup of milk.

I saw a different type of warfare when I spotted a white glare in the sky far to the west. The brilliant spot of light rose straight up in the sky and disappeared. This was not the first time I had seen this phenomenon. I believe what I witnessed were mobile launchers firing long-range V-2 rockets against London. Even at this late stage of the war the Germans were still fighting back with these missiles.

The first two nights of the march I was unable to sleep well. Although I slept fully dressed, the damp and cold from the bare ground would soon work its way up through my thin blanket. In no time I would be chilled through and have to get up and walk around to get warm. It was the same with Ed, so we tried sharing our bedding and slept together with our greatcoats under us and our two blankets over us. This was a marked improvement.

When we were breaking camp next morning the latest bulletin from our radio team was, as usual, circulated verbally. We were thunderstruck to hear that Franklin Roosevelt had died the previous day. The news was even more astounding because we had no indication that he had been in poor health. Nor did we learn the cause of his death. His successor was Harry Truman, a name unknown to me. Later, when we set off, someone who must have been keeping track of the days (perhaps it was Padre Thompson) remarked that it was Good Friday. But for most of us it was just another day on this bloody march to nowhere.

As I trudged through villages and towns I was surprised that I saw no signs of large-scale enemy troop movements. Somehow I had expected that, with fierce battles taking place not too far behind us, there would have been convoys of German troop reinforcements heading for the front. Perhaps, I thought, they only travelled on major roads under the cover of darkness.

However, I did see, on the outskirts of many villages, some feeble defensive preparations by the inhabitants, consisting of felled trees and rubble barricades across the roads. I could not help but feel pleased that after more than five years of war the bastards who had started it all were finally fighting on their own soil. Now they would learn firsthand what it was like to suffer the ravages of war.

At one point in our walk we were hiking through a small town when we came upon a German staff-car parked in front of the town hall. The driver stood stiff and sullen, guarding his vehicle while his officer was inside the building. Not a word or sign passed between us as we sauntered past him. But we had a hard time keeping a straight face because, unbeknown to him, a kriegie was crouched out of sight at the back siphoning gasoline from the gas tank. This urge to steal from the enemy, whether useful or not, was always with us. Hardly a day went by without our pinching something from the goons.

That day ended on a good note because we had walked only eight kilometers. I hoped the Allies were closing in on us at a faster pace. On Saturday, in beautiful spring weather, we meandered through rich farmland. I guessed we were approaching the

Elbe at a lower elevation on the floodplain. Although the war seemed far away, I realized that at any moment we could still become deeply involved with it.

Our painfully slow progress did not seem to disturb our guards much, so no major incidents occurred. We thought that perhaps they, too, did not want to cross the Elbe where, when the war ended, they would become prisoners of their feared enemy, the Russians. That night we camped in a field west of Hamburg, within striking distance of the Elbe. We had walked only seven kilometers, the fewest yet. We hoped the Germans were about to end this foolish march and we would wait on this side of the Elbe for the war to end.

Next day, on Easter Sunday, to our surprise the whole atmosphere of the forced march changed drastically for the worse. Overnight the easygoing older Postens had been reinforced with younger men who quickly let us know they were in charge and would stand for no nonsense. We were roused early for a quick start. We walked at a fast pace and did not dawdle. We stopped infrequently and rested only briefly. There was no doubt that these new troops were under orders to get us to a predetermined destination that day.

Another change was that the villagers along our route were quite hostile towards us. Perhaps it was because they lived in the outer limits of Hamburg and had experienced firsthand the destruction wrought by Bomber Command. For me the day was memorable not because the guards had turned nasty but because it was sunny and hot and the road for miles on either side was lined with apple orchards in full blossom.

Our rapid march brought us close to the Elbe, then right a short distance to a port on the outskirts of Hamburg where we stopped for the night. Presumably we would cross this famous river tomorrow. We had walked eighteen kilometers. I estimated we had covered sixty kilometers in the six days since leaving Marlag and Milag Nord.

That night our mood was one of frustration and disappointment. We had done our best to slow our progress, yet our western Allies had not been able to overtake us. We were sure that as soon as we crossed this wide river we would add weeks, perhaps even months, to the long wait for liberation. We still did not know our final destination – perhaps Denmark or somewhere on the Baltic sea. Surely the damned goons would not keep us walking endlessly inside the rapidly shrinking boundaries of Germany.

On Monday morning, when we were ferried the two kilometers across the Elbe estuary to the large town of Blankenese, I saw no U-Boats or other naval vessels. Thankfully no air raids interfered with the crossing. With the absence of these more obvious signs of war I could almost imagine myself a tourist cruising on the river on a sunny spring day.

The tough extra guards disappeared at the dock in Blankenese, so we quickly reverted to our "go slow" tactics. As we started up a short steep hill into the main part of the town I saw my first German sailor. He came ambling down one side of the shop-lined street as a group of us slowly climbed the other. His thoughts must have been elsewhere because opposite us, much to his embarrassment and our delight, he tripped over his own feet and almost fell.

At the top, as we continued through the city, the guards were so widely scattered we could easily have taken a wrong turn. We did not camp for the night until we were well out into open country. "Just as well," I thought to myself, "because the Hamburg area is a favourite target of Bomber Command." We set off next morning in a northeasterly direction along the Autobahn towards Lübeck. I was not overly impressed by my first experience with one of the much ballyhooed German highways. A wide, grassy, median strip separated two double-lane concrete roadways that seldom ran straight and level for any distance. Undoubtedly they could carry a lot of heavy traffic but for military purposes they were vulnerable to aircraft attack. Perhaps that is why we were the only ones using it that day. The rumour going the rounds was that the famous port of Lubeck on the Baltic sea was to be our final destination. If so, then perhaps it would be the Russians who would eventually liberate us. Not too pleasant a prospect!

After more than a week on the road we still subsisted on our ample Red Cross food because the Germans had nothing for us. The farms along the way had no milk or meat for us to beg, borrow, or steal, and it was still too early in the year for fresh vegetables. We did try swiping last year's swedes, a tasteless root vegetable of the turnip family which was grown in abundance to feed both humans and livestock, but they were hardly worth the effort because they were tasteless and usually full of worms.

We were a dirty, smelly lot of airmen tramping along the Autobahn. We each had only one set of clothing, which we wore constantly because it was too cold to undress at night. Since leaving Milag Nord we had been without an opportunity for a shower or bath. Suffice it to say that in our present condition we would not have been welcome in polite society. That afternoon, with the strong sun beating down on us, we were hot and stinking when our break occurred beside a slow-moving river. It looked like a heaven-sent opportunity to cleanse our reeking bodies. We threw off our clothes and gingerly tested the water. It was frigid! Not surprising, I suppose, close to the Baltic Sea in mid-April. But we could not let the opportunity pass so we splashed ourselves with water and applied soap until we were well lathered. Now that there was no turning back, we had to jump in. My God it was cold! But as usual there were a few idiots with ice in their veins who swam back and forth pretending to enjoy it.

While preparing our evening meal that night, Ed and I discovered we were overstocked with dried prunes. So we soaked all forty-three of them in water for dessert. I won the toss for the extra prune. Surprisingly, neither of us suffered any ill effects. Later, at a nearby farm, some of us made friends with a few captured Russian soldiers who worked there as slave labourers. We had a "bang on" evening together, highlighted by their impromptu concert of fast stepping Russian dancing with accordion accompaniment. I was shocked when these men cheerfully told us that if they returned home after the war they would be shot because they had allowed themselves to be captured. What a difference between Russian and Allied military values!

On Thursday, after more than ten days on the road, we finally met, close at hand, an armoured division of battle-ready enemy troops. These panzers, who overflowed the main street of a town on our route, appeared to be on stand-by while awaiting orders to proceed into combat. We eyed each other warily as they made room for us to pass. They wore a black, English-type of battle-dress top and baggy trousers tight around the ankles. Instead of the usual German high-cut jackboots they had low-cut boots which were quite similar to our Canadian style hiking boot. I was surprised that most of them appeared to be still in their teens, since the panzers were rated among the best of Hitler's front-line troops.

After supper that night, two kriegies from a nearby mess had barely bedded down together when the comparative quiet was broken by a low whistle from the far side of the nearest hedge. "Ah, that must be for me," said one of the two. He threw back the blankets, crawled silently to the hedge and disappeared through it. Sometime later he arrived back just as mysteriously as he had left. His buddy, who was now awake, asked him where he had been. "Just enjoying the finer things of life," was the reply. "Near that last village today I met a German girl who agreed to a rendezvous with me outside the hedge after dark." On hearing this, his companion refused to share the same bedding with him.

About noon next day, while we were in open country, I became aware of the sound of distant aircraft. I searched unsuccessfully for the source. The noise persisted and increased in intensity. This time, I spotted a distant black speck north of us. Then I saw another and still another. Hundreds of scattered black specks, much like a swarm of angry bees, filled the sky. The approaching airplanes could only be RAF Bomber Command on a rare daylight raid.

The thunder of engines became deafening and the sky black with Halifaxes and Lancasters. Some straggled far behind while others were isolated ahead or off to the sides of the main group. They were not as pretty a sight as the sparkling silver American Flying Fortresses in their precise formations. Yet each one of these hundreds of bombers carried many times the bomb weight of the Americans.

Unmolested, they passed overhead, their apparent target the panzer troops in the town through which we had passed yesterday. Minutes later we felt the ground shake as hundreds of tons of bombs hit their target. If the raid had been yesterday, we would have been caught in the middle of it. Later we heard a rumour that the attack had flattened the town and inflicted heavy casualties on the panzer troops.

That evening, when we were setting up camp near a group of farms, I spotted numerous kriegies carrying armfuls of hay to use for bedding. This extra comfort seemed like a great idea so I joined others with the same thought and followed the trail of dropped hay back to its source, a large stack in the middle of a farmyard. By the time I arrived, the farmer had become quite upset about his rapidly disappearing hay and it was now guarded by an armed sentry. However, it was a large stack, so while the Posten was occupied with thieves on one side, other kriegies were out of sight on the far side carting away armfuls of hay. This escapade was similar to the time one of our goon-speakers engaged a farmer in friendly conversation while his kriegie chums crept into his barn and milked his cows.

Another rest day followed. We were in especially good spirits because we heard that the Russians were fighting in the streets of Berlin. Not much longer now! Although Germany was almost finished, there was ample evidence that the younger soldiers were still prepared to fight. Frequently one would bicycle by with a *panzerfaust* anti-tank rocket strapped to the frame of his machine.

As I walked through a small village, one of these soldiers, who did not look old enough to shave, stood with his bike at the edge of the road sullenly watching us pass. His left arm was wrapped with blood-stained bandages and he was obviously in pain. As we passed, a kriegie who had studied medicine and carried some first-aid supplies stopped to offer help. But this Nazi youth, indoctrinated to hate us, snarled at him and angrily waved him away.

The following day, when I was hiking along the autobahn, I was overtaken by a truck full of Wehrmacht soldiers. It was barely a hundred yards beyond me when, without warning, an airplane screamed across the road at treetop level. It was gone before I heard the shriek of its engine so I had no chance to jump into the nearest ditch. It was one of the latest Luftwaffe fighters, the first jet I had ever seen. Just beyond me the soldiers, unaccustomed to seeing their own fighters, were sheepishly climbing out of ditches and reboarding their transport.

At dusk that night we were finishing our evening meal in a field at a crossroad when some fifty to a hundred young boys came by, chattering among themselves in a foreign language. They were only children, perhaps ten to fourteen years old and unaccompanied by any adult. They carried little in the way of food or personal belongings. Our curiosity was aroused.

One of our linguists found a common language for conversation and learned that, early in the war, the Germans had taken these children from their homes in Hungary to work in Holland. Now that the war was over they were walking home. They had already come hundreds of miles, yet still had a long way to go.

They were in good spirits and quite confident of finding their way through war-ravaged Europe although they had no food, no money, and no maps. They did not stay long because they were anxious to continue. We gave them food before they resumed their journey home.

On Monday, April 23 we settled in on a sprawling estate near Walmenau that had many large farm outbuildings. Here we learned that the next day we were scheduled to walk ten kilometers to our final destination, a large, multi services, all-nationality POW camp in Lubeck. Next day our SBO told the Germans that we would not start off before he had been allowed to inspect the conditions at the proposed new camp. His demand was met and his inspection showed it to be completely unsuitable: it was overcrowded, unsanitary, and short on food. Rather than face such sordid conditions we gave our parole not to escape if we were allowed to remain camped around the many buildings of this large estate.

After thirteen days, in which we had walked some 140 kilometers, it was a godsend to know that the mindless, endless walking was finished. We quickly staked out places in and around the barns that we could call home. We made comfortable beds of straw and laid out our few possessions. We discovered running water in nearby farm buildings and washed ourselves and our clothing. We made ourselves snug and comfortable and prepared to wait out the last few days until the end.

Our radio kept us abreast of the rapid collapse of Germany. The only sign of war we saw occurred each evening at sunset when a Luftwaffe jet fighter-bomber circled overhead nearby, selected a target, dropped its bomb, then disappeared for the night. The days passed quickly. We sat in the sun and speculated as to how we would be received by the air force on our return home. Some had worried ceaselessly since their capture that perhaps they had jumped too soon from their flaming bomber or that they had not acquitted themselves properly in the terror-filled moments of battle. Perhaps they had made errors which caused the deaths of their comrades. How did you explain to the next of kin why you survived when their loved ones did not?

We speculated about what plans the air force had for us. Would we be given extended leaves and discharged or would we be retrained and sent to fight the Japanese? Those with steady

girlfriends or fiancées wondered whether their girls were faithfully awaiting their return. Many married men could hardly wait
to hold a child born after they were shot down. Others, after long
absences from home, would meet their grown children who might
ask, "Who is this man, Mummy?" Some less-fortunate married
POWs had already learned by kriegie post that their wives had left
them for other men.

There was so much family news to catch up on. Many would
have lost close family or friends due to aging as well as war
during their long months or years of enforced absence. I was
lucky – I had not been gone a full year. But I had received no mail
or other news since early June of last year. What would I learn
when I received my first letter?

Daily the excitement of returning home increased. We could
hardly imagine sleeping in a real bed with a roof over our heads
and no searchlights or armed guards nearby. We dreamed about
roast beef, fresh vegetables, fresh fruit, and food which did not
come from a can. We tried to remember the taste of fresh white
bread and milk. What was it like to sit in a real chair, to have
running hot water, real soap, daily changes of clothing?

What would we talk about when we met people, especially those
of the opposite sex? We did not know the latest popular music, the
latest movies, the latest fads, and, other than war news, the latest
current events. All we could talk about was war. Surely no one
would want to hear our stories. We noted each others' addresses
on scraps of paper and as at Buchenwald, made grandiose plans
for reunions and keeping in touch with each other.

The Allied armies reached Hamburg and prepared to cross the
Elbe. The thunder of a massive artillery barrage kept us awake
during the night of April 30. Next day our radio brought the
exciting news that the Allies had crossed south of Hamburg and
swung north towards Denmark. We were directly in the path of
their rapid advance. It should only be a matter of days before we
would be liberated. I wondered if lines of tanks would sweep
across the fields in pursuit of the retreating Germans. On May 1
we optimistically studied the distant countryside to the south for
signs of fighting, but nothing unusual occurred.

Wednesday, May 2, started dull and overcast with a threat of
showers later in the day. After nine days of waiting here, we felt
sure this would be the day. Again we kept watch on the main

road about a mile south of us. Late in the morning three Spitfires flew low across the farm buildings and waggled their wings as a sign of recognition. We cheered madly at this signal that our people knew where we were and would not accidentally fire on us. Our German guards discreetly kept out of sight.

Just before midday, after many false alarms, we spotted some armored cars moving slowly in a northwesterly direction along the road that passed by the farm. At the farm entrance one of them turned right onto it and came towards us. We could see the large white star of the Allied invading troops painted on its side. It drew to a stop in the middle of the farmyard. Two British officers climbed out and were quickly mobbed by jubilant ex-kriegies.

It was noon, May 2, 1945. The scout car was from General Montgomery's 11th armoured division.

At last it was over.

CHAPTER TWENTY

Germany Kaput

Never in my wildest dreams had I imagined that our liberation would be such an undramatic business. Not that I had any regrets – far better for it to happen like this than to be caught in the middle of flying bullets as the enemy retreated with our forces in hot pursuit. As it was, we all seemed dazed by how quick and simple it had been.

When it slowly dawned on us that we were free, we mobbed the two British officers from the scout car, as though they alone had liberated us. The two of them seemed embarrassed at being the centre of attention of our excited crowd. Laughing and joking, we plied them with question after question, hardly waiting for the answer to one before asking another. But after a few minutes they reminded us that the war was not yet over and said they must rejoin their units in pursuit of the retreating enemy. They had only stopped by to see the state of our health and if we had urgent needs. Others, they said, would arrive shortly to brief us about plans for our welfare and return to England. Before driving off, they cautioned us not to leave the farm because of the many armed Germans still in the area who had not yet surrendered.

Soon afterwards a British truck arrived with soldiers to take away our former guards. One of the first questions they asked us was which of the Germans we wanted shot. We were astounded by this cold-blooded suggestion, so casually offered. We protested vehemently that we had been reasonably well treated by the Luftwaffe and that they, too, should receive a fair deal. Had our soldiers asked me the same question about the murderous ss I had encountered on the train from Fresnes and at Buchenwald, my reply might have been different. But I forced this thought from my mind. The war was almost over and I had survived, against tremendous odds.

At the moment I was overwhelmed by the many exciting events taking place – good ones that I had not dared dream about. I could hardly believe I was about to leave Germany and would soon sleep with a roof overhead in a real bed. That I would have a choice of all the food I could eat while sitting on a chair at a table. That I would have clean clothes to wear and a selection from which to choose. So many times this last year I had thought I would never make it back. Even these last few weeks we had lived with the real possibility that a fanatic ss squad might arrive to murder us, the final defiant act of a defeated enemy.

My high spirits were momentarily dampened when I heard that it might be a few days before transport would be available to move us from here. But I was in safe hands with nothing to worry about, so a few more days here would be of little consequence. In the meantime, in spite of the warning about staying close to the farm, I could hardly wait to explore the adjacent countryside. Others with the same idea were already drifting away.

My first sortie was with Ed Beaton. We crossed the fields to watch the army convoys on the nearby road heading for the battlefront. The trucks were bumper to bumper, stop and go, just like city rush-hour traffic. And they seemed to be loaded with an incredible supply of munitions and goods. During a brief pause in the flow, one truck crew told us they were even carrying the sections of pontoons to bridge the Kiel canal near the Danish border.

Later, when we were chatting with still another crew, I was startled to hear the unexpected roar of an approaching single-engined airplane. I saw a German Messerscmitt 109 fighter flying directly towards us at treetop level. It was so low that I could virtually see the whites of the pilot's eyes. I went numb with shock. "This is it," I thought to myself, "caught like a fool in the open!" The Tommies scrambled for their automatic weapons, but before they could pick them up the fighter had swept by overhead.

Fortunately for us, the pilot had chosen not to shoot. This incident, a stern reminder that the war was still not over, shocked us out of the euphoria of our liberation. Needless to say, Ed and I were extremely alert to further threats while we walked back to the farm.

As the day drew to an end, I was amused to see assorted German jeeps, scout cars, and civilian automobiles appear at our farm. Each one had an ex-kriegie behind the wheel and the white star of the invading Allied armies chalked on its side. This commandeering of enemy vehicles was a new diversion for kriegie energies. Even the fire truck from a nearby town was taken over by one of our "bods." The only hitch to this new sport was the shortage of petrol. The easiest solution, if a vehicle ran out of gas, was to abandon it in the nearest ditch and confiscate a new set of wheels.

Late next morning Ed and I walked into the closest town. We thought that walking around as victors among the vanquished would be an exciting new experience for us. Perhaps we might also share in the spoils – not that there was really anything we wanted. On the outskirts of the town we met up with British soldiers near a mess tent. They gave us each a slice of a light, fluffy, white substance to eat. It was only on closer examination and taste that I realized that this was REAL WHITE BREAD, a food which was nonexistent in Nazi Germany. This delightful surprise was for me the first of many long-forgotten pleasures.

When we continued into town, a British Sergeant joined us. He said if there was anything we wanted he would confiscate it from the Germans. We welcomed his company because neither of us were comfortable about taking other people's belongings, even if only yesterday they had been our bitter enemies. I told him that I could probably do with a pair of new boots. I was wearing the only ones I possessed, issued some seven months ago at Stalag Luft III. The constant use, including two forced marches, had worn large holes in the soles.

Few of the townspeople were to be seen when we strolled down the main street. Presumably the inhabitants were cowering fearfully indoors. Occasionally an old automobile filled with civilians rattled past. Our companion said these were residents of the area who were trying to escape westward because this district was scheduled to be administered by the Russians, their hated and feared enemies. I watched one such motorcar pass, its interior full of fleeing refugees; their remaining worldly possessions were packed inside with them or tied to the sides and high on the roof. The vehicle was so overloaded its bottom seemed to scrape the road. When it turned down a side street just ahead of us, we heard a short burst of gunfire. We hurried to the corner and looked for the reason for the shots.

Two ex-kriegies were perched on top of a massive British tank, which blocked the road to all vehicles. Our two men had enlisted the army's aid to commandeer a set of wheels for a few hours joy-riding. The unfortunate refugees happened to be the first to come along, abruptly ending their flight to a safer haven. Threatened by the mighty tank guns, they were hurriedly unloading their jalopy. I felt sorry for the fleeing civilians, although I could not help laughing at the unequal confrontation of mighty tank and automobile.

We continued our foray. Farther along the road an unarmed German Army private trudged towards us. A loud shout from our Sergeant brought him to a frightened standstill, apparently expecting to be shot. At first I did not know the purpose of stopping him. It was only after he was ordered to lift his foot that I realized that the Sergeant wanted to examine the condition of the soles of his boots.

The unfortunate man did not understand English so the Sergeant yelled louder, and then still louder, apparently thinking the louder he yelled the easier it would be for the German to understand. Instead he became even more frightened. Impatiently the Sergeant grabbed his foot and lifted it, much as one does when examining the shoe on a horse's hoof. Then I realized that if the boots passed my inspection, I would become their new owner and the unfortunate soldier would leave barefooted. Since I expected to be issued new British footgear a few days hence, it seemed ridiculous to impose any more hardship than was necessary on this former enemy. I quickly invented the excuse that the boots were obviously much too small for me.

Undaunted, our aggressive NCO then led us to a nearby house where he thought I might find a suitable pair. Without knocking or ringing the bell, he pushed the door open and walked in as though he owned the place. The occupants, two women and a small child, were scared to death by our sudden invasion of their home. Their obvious fear of us helped me decide to see it through with my comfortable but worn old boots. Nor did foraging in the home of frightened people seem like much fun anymore. We poked around the front living room for about fifteen minutes. I kept a German road map of the area through which we had travelled since leaving Milag Nord as well as a small snapshot of a German soldier beside an antitank gun in a snow-covered landscape. As soon as we were back on the street, Ed and I found an excuse to leave our helpful Sergeant and head back to our farm quarters.

Events moved fast. The next day, May 4, we climbed into the back of army trucks and were driven to Lüneburg, southeast of Hamburg, the first stage of our journey home. Here we were given postcards on which were printed six formal sentences we could tick to indicate whether or not we were in good health. This scrap of cardboard was the first personal message that I had sent home since I walked out the gates of Stalag Luft III.

That night and the next day we were billeted in former German army barracks. Here we were separated into RAF and RCAF. On May 6, army transport drove us via Sulingen to an airfield at Diepholz, where the next day we boarded RAF Dakota transport aircraft. I was so anxious to get home that I conveniently forgot that when I landed by parachute in France I had sworn to myself never to fly again. I left Germany for the last time, hopefully leaving behind many unpleasant memories. We made one brief refueling stop in Brussels before resuming our homeward journey.

It was a long flight of several hours. I was no longer with my many RAF friends. Sitting on benches along the length of the noisy, smelly airplane, there was little talking. I was exhausted and filled with my own emotions and private thoughts. Late in the evening the aircraft touched down at an airfield just north of London. Dazed and confused by the pace of events, I was back in familiar, wonderful England.

On disembarking we were directed to a nearby large hangar. As we entered, we were liberally doused with delousing powder. Although in ragged uniforms, we were now acceptable to civilized company. The many military and service organization people who awaited us greeted us as though we were conquering heroes. It was such a warm feeling to be welcome again. I seem to remember that we were plied with coffee, doughnuts, and refreshments, checked by medical staff, and identified by name, rank, and number before boarding trucks for London where billets awaited us.

Next day, still in our POW rags, we were assigned first-class accommodation on the morning train to Bournemouth. Fellow civilian travellers, when they learned who we were, treated us royally, plying us with drinks, cigarettes, and food. At this point we still had no money and had to depend on military vouchers for our immediate requirements. I remember I was worried that some of us might continue the kriegie practice of stealing anything that was not fastened down.

It was May 8, the official end of the war in Europe. Hardly an English home had not lost family members in air raids or foreign battles. Their houses had been bombed and they had endured severe rationing of food, clothing, fuel, and all the common necessities of life.

We arrived in Bournemouth early in the afternoon. In the summer of 1943, this RCAF transient depot had been my first stop in England. The wheel had now turned full circle. No longer a fledgling airman to be billeted in a secondary hotel, I was assigned a private room in the posh Royal Bath Hotel, the hotel patronized by royalty. Here a dining room, serving only the best food, available in unlimited quantities, had been set aside for the exclusive use of ex-POWs. Unfortunately, our stomachs were not accustomed to such a rich diet and we could not fully appreciate it.

It was VE Day and all of Britain was celebrating. Mobs of soldiers, sailors, airmen, and civilians overflowed the streets, parks, and public places. It was great to watch the excited, happy, cheering, and often drunken throngs. My leg, which still bothered me, forced me to walk with a slight limp. Otherwise I was in good health. I had much for which to be thankful.

After ten months in enemy hands all I had as souvenirs were my "lucky" piece of parachute, my tin coffee mug, and scraps of paper with addresses of POW friends. Although I was clean, I was still wearing the same ragged, dirty clothes which I had worn without change for the last few months. After supper I walked alone up through the crowded Public Gardens. All about me were celebrating. But somehow I was not in a festive mood; I felt very much out of it. Perhaps too much had happened in the last few days and I was still in a state of shock. Perhaps it was that I had experienced and seen too much deprivation and hardship to think of celebrating, or that I felt I was still in Germany. Or perhaps I was dreading the task of writing the six letters to the next of kin of my fellow crew members and trying to explain why I alone was the sole survivor.

I had not heard from home for almost a year and I was worried about what the first news might bring. I retraced my steps to the hotel and went to bed.

Epilogue

I chose to write this story in the first person singular without reference to concurrent events beyond my restricted sphere of knowledge at the time because it is about my adventures as I saw them. As I progressed with my writing and research I obtained many private and official documents that complement the story. In this epilogue I draw on the most interesting of this material to pull together many loose ends.

My only return to the region where it all began was during a 1991 holiday in France with my wife, Elizabeth. We had set aside one day in which to visit the graves of my bomber crew in Laons, relive my adventures in the village of Blévy, and make a quick search of the nearby countryside for the Demusois farm. No one was aware of my planned pilgrimage.

As we drove towards Laons, I was surprised to see that this area had hardly changed since the war. The farms and villages appeared the same, no modern highways cut through the recently harvested wheat fields, and, as we soon learned, the next generation own and farm the same land while those of my generation live close by. The village of Laons appeared deserted on this late August day, its houses tightly shuttered against the scorching noontime sun. Near the church we asked a solitary person for directions to the graveyard "where the Canadian airmen are buried."

In the walled cemetery it was easy to find the six identical white gravestones, standing upright as if at attention. On the rectangle of white gravel defining the plot lay a spray of barely withered flowers. I stopped at each headstone to check the name and to conjure up a mental picture of my fellow airman. "Oh God," I thought to myself, "Why did all this have to happen?" Again I asked myself the question that haunts all survivors, "Why was I the only one?"

Through the cemetery gate, an out-of-breath, middle-aged woman hurried up to me and asked if I knew the bomber crew buried there. On hearing that I was the only survivor, she invited us to her home for a delightful light lunch in the parlor-dining room. While we were toasting the occasion, prominent village personalities were notified that the Canadian airman had returned.

Afterwards, three helpful local residents joined my wife and me in our Volkswagen as guides while I continued my pilgrimage. Our first stop was at the edge of the wheat field in which my bomber had fallen. This turned out to be about a kilometer north of the spot where I landed by parachute, not where I had seen aircraft wreckage the following morning.

One of our guides, as a boy of fourteen, had been first at the crash site. He said that one other member of my crew had jumped but his parachute had not fully opened. I assumed it was Don Wilson, our replacement bomb aimer and the only other person near the nose escape hatch. Perhaps if Don's chute had been beside him, instead of a few feet away, he might still be alive. Ironically the man he was replacing, Hugh Fraser, completed a tour of operations with another crew and, as far as I know, survived the war.

Apparently once the Germans had examined the crash local residents shrouded each of the crew in his parachute and laid him to rest in this cemetery at Laons, a few kilometers to the north. Three times a year, ever since the war, a spray of fresh flowers has been placed at the grave site. A week after the funerals an airman's boot, encasing a severed foot, was found by a farmer while he was threshing his field.

We drove on, passing the dip in the road and the high bank on the left where I spent my first night in France and, further on, the water tower that I had first believed to be an enemy lookout. In Blévy we stopped at the bridge so that I could relive the fearsome moments when the German truck stopped so close to me. Here I had to recount my narrow escape all over again.

I had destroyed the address of the Demusois farm when I feared capture by the Gestapo, and we crisscrossed the countryside all afternoon in fruitless search for it. Any landmark I dredged from my memory sent my passengers into a frenzied discussion as they tried to match existing spots to my hazy descriptions. Our party finally returned to Laons, where the mayor awaited us at his home with his father, on whose farm one of my bomber's engines had fallen. We celebrated with champagne.

That hot summer night we sat on the terrace of the home of more newfound friends in Châteauneuf-en-Thymerais, drinking bottle after bottle of wine and dining sumptuously on freshly caught salmon. Before retiring for the night in this beautiful home, our host contacted Gérard Renault of the Garde Mobile in Chartres. Next morning we met Gérard and two reporters at his office. We learned that his hobby was researching Allied war planes that had crashed in the Eure-et-Loire district of France. He provided me with most of the documentation about the crash of my bomber, the redheaded traitor, the Gestapo agent, and the Resistance operations in the Chartres area. He also dug up and sent me pieces of "W" Willie and located the propeller spinners from two of its engines. Gérard and I corresponded regularly until his untimely death in January 1994.

The Demusois and Rothiot families who had sheltered me had returned to Paris a few weeks after I left them. Following the war they wrote from Paris and we exchanged correspondence briefly before losing touch again. When I tried to re-establish contact some thirty-five years later their Paris addresses were no longer valid. Then in the fall of 1993 I was most fortunate in locating Antoinette ("Venette"), who had remarried. She supplied me with the missing details concerning her family.

Vennette's first husband, who was in Buchenwald, had been put on a train headed east a few days before the camp was liberated. He was never seen again. Her brother (husband of Marthe) died in 1945, soon after returning from Mulhausen

Concentration Camp weighing 63 pounds. Two years after the war her daughter died. In 1958 Venette remarried.

The small house in which I was hidden was located in the hamlet of Chappes, just west of Châteauneuf-en-Thymerais. Because it was in poor repair it was torn down after the war. Although the nearby large farm still exists, new housing has changed the appearance of the area. Not surprisingly, the tone of Venette's last letter indicated she was not particularly overjoyed to be reminded of those bad times.

There were several branches of the Resistance in the Chartres area. The best-known, perhaps, was the Picourt group, which was centered there. The branch to which Colonel Lecointe belonged had been penetrated by the Gestapo and he, along with others, was arrested a few weeks after Grenon, Scullion, Hetherington, and I were put in its care. He was severely tortured and left paralyzed in both legs, unable to move about except with great difficulty. In 1963 he was eighty years old and on a full wartime disability pension.

The traitor who betrayed the Picourt Resistance group to the Gestapo was the redheaded woman, Madam Orsini, wife of the manager of the Buffet Hotel at Chartres station. When Picourt was looking for volunteers to help evading airmen, she introduced him to Jacques Desoubrie, alias "Jean Jacques," alias "Pierre Poulain," alias "Jean Masson," a Belgian agent of the Gestapo. He was the driver of the car that took us to Paris. He disappeared after the war but in 1947 was discovered hiding in Augsburg. In 1949 he was tried in Paris by the French for war crimes, found guilty, and executed by firing squad.

Orsini was always with Jean Jacques, probably as his mistress. The Picourt group was allowed to keep operating and unwittingly delivered Allied flyers to the Germans until the area was liberated by the Allies. Orsini and Desoubrie drove more than sixty Allied evaders to Paris and delivered them to the Gestapo, who paid about $150.00 U.S. for every airman betrayed. Orsini was brought to trial in Paris in May of 1946 and acquitted, supposedly because she was related to a high-ranking French army officer and because most of the witnesses for the prosecution were absent.

Fresnes, an antiquated, Napoleonic, civilian prison in the Paris suburbs, just north of Orly Airport, is still used. During the summer of 1944 Allied airmen captured in non-military attire were collected in Fresnes. While according to the Geneva Convention it was permissible to wear civilian clothes when trying to escape or evade capture, the Gestapo chose to ignore our identity discs and classified us as police prisoners. Consequently they did not advise the Red Cross that we were alive nor treat us humanely. As police prisoners, many of my fellow airmen were beaten and/ or locked for varying lengths of time in unlit, below-ground, solitary cells.

When Paris was liberated, the inscription I had written on the wall on August 10, 1944 was found and photographed by the French Ministry of Prisoners and Deportees. Copies of it were sent to the Air Ministry in London, which held them until after the war before sending me one in Canada. General Georges Vanier, the first postwar Canadian Ambassador to France, must have received a copy because it is reprinted on page 301 of his biography, *Vanier* by Robert Speaight.

On August 15, 1944, five days after I wrote on the wall of my cell, all 169 Allied airmen held as police prisoners were packed in cattle cars and shipped to Germany. The Fresnes contingent of Allied airmen and other prisoners was loaded aboard boxcars in the Pantin freight yards on the eastern outskirts of the city. It was the last train of boxcars to leave before Paris was recaptured. Its approximate route to Germany was through Nancy and occupied France to the Rhine, down the Rhine to Frankfurt, northeast through Erfurt to Weimar, and up the short northward climb to Buchenwald. By passenger train in normal times this trip took ten hours.

Reportedly, the French Resistance had 2,000 armed men ready to attack the train while it was still in occupied France and free all prisoners. This may account for our erratic progress and the extreme alertness of the ss guards until we crossed the German border. At Nancy, the railway bridge across the river had been sabotaged before we arrived. This was why we disembarked, crossed another bridge, then re-embarked on another string of cattle cars.

My family received its first glimmer of hope about me in late September 1944. Mrs Grant, the mother of one of my old school chums, stopped my mother after church to say how wonderful it was that I was now a POW. My parents, who I imagine must have thought I was dead, were astonished to hear this because they had heard nothing from either the Red Cross or the RCAF Casualties Officer. Mrs Grant's source of information was her son, Ian, from my squadron.

Ian wrote that by a strange quirk of fate he had met a bomber pilot who was just back from occupied France and been told that there had been a John Harvie from Ian's squadron on the prison train from which he had escaped. With the help of senior air force connections in Ottawa my parents learned that this airman was Joel Stevenson. Flying Officer Stevenson, pilot of a Lancaster bomber from 431 Squadron that had been shot down on July 4/5, 1944, had been captured but escaped successfully to Allied lines. He returned to England with the first news that I had survived the destruction of my bomber.

On November 8, after his return to Canada, the RCAF arranged for Stevenson to visit my family and tell them about meeting me in the boxcar. The official telegram from Ottawa saying that I was now a POW did not arrive until December 8.

At the 1989 RCAF POW reunion in Ottawa, my first, I met Dave High from Edmonton. Dave said he was one of those two prisoners ordered out of my boxcar stark naked to bury the murdered young Frenchman. With bare feet, they were only able to scratch a shallow grave beside the track. Dave was sure that he, too, was going to be shot. Dave also said that one of the escapers from our wagon was run over by the train and this was how the SS first learned that prisoners were getting away.

Buchenwald (Beechwood), until recently in communist East Germany, is about eight kilometers north of Weimar, a smallish city between Erfurt and Leipzig. It was the first concentration camp to be liberated (on April 11, 1945) by the Western Allies. The notorious mass extermination camps, which were mainly in occupied Poland, were freed by the Russians.

Construction of Buchenwald had been started in 1937, using political undesirables, habitual criminals, and Jehovah's Witnesses. In 1938 this small work force had been increased by the addition of several thousand persistent offenders, vagrants, social misfits, and homosexuals. The German nationals imprisoned at

Buchenwald, who were serving life terms for robbery or murder, lived in a separate barrack. On Sundays and holidays they were allowed to mingle with the other inmates.

Initial priority was given to the building of ss barracks and facilities, houses for ss commanders, a falcon house, and a zoo. The camp had not been designed for mass exterminations and consequently did not have gas chambers. Over the years various additions and modifications were carried out until construction was essentially complete by 1942.

The first 13,000 Jews, mainly from Germany and Austria, arrived at Buchenwald in 1938. In 1942 most of them were transported to "Final Solution" camps, set up to handle mass exterminations. Several hundred skilled workers were retained. A new influx of more than 30,000 Jews arrived at Buchenwald in late 1944 and 1945. Few of these lived to see the camp liberated.

Buchenwald slave workers operated camp munition factories or toiled long hours in a nearby quarry under the whips and guns of ss men and the snapping fangs of guard dogs. Camp inmates were the source of slave labour for more than 136 other small labor camps across Germany. Captured Russian soldiers, who were treated as common criminals instead of as POWs, formed a large percentage of the labour pool.

Buchenwald, which covered 190 hectares, was a place of sharp contrasts. Starving prisoners fought to survive in the overcrowded huts and filth of the main camp while ss commanders distanced themselves in elegant villas away from the isolation cells, gallows, and crematorium. Incredibly, the officer in charge of the crematorium lived with his wife and children in a substantial home only a stone's throw away.

The Prisoners' Camp occupied the largest area. Behind electrified wire and watch towers were the big and small camps, the main parade ground, main prisoner barracks, laundry, stores, personal property storage, disinfection building, gallows, pathology, prisoners' canteen, crematorium, cinema, special cell block hospital, piggery, rabbit barns, fowl yard, horse barns, bunkers (high security cells), locksmith and electrical shops, optical workshop and prisoners' brothel. The next largest section, also heavily guarded, was the extensive Gustloff Munition Works. It used slave labour to manufacture parts for the V-2 long-range rockets which were fired against England during the last years of the war.

The camp centre was dominated by seventeen multistoried ss barrack blocks grouped in a semi-circle around a canteen. During the war years these buildings housed as many as 3,000 soldiers. The villas for the most senior ss leaders and their families were along the crest of the slope at the southern camp boundary. The Camp Commandant (Koch) with his murderous wife Ilse, the "Bitch of Buchenwald," lived in one of these.

The single-storey prisoner barracks were intended to house a total of about 18,000 men. However, by the end of September 1944 there were 84,505 prisoners in Buchenwald, including the several thousand sleeping on the bare ground in the open area of the small camp. On August 24, 1944, during the American air raid, reportedly 315 prisoners were killed and 525 wounded.

Buchenwald was infamous for Block 50, the Hygiene Institute, in which inhumane experiments were carried out on human guinea pigs. Few of the victims survived these incredible procedures.

The crematorium, which employed thirty-five men, had a twelve-meter high chimney that never stopped smoking. Six ovens consumed the corpses from the multiple hangings on evening roll call, hangings on piano wire in the crematorium basement, and murder victims thrown down a chute to the floor of the crematorium. This was in addition to the many who expired each day from starvation, disease, beatings, and random shootings. During the period from October 1944 until April 11, 1945, when the camp was liberated, 45,000 prisoners died, largely from malnutrition, disease, and freezing.

When at Buchenwald, I did not believe the Germans kept personal records. In actual fact they were quite meticulous about it. I did not know I had been assigned prisoner number 78412 until recently.

On August 20, 1944 our group of air crew from Australia, Britain, Canada, Jamaica, New Zealand, and the United States arrived at Buchenwald in a party of 1,650 prisoners, mostly French. We were unaware that our camp documents had been annotated DARF IN KEIN ANDERES LAGER – Not to be transferred to any other camp. A more liberal translation was that we were not to leave the camp alive. Squadron Leader Lamason, our New

Zealand CO, recently revealed that just before we were transferred to the POW camp the SS had received orders we were to be hanged, as were the Allied Secret Agents we had met.

It turns out that our disciplined military behaviour had convinced the secret prisoner underground that we were indeed Allied airmen. This group alerted the Luftwaffe, whose responsibility it was to guard enemy airmen. The Luftwaffe, who hated the SS, immediately set in operation the process for our transfer to POW camps.

Before I left Buchenwald one airman (RAF) died. Eleven were too sick to leave with the main party on October 19, 1994 and one of these, an American, died. The remaining ten reached Stalag Luft III on November 29, 1944.

The KLB Club that we formed in Buchenwald exists today. In 1979, at a meeting in Halifax, Ed Carter-Edwards, Bill Gibson, Stan Hetherington, and Jim Stewart resolved to make a serious attempt to trace all members. At last count the current addresses of all but fifty-four were known. Art Kinnis of Victoria, BC, is the volunteer president and secretary-treasurer of the Canadian branch. We are represented internationally by Ed Carter-Edwards of Canada and Jim Hastin of the U.S. We have stationary with the KLB logo on the letterhead and some members have had gold pins crafted with the club emblem of a winged foot chained to a KLB star.

The Danish police who arrived at the camp in late September 1944 have their own *Buchenwald Klubben* and a police flag that is carried at official Danish ceremonies. Following "The Oath of Buchenwald" on April 19, 1945, the internees from most other countries also formed national clubs. All of these groups are now represented by an International Buchenwald Committee.

Of the KLB members I knew best, Tom Hodgson and Pat Scullion have passed on. Léo Grenon died in early September, 1994, at his home in St-Jean, Quebec. The Gestapo accused him of being a spy, possibly because of his French name and the forged passport that he carried. He was badly beaten and, as a result, spent the rest of his life with a metal plate on his skull.

Whitey McLaughlin resides in Florida. Harry Bastable is a vocal member of the Canadian Legion in Winnipeg. Dave High lives in Edmonton. No one knows what happened to Stevenson after the war.

Stalag Luft III has been preserved and some former POWs have been back as tourists.

I do not know if the tunnel completed by my hutmates in East Compound was ever discovered.

My first letter from Stalag Luft III, written on October 23, 1944, arrived home two months later. The last of eight which got through was dated December 27, 1944. No mail from home caught up with me.

Lieutenant Gregory, who was repatriated from Sagan, sent my parents a mimeographed sheet describing in detail day-to-day life in Stalag III. A short personal note was attached.

In June 1947 I received from the RCAF in Ottawa my POW identity card, one of 400 found among captured German documents.

I have little up-to-date knowledge of my RAF roommates and friends from Luft III days. Recently I have tried to contact them through their POW Association but with no success.

I do know that Tut married soon after he arrived home. I was invited to the wedding but could not attend because I was on a troopship for Canada. Padre Thompson wrote a book, *Captives to Freedom*, about his extensive religious and psychological work as a POW. He passed away a few years ago. Percy emigrated to New Zealand. For a few years we kept up a desultory correspondence. Timmie Timmins received his medical degree and practiced in England.

I have not heard from the only other Canadian in Room 13, Ed Beaton. Perhaps at this moment he is curled up under a blanket having a nap!

In the early fifties I read that the Canadian Government had a large amount of money from seized German assets that it planned to distribute to any who had been maltreated by a criminal organization. I applied for consideration, and after lengthy delays the War Claims Commission judged that:

the claimant was in custody a total of 307 days. He was forced to participate in a capture march. He was transported by box-car on 3 occasions. He was in direct custody of the Gestapo a total of 94 days. He was forced to participate in a "hunger march" of early 1945 for about 29 days after a preceding period of severe malnutrition.

In all the circumstances of the case I recommend that the claimant be awarded $289.80.

When I returned from Germany in 1945, I gave the tin coffee mug I made, and of which I was so proud, to a WAAF I knew in Bournemouth.

The piece from the parachute which saved my life is one of my valued war souvenirs.

KLB Fiftieth Anniversary

In September 1994 Denmark hosted a meeting and reunion of Buchenwald clubs in Copenhagen. The timing was chosen to commemorate the fiftieth anniversary of the arrest of the Danish police force. In addition to Denmark's large representation there were members from fourteen other countries including Belgium, Canada, France, Germany, Hungary, Norway, Poland, Russia, Sweden, and Yugoslavia.

The International Buchenwald Committee concluded its business early in the five-day program. Afterwards, my wife and I attended a service at the Lutheran Godthaabkirken where I noticed a menorah on the low alter to the side of the chancel. I wondered whether prayers of thanks had been offered here during recent High Holidays for the rescue of the Danish Jews from Nazi persecution.

September 19 was a Danish patriotic day. Early in the morning we laid wreaths at the base of a monument in a cemetery in honour of fallen police. We moved to a Memorial Park which honoured all those who died for Denmark, where we again laid wreaths. Next, at police headquarters, a memorial service for the ninety or more police who died in German hands began with an air raid alarm at 11 A.M. The same alarm was sounded exactly fifty years ago by the Germans to assemble the Danish police for surprise arrest. After lunch we assembled at the Frederiksberg

City Hall for a commemorative ceremony. Speakers lauded those who had died for world peace and liberty and reminded the living that these ideals must always be defended. Queen Margrethe II was the honoured guest. That evening some 500 persons, former Buchenwald prisoners and wives, attended the final dinner. At this elegant black-tie affair an official message from Jean Chrétien, prime minister of Canada, was read, as was one from Bill Clinton, president of the United States.

After Copenhagen, I returned to Buchenwald for the first time. At the top of the hill overlooking Wiemar the bus-load of club members and wives stopped at the memorial area outside the camp. We descended the steps to the broad, cobbled terrace on the face of the hill called "The Road of Nations." On the way down we paused at each of the seven upright stone sculptures to study the relief scenes depicting the many horrors of life in the camp. We walked along the "Road of Nations" where a row of eighteen stark, vertical, granite block monuments jut in from the curved parapet. Each is topped with a massive, unlit saucer-shaped lamp and each carries the name of a country whose nationals perished in the camp. Neither Canada nor the United States are included.

Along the terrace we stopped in reverence at the three large, circular, granite-walled, grass-covered pits containing the remains of bodies from the crematorium. Then we climbed back up another set of steps past a group of statues at the base of the monumental bell tower. At this memorial we laid a wreath and one of the Canadians read a prayer composed by Rabbi Ginsburg of Beth Israel Synagogue in Calgary.

As we left the memorial area we encountered a group of German students. We learned from their teacher that all local high school students are required to visit Buchenwald. Since our KLB clubs are dedicated to preserving Buchenwald as a reminder that what happened here could easily happen again, we stopped to talk with them. We tried to make them understand the significance of our pilgrimage – that we had been inmates. We let them know we were upset to hear that neo-nazi youths had recently spray painted Nazi symbols here and threatened the staff.

Inside the main prisoners' compound all the buildings have been demolished except the prisoners' canteen, one of the hospital blocks, the personal property storage and disinfection building, the crematorium, and the main gate with the bunker solitary cells. A memorial to the Jews who died in Buchenwald has been created at the site of Block 22. Here a concrete wall containing exposed pieces of olive wood from Israel has been built under one long side of the former hut. From the centre of its base white rock from the quarry rises to ground level at each of the other three sides. As I stood there looking down at it, I imagined it as the site of a mass grave.

The site of our barrack, Block 58 in the small compound, is overgrown with trees.

The clock in the main gate tower shows the hour at which the camp was liberated. The dirt, filth, smells, vermin, as well as the dying skeletal humans in striped suits are long gone. When I looked down the slope to the distant countryside, I was pleased to see that it remains as beautiful as I remembered it was fifty years ago. My ghosts of the past were put to rest.

When I asked one of the Danes who had already made the trip to Buchenwald three times why he was here yet again, he replied that each time he comes he re-experiences the exhilaration brought about by the contrast of the freedom he knows now and the degradation he knew then.

Today Buchenwald is a clean, well-maintained historical site open to visitors.